THE CURIOUS FRAME

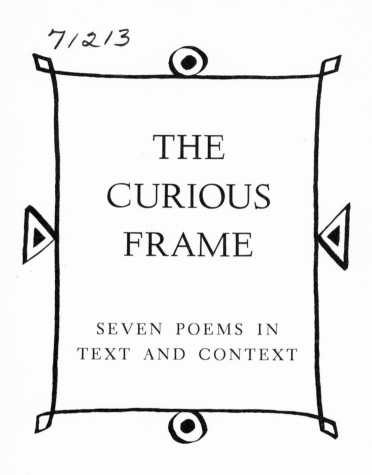

THE CURIOUS FRAME

SEVEN POEMS IN TEXT AND CONTEXT

JOHN EDWARD HARDY

THE UNIVERSITY OF NOTRE DAME PRESS · 1962

Copyright 1962

UNIVERSITY OF NOTRE DAME PRESS
NOTRE DAME, INDIANA

Publication of this volume was made possible by a grant from the
Ford Foundation, and grateful acknowledgment is hereby made
to that institution.

Library of Congress Catalog Card Number 62-12465

Manufactured in the United States of America by North State Press, Hammond, Ind.

TO THE MEMORY OF

LEO SPITZER

Lover of Language — Philolog, Philologue, Philologist

Acknowledgments

It was all done, all done over, in the space of a few weeks. And yet, whether it looks it or not, this little book has been a long time coming from a great way off — to get done over. I believe I should extend my thanks to as many of those as I can at the moment remember, who have given it a handout, cautioned it on its wayward ways, paid its fare from there to here: to John Kyle, who recommended it, and to Jean who read its beginning; to George Boas, a gentleman of the mind; to Elliott Coleman, who thought it insufficient; to Emily Greenslet, who was always at least distracted by it; to Earl Wasserman, who demurred, but did it shrewdly; to Georges Poulet, who sent me with a note to Constantin Guys; to Professor Anna Hatcher, who asked me about Marie de France; to Richard Macksey, for poetics and Packards; to Bruce Wardropper, who offered a beer; to Patrick Quinn, for being wrong about Baudelaire; to Jean Farley, who made me see Rilke; to Karl Klüwer, who brought me back; to Father Chester Soleta, who was more than agreeable; to John T. Frederick, who thought it a good idea; to Paul Baumgartner, who thought he saw what I meant even about Wordsworth; to Frank O'Malley, who asked where I had been; to Joseph Duffy, who humphed; to Mortimer Donovan, who liked the Marvell; to Louis Rubin, whom I have quoted; to Marvin LaHood, who suffered neglect; to Joseph Roberts, who drove me to distraction but also to books; to Ernest Sandeen, who listens; to John Logan, who urged the necessity of chance; to Alan Pollock, who advised restraint; to James Degnan, for the bitter charity of his mind; to my oldest daughter, Margot, who furnished a diversion; to Michael Murray, who had ideas; to John Murphy, who always had a better idea; to Ben Allen Park, who escapes the frames; to Cleanth Brooks and William Wimsatt, if it seem not an impertinence; to Marie.

Thanks are also due the University of Kentucky Press for permission to quote from William Wimsatt's *The Verbal Icon*, and the Yale University Press for the quotation from Elizabeth Sewell's *The Orphic Voice*. The quotations from T. S. Eliot are from "Burnt Norton" and "East Coker" in *Four Quartets*, copyright 1943, by Harcourt, Brace, and World, Inc., and are reprinted with their permissions.

The book, literally and physically, could not be but for the kindness, intelligence, and patience of Emily Schossberger, Charles McCollester, and Thomas Donohue, of the University of Notre Dame Press.

Preface

This book is concerned with poetry, and the ways of reading it. Anyone who wants to read poetry, for whatever reason, may find here something of interest.

I should, however, say something about the rather strange organization of the volume. First, there is, so far as I am aware, no occult significance in the fact that seven poems are treated. It is, after all, with the second text of "Young Waters," eight not seven. Second, the chronological arrangement of the studies is only approximate. "Young Waters" is dateless, but it was first published in the 18th century. The poem "A Prayer for My Daughter," which comes last, was written three years before Rilke's sonnet of the horse.

In other words, I have made no pretense to covering the succeeding "periods" of literature from the 17th century to the present. The question of the poet's and our historical awareness is here and there much to the fore. But the book's organization is not basically historical, and it makes but perfunctory bows to literary history. Nor have I started out to get samplings from various languages, and stopped short by including only French and German besides English.

The poems by Baudelaire and Rilke are here, not *because* they are in French and German, but so to speak in spite of that fact. The book is addressed primarily to an English-speaking audience, and to those who are students primarily of English literature — although I hope that students of French and German poetry, including native speakers of those languages, will not find my readings of these poems entirely ludicrous. These two poems are here, like the other poems, first of all because I like them. They say something.

This, then, was my first "rule" of selection. I wanted to write something about some poems that had excited my attention, no matter in the beginning why they had excited it, or what precisely I might find to say about them.

But, then, a second rule gradually established itself, almost simultaneously with the first. And this is the one which I offer as justification for the book, to those readers who may find the first principle no principle at all, but only egotistical self-indulgence.

I was brought up to read poetry in the school of "The New Criticism,"[1] especially in the explicationist department of the school. It was a good school, and I thought and still think I learned a lot there. But after so long a time, as I continued to read poetry, and to write it, I developed the uncomfortable awareness that I was feeling things I was not supposed to feel, according to the canons of the school as I understand them; thinking things I was not supposed to think; being excited by the poems to interests (in the biographies of Wordsworth and Baudelaire, for example) that I was not supposed to have — and yet, all the while, continuing somehow to retain the notion that I was reading the poem.[2]

This experience put me, as I think it might put any man, in something of a quandary. And this book is the result of the effort to get out of the quandary. It is not, I trust, the only result. But it is one of the results. After a good deal of sometimes aimless, sometimes concentrated thought on the subject, I eventually felt that there was one thing and one thing only, distinctly salvageable from the wreckage of my former convictions. This was the notion of reading poems individually, reading them close, "explicating" them, first to myself, then perhaps to and with other people, then again to myself. What had been the department became all I had left of the school.

But, this might not have been so disturbing, except for the fact that I was still left also with the poems. Since however closely and absorbedly one might read, it was apparent that he could not stay forever within any one poem, I felt that I should try to account to myself in some organized fashion for this necessity of going from one to another. To what extent, and how, might one ever satisfy him-

---

[1] See footnote, p. 152, Chapter VIII.

[2] I even felt that I *had* been doing all this long before, when I had thought I was doing something else; and it is principally for this reason that I have included in this volume, without much additional comment, the essay on "Lycidas" from the earlier book I wrote with Cleanth Brooks. It seems to me an interesting piece of evidence.

X

self that he had got sufficiently *into* a poem to justify himself in getting out of it? I realized — just from the fact that one keeps doubling back,[3] reading some of the same poems over and over, with periods of respite in between when he attempts to read other poems, or to occupy himself altogether with activities other than poetry-reading — that I should probably never get a full answer to that question. But, I had come not to expect full answers, ever, to any question of any importance. An approximate one would do.

It seemed, then, that there were some "typical" problems that kept coming up. Here was a poem that seemed at length to send one away from it, at least temporarily, to other poems that shared with it some definable "convention" of form, or theme. Here was another that seemed to have some special relationship to the ascertainable facts of the author's life. Here was another that was part of a consciously organized sequence . . . a "sonnet sequence." And so on. Of course, the problems overlapped, and some of the poems yielded not one but several of the problems. But still, it occurred to me that one might organize a book, if he were not too pretentiously precise about the organization (for none of the poets, I was sure, had written his poem to be put in my book), by selecting for study several poems each one of which had seemed *dominantly* to yield one or another of these approximately definable, "typical" problems.

In any event, I tried it. And that, if anything, is the approximate principle of this book's approximate order. It brings up, poem by poem, some of the typical problems of "escaping" from the poet's enchantment — which happen, it appears to me, strangely to coincide with some of the familiar issues of dispute between the New Criticism and other schools of "approach" to poetry. And some readers may find to their satisfaction, or dissatisfaction, that this latter is the "subject" of the book. But I have always felt, in reading poetry, much more the pursued than the pursuer. And for me, the main thing was and is that question of escape. For, of course, if you do not acknowledge the enchantment in the first place, if you *are* not enchanted, then there simply are no problems — of any kind.

---

[3] I don't know that the meaning of this term, "doubling back," will be apparent to a general audience. It is what a fox does when he turns back and re-crosses his trail. The fox is a lovely animal, once much admired and pursued by Southern gentlemen of blood. John Crowe Ransom calls him a "lovely ritualist"; but that is getting quite literary.

Perhaps the enchantment will seem to have worked all too well on me. There are remarks here and there, and especially in the final chapter of conclusions, on poetry and academic responsibility, poetry and language, poetry and belief, that some readers will put down as the merest effect of enchantment, the lunacy that comes of entertaining too long the conversation of that in Jacques Maritain's phrase "moon prince," the poet.

And the very length of the individual studies will seem intolerable. Is not, especially, the gigantic chapter on "A Prayer for My Daughter" really an insufferable demand upon the reader's patience with the explicationist method? Perhaps it is. Probably I can claim with it the world's endurance record in this esoteric art of ballooning. I have tried to help the reader out there, and also in the Wordsworth chapter, by dividing the essay into numbered sections, so that he may the more conveniently put the book down for a time (as I did), when he finds either the tedium or, as I hope, the mental strain, too much for him, and come back later. But even this may not be enough. I don't know.

As for the poem by Yeats in particular, I can submit only that I had to make a choice between the risks of saying too little or too much. I made the choice, and risked too much. But I hope it may astonish some to know that the present study was cut by almost half from an original draft, and that even in the original I was at every point having sternly to reject preoccupations with the text that seemed to me of great importance. If the essay is insufferable, so for me has been for many, many years the terrible hold upon my mind of this great and beautiful poem. If any one of them, this was the poem that at last broke the frame.

Table of Contents

"Young Waters"

A Version of Anonymity

1   *About Yule, when the wind blew cule,*
     And the round tables began,
   A there is cum to our king's court
     Mony a well-favord man.

2   *The queen luikt owre the castle-wa,*
     Beheld baith dale and down,
   And there she saw Young Waters
     Cum riding to the town.

3   *His footmen they did rin before,*
     His horsemen rade behind;
   And mantel of the burning gowd
     Did keep him frae the wind.

4   *Gowden-graithed his horse before,*
     And siller-shod behind;
   The horse Young Waters rade upon
     Was fleeter than the wind.

5 *Out then spack a wylie lord,*
   Unto the queen said he,
  'O tell me wha's the fairest face
   Rides in the company?'

6 *'I've sene lord, and I've sene laird,*
   And knights of high degree,
  Bot a fairer face than Young Waters
   Mine eyne did never see.'

7 *Out then spack the jealous king,*
   And an angry man was he:
  'O if he had bin twice as fair,
   You micht have excepted me.'

8 *'You're neither laird nor lord,' she says,*
   'Bot the king that wears the crown;
  There is not a knight in fair Scotland
   But to thee maun bow down.'

9 *For a' that she could do or say,*
   Appeased he wad nae bee,
  Bot for the words which she had said,
   Young Waters he maun die.

10 *They hae taen Young Waters,*
   And put fetters to his feet;
  They hae taen Young Waters,
   And thrown him in dungeon deep.

11 *'Aft I have ridden thro Stirling town*
   In the wind bot and the weit;
  Bot I neir rade thro Stirling town
   Wi fetters at my feet.'

12 *'Aft I have ridden thro Stirling town*
   In the wind bot and the rain;
  Bot I neir rade thro Stirling town
   Neir to return again.'

13   *They hae taen to the heiding-hill*
                His young son in his craddle,
                And they hae taen to the heiding-hill
                His horse bot and his saddle.

14   *They hae taen to the heiding-hill*
                His lady fair to see,
                And for the words the queen had spoke
                Young Waters he did die.

This poem is, in many obvious respects, faithful to the ballad conventions.[1] Its themes are familiar — jealousy among the great, the ruthless abuse of power, the curse of woman's favor, the untimely death of the young, proud, and beautiful. And so is its general form — a rapid narrative, with very little attention to setting; interpolated speeches by the characters, with a minimum of introduction; the whole tendency, in short, toward a *dramatic* form. It offers examples of the familiar devices of incremental repetition, of question-and-answer dialogue, and so on. Even in many of the particular details, it is reminiscent of a great many other of these Scottish and English ballads.

In its use, for example, of emblematical reference to the season of the year in which the action takes place — "About Yule, *when the wind blew cule*" — we may compare the opening stanza here to that of "Bonny Barbara Allen" . . . "It was in and about the Martinmas time,/ When the green leaves were a falling"; or of "Robin Hood and the Monk" . . . "In somer, when the shawes be sheyne,/ And leves be large and long"; or of "Edom o Gordon" . . . "It befell at Martynmas,/ When wether waxed colde"; or to the opening or transitional lines of any number of other ballads. The generalizing, al-

---

[1] The ultimate, popular origins of this ballad, if indeed it ever existed in a popular, or "traditional," form, are uncertain. According to some editors, there is a Scandinavian version of its story — which might argue a history of oral transmission and gradual revision. At any rate, the present poem has the look of being "edited," if not wholly composed, with conscious care by a single author — although, of course, a part of what he is conscious and careful of are the characteristics, prosodic and rhetorical, of the traditional ballad form. It was first printed in 1755. In the *Reliques*, Percy printed a text differing very little from that of the 1755 edition. Buchan's "version," 1828, is discussed later in this chapter.

literative phrase, like "dale and down," in stanza 2, is out of the common stock. Such properties as the horse are, of course, familiar attributes of the knightly office. And the detail of the riderless horse brought to the execution — "His horse bot and his saddle" — is related in its effect to a conventional pathos; cf. stanza 2 of "Bonnie James Campbell" — "Hame came horse, hame came saddle,/ But neer hame came he." An example of a stock, descriptive comparison is that of the horse's speed to the speed of the wind — cf. stanza 16 of "Lord Thomas and Fair Annet," where "the horse fair Annet rade upon,/ He amblit like the wind."

Further, these conventionalities — there is no need to catalogue them exhaustively — attest to what is sometimes called the communal authorship of the popular ballads. Such poems are the work of gradual revision, conscious or unconscious, through many retellings by many different performers, over a long period of time. There is a tendency to use the same phrases and poetic devices, the same basic story situations, in ballad after ballad, with only a slight revamping or reshuffling of the materials each time — so that, as has happened in the case of the present story (see p. 18, below), it often occurs that one poem is actually for a time confused with another.

And, although this present version has the look of being the rather carefully finished result of one author's work with some traditional, basic materials, still the poem is not individualized in the sense of carrying any stamp of that author's personality. In line with the whole tendency toward the dramatic form, the author stays almost entirely out of it, letting the story tell itself, explaining nothing, interpreting nothing. Neither his name nor anything of his personal identity is known to us from other sources, nor can we, from the evidence of the poem itself, tell much about him.

And it is important that we recognize these characteristics of the commonplace in the poem. For its conventionality is an essential part of its effectiveness. We cannot recover the state of mind in which the audience received these poems when they actually were part of an oral tradition. For as soon as such poems begin to be "collected," and different versions "compared" even with such relatively genial diligence as the hobby-scholars of the 18th century practiced, the oral tradition is at an end. It has already ended, perhaps much earlier still, when someone like our anonymous author here sits down to "compose" a single version of the poem which can be committed to writing. We see only a ghost of the old carelessness, in such things as the uncertainty of spelling — with the same word being rendered "but" in one line and "bot" in another, and again "bot" meaning "but" in one place and "both" in another. We can only speculate, how the ancient ballad-singer's audience must have delighted precisely in the conventionality of story and phrasing, of rhetorical devices, welcoming perhaps only the slightest originality on the part of the individual performer, a few slight tricks of improvisation, as a spice to the principal joy of hearing over again what they had heard a hundred times before — and how, on the other hand, they must have been altogether free of the anxiety which a modern audience feels when a reader violates the particulars of a known, "established" text. But still, the poem has some effect upon us. We feel, for one thing, its sadness. And to a great extent our sympathy with Young Waters in his fate, the sadness of this particular incident, depends upon recognition of its conventionality, at least in the sense of its being only one incident, one in a world full of such happenings. Our author, if not quite in the old way of the oral tradition, is in another way still more "anonymous," as we have seen. Unlike the ballad-singer to his audience, he is completely lost to us, completely invisible. And the peculiarly modern melancholy of our reaction to Waters' fate, our sense of its universal significance, is produced just by our unique awareness: of the conventions which are now *only* conventions, the familiar, typical phrasing, the commonplace dramatic devices, the stock imagery and symbolism; and of the wholly impersonal aspect of the work, without any stylistic or other mark of an author's conscious individuality.

Yet, simply to note in this way how the poem appeals to the "historic melancholy" of the modern mind, is not to deny that it is something in itself — one, whole, and complete. Even for us, perhaps especially for us, it has this unity. It is made up of readily identifiable, conventional elements. But what cannot be defined simply by identification of the several conventions, is the exact pattern of relationships into which these elements are brought. We may begin with a consideration of the way in which the poem is so contrived as to center interest upon one, strong effect: the outrage of a king's exercising his power of life and death on the strength of a caprice of jealousy and personal vanity. As theme, this outrage is itself quite familiar, a ballad convention. But as an actual, achieved effect, in the poem, it is something arrived at through a peculiar *arrangement* of conventional devices.

As is characteristic, again, of most of these ballads — but we shall see the fact also as having a special significance in the way the situation of this particular story is worked out — the persons of the action are not highly individualized. The poem's final effectiveness is in its presentation of an *action*. From this action, no detail of description, none of the metrical or rhetorical devices, is calculated to divert attention. And the same is true of the characterizations. What the king, for example, does — his outrageous act — is the matter of final importance; why he does what he does, beyond the immediately effective motives, what he might be like as a whole personality, are questions that the poem provides no grounds for entertaining.

We recognize the king's motives as "personal" — he is jealous, vain of his beauty of person, petulantly demanding of his wife's exclusive, personal admiration and affection, and this personalism is one of the two elements of the central dramatic conflict as we have defined it — but not as part of a "personality" in which we are permitted to become very much interested. These motives are "personal," rather, and significant as such, only by contrast to the official, "impersonal" motives he might have as a king, proper to his political office, for such an act as this. And the situation is similar with the roles, and implications of motive, of the other characters. They are characterized sufficiently only to make probable the action which their meeting precipitates.

Not only is anything very precise in the way of personal characterization missing, but historical data are largely excluded. The country is Scotland. From this fact, and such references in the poem as that to the Yuletide celebration, and the council table, as well as the queen's identification of the king's position, we can make certain inferences about the general cultural and political milieu — just as we have already inferred the code of behavior in terms of which the king's action becomes an "outrage," and the story's effect is calculated. But beyond this, all of which together is little enough, the historical circumstances of the action are not stated. The action itself is the poem's ultimate concern. And the time of the action is its own, all but wholly abstracted from history.

Or, it might be better to say, the possible historical *consequences* of the action — political and social — are left unexpressed. The principals are a king, a queen, and a man who is evidently a lord of considerable importance. And we do have one small hint at a background of intrigue. The man who asks the queen the fatal question — "O tell me wha's the fairest face/ Rides in the company?" — is described as a "wylie lord." He has, it is implied, noticed her excitement as she watches Young Waters, and shrewdly puts his question to trap her into an open expression of the meaning he has read in her glance. But the "wylie" perhaps implies that he has some design in doing so. Perhaps he anticipates the outcome of the incident, and has some reason for wanting Young Waters done in. However, if the action is one that arises from, and is to have consequences in, an interplay of forces in the society as a whole — the state — we are not told so. Beyond this single hint at the possibility of intrigue, the poem is not burdened with any suggestion of such complications in motive and plot. And it may be that the lord is "wylie" only in the sense of being shrewdly bad-tempered enough to put the queen in an embarrassing position, a villain for the sake of villainy.

But let us go back now to the first, and attempt to define more positively the limits of the poem's statement — to look at what definitely is going on in the story as it is told, rather than at what, like the possibility of political intrigue, might or might not be implied. The mention of Yule, and of the large company gathering at the castle, indicates a festive occasion. The king and queen and their companions have apparently come out to the battlements to watch the brave progress of the approaching guests. Young Waters is only one of a great number of visitors who are arriving — although, of course, principal attention is given to him and his retinue. In any event, the queen's answer to the lord's question is clearly to be taken in the context of the occasion as a whole, is the sort of thing that might normally be interpreted only as an expression of her appreciative excitement in the festivity. The lord's question catches her unaware. "Of all the fine, handsome lords who have arrived today, who is the fairest?" And she answers quite simply and naturally. To be sure, she says that she has "never" seen a lord so handsome as Young Waters; and this is the excess of her enthusiasm which the "wylie lord's" question anticipates and which provokes the king's fatal jealousy. But her remark is evidently made before the whole company, including the king, so that it is clear she could not have been conscious of any impropriety in her attitude. In this sense, then, of her unawareness at the moment — regardless of how right the lord, or the king, might be about the ultimate waywardness of her thoughts on Young Waters — she is innocent. We have, as a setting for the dreadful event of the beheading, an occasion of pomp, the brilliantly dressed company, the caparisoned horses, the brave procession. But more, it is a festivity which appears, so far as the description goes, wholly innocent and happy. And the queen's words, for which Waters must die, would seem to be a part of that innocence and happiness, to arise directly out of it.

Of course, it is *Waters'* innocence on which the pathos principally depends. For nothing that he has done, for no fault except the passive one that he is too handsome, cuts too fine a figure in his golden mantle and on his prize horse, he dies — in short, as the poem insists by a repetition of the line, solely "for the words the queen had spoke." But the pathos is heightened by the further implication of the queen's innocence. Allowing the guilelessness of her first remark, her plea to the king too must be taken as relatively innocent — as an attempt to cover up only her embarrassment, not any deep sense of guilt. It is an ingenious quibble, a protest on the implied limits of her statement. She would protest that she has meant to say only that Waters is the fairest of "the company" who are arriving now at the castle (just as the lord's phrasing of the question has indicated); or, at the most, that he is the fairest of all *such* as these, i.e., of the lords, lairds, and knights who owe the king fealty, and that the king himself is automatically excluded from the field of comparison. "A fairer face . . . mine eyne did *never* see," she would argue, is only an exaggerated manner of speaking, within the assumed limits of literal reference. The quibble is fatally unsuccessful; and, reminiscent as it is of the kind of quibble on which so many riddles and oracles turn, there is a hint here at the *fateful* — which is borne out later in the way that Waters accepts his death. Again, there is a tendency to put the emphasis on what happens, and ultimately to refer the question of why it happens to forces beyond human control. But, in the immediate situation of human relationships, there is also implicitly at work the theme of the king who would be a man, who wants more than anything to be admired for his personal qualities. And we might see the queen's last words — "There is not a knight in fair Scotland/ But to thee maun bow down" — as those that most infuriate him. He *knows* this; but what he wants is not recognition of the rights and powers of his office, but, as a man, the undivided admiration of his queen as a woman. And she never does, in fact, say directly that he is more *handsome* than any of his underlings. But, in any event, the very, desperate ingenuity of the queen's device — the fact that it is not after all ingenious enough — stamps it as an expedient of the moment, not as part of a practiced strategy of deception.

The queen is evidently guilty of a fatal failure to *understand* just how the king's mind is working, or perhaps finally of a certain stubbornly honest refusal to give in completely to the demands of his fatuous vanity. But there is no evidence that she ever feels guilty about her first outburst of admiration for Young Waters, which was entirely natural, instinctive, of the moment. Since she clearly does not appear to be unintelligent — although it fails, the ingenuity of her reply to the king is evidence enough of a ready wit — she could not so easily have been led into her extravagant compliment to Young Waters before the group, if she had had conscious guilt to hide. Guilt is more artful than this. The frank statement that Young Waters' is the fairest face she ever saw is reminiscent almost of the kind of innocence displayed by Moliere's Agnes, in *L'École des Femmes*, when she tells old Arnolphe of her love for Horace. And although the queen, when the king speaks, senses the damage she has done, and is anxious to repair it, there is nothing of the guile of deception in her rejoinder.

But whatever we can legitimately read here of the character of the king and queen — and the poem is richer in this respect than would appear at first glance — the poet does not linger, but comes back strongly to his central concern, with the deed. The relationship between the king and queen is only an instrument to precipitate the action. We know least of all about Young Waters; and yet, although entirely passive, he is, as victim of the outrage, the central personage; it is his story. The "hero" is as anonymous as the author.

We come back to a restatement of the situation in terms of the impersonal symbols which appeared early in the poem. The wind, for example, when first mentioned, is only a conventional, descriptive tag — "About Yule, when the wind blew cule." But something of its final symbolic function is anticipated in the description of Young Waters in stanza 3 — "And mantel of the burning gowd/ Did keep him frae the wind." The wind is symbolic of hardship, of danger, of threat, of the forces of fortune against man's progress. The golden mantle is emblem of protection, of the pride of the knight's position, of his assurance as he rides up to the castle to do homage to his lord. And in the final passage of the poem, the mantle is eloquently *not* mentioned; and Young Waters speaks, with the detached irony which befits a hero's acceptance of his fate, of the weather only, "the wind bot and the weit," through which in times past he has ridden through Stirling town. Through all sorts of hardships, in other words; and, perhaps the implication is, on the king's service; but, in any event, before now he has ridden always choosing his own course, with or against the wind, so to speak — never before helplessly moved by so ill a wind as this, never disgraced, with fetters at his feet, and not free to return. For the natural wind, of course, is a force to be reckoned with, but on something of equal terms, if one is free. It *symbolizes* the ultimate animosity of fate, or the caprice of tyranny, but only symbolizes it. And the final sense here is somewhat that of "Blow, blow, thou winter wind,/ Thou art not so unkind/ As man's ingratitude," or of Lear's welcome to the storm, preferring its terrors to the horror of human relationships. Young Waters reflects, sadly but drily, upon the relative comfort of whatever other trials he has faced, as a fighting man, by contrast to his present helplessness.

The king has Young Waters beheaded. The method of execution is ironically appropriate, not only to the nature of his "crime," with the beautiful head which the queen has so much admired being lopped off, but also, traditionally, to his exalted rank. It is a death for a nobleman. But it is a sorry kind of tribute, of course. And, again with ironic appropriateness, he is accompanied by a vestigial reminder of his former glory. He is a knight, a cavalier; and so his horse is there, and saddled, but not bearing its master. Waters is made to walk, presumably, or perhaps to ride in a cart. Or we may observe, as negative reinforcement of this humiliation of the once proud man, the contrast between the bareness of the final reference, simply to "horse," and "saddle," and the magnificence of the earlier description — "Gowden-graithed his horse before,/ And siller-shod behind;/ The horse Young Waters rade upon/ Was fleeter than the wind." (It might be noted in passing that this, in the simile, is another mention of the wind, and again with something of the same sense it has elsewhere. Young Waters can outrun the wind, but only so long as he has the king's favor and is allowed to keep the properties of his knightly office, so long as he is mounted; or, he can outrun the wind, but not the king's vengeance.)

And although we learn at the very last one further, startling fact about Young Waters — that he is not the lusty young bachelor we might at first have taken him for, but married, and a father — these too are in a sense impersonal matters. (As a point of narrative technique, the information can be furnished only at the end, since Young Waters has to ride in alone at the beginning in order that he may claim undivided attention — or alone, at any rate, except for the generalized "horsemen" and "footmen.") The pathos is thereby heightened, and the impression of the king's consummate hatred — not only Waters' wife, but even the infant, being forced to witness the cruel spectacle. And, again like the king's jealousy as against the proper concerns of his office, these are matters of "personal" relationships as against the "impersonal" pomp of the procession in which Waters enters. The effect is partly that of our seeing the "public man" reduced to the pitiable humanity of his private role. But it is, in fact, best to put it in terms of "public and private" rather than "impersonal and personal." For, once more, we learn nothing of Waters' "personality" from these details. And, finally, one of the principal significances here is simply the formal irony — that this procession, this retinue, of the woman and the child and the one saddled horse, have taken the place of that in which "His footmen they did rin before,/ His horsemen rade behind."

Or, perhaps it is not after all so simple an irony; for what it ultimately comes to is that with whatever company of retainers, many or few, and whether his by virtue of office or of affection, the hero in the view of fate is always alone. In the tragic effect of all these ballads, this sense is paramount — of man's meeting his fate alone, in his loneliness most brave. That quality of "anonymity," which we have discussed, paradoxically defines the hero's "individuality." The hero is "man"; his individuality is more that of "soul," let us say, than of "person"; but he is individual, one.

To sum up, however, on the point of the *poem's* individual integrity: The observations we have made on the fact that primary emphasis is put upon the presentation of an action; that personal motivation is relatively uncomplicated, the revelation of character left principally to secondary implications of described action, and of dialogue that chiefly serves to advance the action; that the significance of the hero's fate is stated more in terms of a typical symbolism than in terms of his peculiarly personal reactions — all can be reduced to generalizations which would apply equally well to a great many ballads. But, again, the precise way in which the management here of the symbolic properties, for example, reinforces the sense of the hero's final alone-ness — the kind of effect produced by the contrast of Waters' grand retinue at the beginning with that pathetic one at the end — is something that cannot be anticipated from the generalizations. And it is precisely by means of this, and other patterns of relationship we have discussed which can be discovered only in examination of the one text, that the poem actually achieves its effect. We can generalize, after the fact, about the nature of the effect, and the nature of the devices by which it is accomplished; but in the actual working of the poem, both means and end are most particular.

But perhaps some of the points I have brought up in this commentary, and a few further ones, can be clarified with a brief consideration of another version of the ballad — or, at any rate, another poem with the same title, and one that incorporates a good deal of the same story. Peter Buchan, in his *Ancient Ballads and Songs of the North of Scotland*, presents a "Young Waters" almost three times the length of the poem we have read. It is tedious, but simply for convenience of reference, Buchan's text is reproduced here:

1   *It fell about the gude Yule time,*
        When caps and stoups gaed roun',
     Down it came him young Waters,
        To welcome James, our king.

2   *The great, the great, rade a' together,*
        The sma' came a' behin';
     But wi' young Waters, that brave knight,
        There came a gay gatherin'.

3   *The horse young Waters rade upon,*
        It cost him hunders nine;
     For he was siller shod before,
        And gowd graith had behin'.

4   At ilka tippit o' his horse mane
         There hang a siller bell;
     The wind was loud, the steed was proud,
         And they gae a sindry knell.

5   The king he lay ower's castle wa',
         Beheld baith dale and down;
     And he beheld him, young Waters,
         Come riding to the town.

6   He turn'd him right and round about,
         And to the queen said he, —
     "Who is the bravest man, my dame,
         That ever your een did see?"

7   "I've seen lairds, and I've seen lords,
         And knights o' high degree;
     But a braver man than young Waters
         My e'en did never see."

8   He turned him right and roun' about,
         And ane angry man was he;
     "O wae to you, my dame, the queen;
         Ye might ha'e excepted me!"

9   "Ye are nae laird, ye are nae lord,
         Ye are the king that wears the crown;
     There's nae a lord in fair Scotland,
         But unto you maun a' bow down."

10   "O lady, for your love choicing,
         Ye shall win to your will;
     The morn, or I eat or drink,
         Young Waters I'll gar kill."

11   And nevertheless, the king cou'd say,
         "Ye might ha'e excepted me;
     Yea for yea," the king cou'd say,
         "Young Waters he shall die.

12   "Likewise for your ill-wyled words
            Ye sall ha'e cause to mourn;
        Gin ye hadna been sae big wi' child,
            Ye on a hill su'd burn."

13   Young Waters came before the king,
            Fell low down on his knee;
        "Win up, win up, young Waters,
            What's this I hear o' thee?"

14   "What ails the king at me," he said,
            What ails the king at me?"
        "It is tauld me the day, sir knight,
            Ye've done me treasonie."

15   "Liars will lie on sell gude men,
            Sae will they do on me;
        I wudna wish to be the man
            That liars on wudna lie."

16   Nevertheless, the king cou'd say,
            "In prison strang gang ye;
        O yea for yea," the king cou'd say,
            "Young Waters, ye shall die."

17   Syne they ha'e ta'en him, young Waters,
            Laid him in prison strang,
        And left him there wi' fetters boun',
            Making a heavy mane.

18   "Aft ha'e I ridden thro' Striveling town
            Thro' heavy wind and weet;
        But ne'er rade I thro' Striveling town
            Wi' fetters on my feet.

19   "Aft ha'e I ridden thro Striveling town,
            Thro' heavy wind and rain;
        But ne'er rade I thro' Striveling town
            But thought to ridden't again."

20   *They brought him to the heading-hill,*
            His horse, bot and his saddle;
      And they brought to the heading-hill
            His young son in his cradle.

21   *And they brought to the heading-hill,*
            His hounds intill a leash;
      And they brought till the heading-hill,
            His gos-hawk in a jess.

22   *King James he then rade up the hill,*
            And mony a man him wi',
      And called on his trusty page,
            To come right speedilie.

23   *"Ye'll do' ye to the Earl o' Mar,*
            For he sits on yon hill;
      Bid him loose the brand frae his bodie,
            Young Waters for to kill."

24   *"O gude forbid," the Earl he said,*
            "The like su'd e'er fa' me,
      My bodie e'er su'd wear the brand
            That gars young Waters die."

25   *Then he has loos'd his trusty brand,*
            And casten't in the sea;
      Says, "Never lat them get a brand,
            Till it come back to me."

26   *The scaffold it prepared was,*
            And he did mount it hie;
      And a' spectators that were there,
            The saut tears blint their e'e.

27   *"O had your tongues, my brethren dear,*
            And mourn nae mair for me;
      Ye're seeking grace frae a graceless face,
            For there is nane to gie.

28   "Ye'll take bit o' canvas claith,
       And pit it ower my ee;
    And Jack, my man, ye'll be at hand,
       The hour that I su'd die.

29   "Syne aff ye'll tak' my bluddy sark,
       Gie it fair Margaret Grahame;
    For she may curse the dowie dell
       That brought King James him hame.

30   "Ye'll bid her make her bed narrow,
       And mak' it naeways wide;
    For a brawer man than Young Waters
       Will ne'er streek by her side.

31   "Bid her do weel to my young son,
       And gie him nurses three;
    For gin he live to be a man,
       King James will gar him die."

32   He call'd upon the headsman then,
       A purse o' gowd him gae;
    Says, "Do your office, headsman, boy,
       And mak' nae mair delay."

33   "O head me soon, O head me clean,
       And pit me out o' pine;
    For it is by the king's command;
       Gang head me till his min'.

34   "Tho' by him I'm condemn'd to die,
       I'm lieve to his ain kin;
    And for the truth, I'll plainly tell,
       I am his sister's son."

35   "Gin ye're my sister's son," he said,
       "It is unkent to me."
    "O mindna ye on your sister Bess,
       That lives in the French countrie?"

36   *"Gin Bess then be your mither dear,*
                    As I trust well she be,
                Gae hame, gae hame, young Waters,
                   Y'se ne'er be slain by me."

37   *But he lay by his napkin fine,*
                   Was saft as ony silk,
                And on the block he laid his neck,
                   Was whiter than the milk.

38   *Says, "Strike the blow, ye headsman, boy,*
                   And that right speedilie;
                It's never be said here gaes a knight,
                   Was ance condemn'd to die."

39   *The head was ta'en frae young Waters,*
                   And mony tears for him shed;
                But mair did mourn for fair Margaret,
                   As raving she lyes mad.

Sargent and Kittredge remark that "everything in this copy that is not in the edition of 1755 . . . is a counterfeit of the lowest description."[2] Now, what "counterfeit" means in an historical sense — whether Sargent and Kittredge are accusing Buchan of having doctored the poem himself, or only of having accepted a fraudulent version (whatever *that* is, among ballads!) as genuine — is not clear. Nor is it possible to say precisely what features of the poem strike them as somehow false. But simply by comparing the longer and the shorter versions on a few points, I think we may easily make out a case for agreement at least with the attitude expressed in the remark.

The whole thing is overdressed, in Buchan's version. The horse, for example, is grand enough in the shorter poem; but in the longer, besides the silver shoes and the golden graiths, he must have bells. And the quaintness of language (the apparently "contrived" archaism is possibly some of the evidence of "counterfeit") is worked on without restraint . . . "At ilka tippit o' his horse mane," and the like. The length of the speeches is extended at almost every point. In his

---

[2] *English and Scottish Popular Ballads*, edited by Helen Child Sargent and George Lyman Kittredge, p. 199.

exchange with the queen, the king is excessively and pointlessly repetitious. And Young Waters, the fine dryness and brevity of whose
comments we have noted in the shorter poem, is here loquacious and
even maundering. He says so much, that it is impossible finally to tell
just what point he is trying to make. But the character revealed, at
any rate, is entirely different from that in the shorter poem. Here he
is self-dramatizing, drawing the last possible pathos from his situation, thoroughly priggish in his consciousness of his virtue — obviously deriving so much pleasure from the prospect of his death, that it
seems finally the kindest thing to have him hurried to it. And the
same kind of pumping-up of the emotional charge is provided elsewhere by the narrator; for example, in the treatment of the women
— with the queen pregnant, and Lady Margaret going mad.

Or, we may consider the handling of the symbolic properties. A
part of the shorter poem's effectiveness in presenting the final procession, its ironic reminder of that at the beginning, lies in the econ-
omy of the reference only to the knight's saddled horse. But here,
hyperconscious of the tradition perhaps, the narrator provides also a
hawk and hounds; and thereby the whole symbology becomes *merely*
conventional. The effect of recurrent reference — to the horse in one
situation at the beginning, and to the horse, alone, at the end — is
entirely lost. (It might be interesting to compare, on this point, the
use of the hawk, hound, and horse in "Edward," where the conventional trio do have a precisely definable function in the dramatic
development.)

But perhaps the principal fault of the Buchan poem is in its narrative confusion. What we have here is actually an effort to tell three
stories under one title. It is not a *complication* of plot, in any legitimate structural sense, but an uncontrolled piling up of diverse elements. Francis Child, in his headnote to the shorter version, remarks
that "this ballad has been supposed to refer to the fate of the Earl of
Murray (see "The Bonny Earl of Murray"). Additional circumstances
furnished by Buchan's copy, however, have led Chambers to suggest
that the unfortunate hero was Walter Stuart, second son of the Duke
of Albany."[3] Child goes on to say that he himself does not consider
the evidence adduced by Chambers "sufficient to establish the his-

---

[3] *English and Scottish Ballads*, edited by Francis Child, vol. 3, p. 88.

torical character of the piece."[4] And Child's judgment is probably the sounder here. But even if we could, which seems unlikely, justify as allusions to some historical actuality the digressive references in Buchan's "copy" of the poem — such as his provision of the names of Mar, and Graham, and the allegation of the uncle-nephew relationship between the king and Waters — there would be nothing here to redeem the disunity of the piece as fiction.

The singleness of effect in the shorter version is quite lost here. Motivation, for example, is not merely complicated, but obscured. Does the king have Waters killed out of jealousy, with the treason charge as an excuse, or for treason, a suspected intrigue, with the jealousy as an excuse? And why, we might ask further, does Waters tell the king the far-fetched story of his being James' nephew, son of a long-lost or long-forgotten sister, and then refuse to accept the advantage it gives him? Second thoughts? Or has he told with the intention, all along, simply of punishing the king with remorse for slaying his relative? This suicidal nobility of Waters' is not only unpleasant, making him here, as we have already observed, too self-conscious a hero to compel much sympathy; it is also highly improbable. We have here a clear instance of the kind of connection that always exists, for good or ill, between characterization and plot structure — impropriety in the one necessarily resulting in improbability and confusion in the other. Inevitably, the introduction of the long-lost-relative story is a mistake. Obviously it would not have done to allow Waters to get off on such an excuse. This would quite have destroyed him as a sympathetic character, and also have avoided resolution of the issue (whatever by now we might suppose that to be!) between him and the king. But to have him refuse the excuse, once he has prepared it, does not much help matters. If it somewhat redeems his character (and it can be only somewhat), it does nothing to settle any issues previously defined, but only abandons these, and leads off into what we soon discover is still another blind alley.

The poem proceeds like the conversation of a man who has made some foolish remark and who, in his embarrassment, trying to patch it up into a semblance of fine significance, only makes himself more and more absurd. In addition to other questions that the poem raises

---

[4] *Ibid.*, p. 89.

but leaves hanging — as, for example, who the Earl of Mar might be, and why he will not execute Waters as he is ordered to do, and what is to happen to him for his refusal — we have in the end yet another one, why it is that the king does not simply stop the execution, regardless of Waters' wishes in the matter. And for all his histrionics, and the king's coöperation, just at the last Waters is forced to relinquish his place as the center of attention. We are told that the madness of his wife has stirred more sympathetic grief among the people than the death of the poor knight himself. The poet, as if realizing that his hero has somehow ceased to be heroic, that the tragic effect has failed, abandons him altogether, and falls back upon a frantic pathos.

The long version of the poem, then, is in every respect sprawling, bulging, distorted. The stylistic effects are excessive and gaudy, the symbolic structure confused, the characterizations at once vague and over-elaborated, the speeches pointlessly repetitious, the plot wandering and burdened with irrelevancies, leaving the dramatic issues unresolved.

If it is "counterfeit," it is not that any particular one of its devices violates the ballad conventions. If we were trying to make up a catalogue of "authentic" balladic effects, there would be plenty of good material here. And in *some* of its details — principally the name "Young Waters," and the initial story situation — it resembles the shorter one.

But, finally, even the story is not really the *same* as in the other ballad. And in so far as a poem has its single identity in a certain organization of many elements — of diction, metaphor, rhythm, and so on, to one effect, the narrative being ultimately inextricable from the total complex — it makes little sense to speak of the two here as "copies," or even "versions," of the same poem. I am inclined to doubt that even the illiterate audience of the ballad-singer was so uncritical as to accept indifferently two such poems as the same, and not to prefer one to the other. Perhaps for them, almost as much as for us, an anonymous author and anonymous hero; but I doubt that the *poem* was anonymous, even in that forgotten time. Certainly for us, it cannot be. The case is a strange reversal, or inversion, of the situation with modern poems, in which we know the author, but strive to make the poem itself anonymous.

The poem in Buchan's collection might turn out to be the earlier of the two, and so, also in a purely historical sense, the more "authentic." But this would not alter the critical situation. And yet, there is a distinct critical advantage offered by the historical scholarship which preserves the different "versions" of the ballads. Such scholarship is obviously in itself not a complete critical method. But neither is the kind of approach which would confine our attention *only* to the "preferred" text. The advantage, in our having both pieces and in studying them together, is just that to which I have tried to turn the evidence here — showing the tightness of the first poem by contrast to the looseness of the second, indicating more clearly what the shorter poem is, by determining what the longer is not.

Milton's "Lycidas"

The Sublime Pastoral[1]

In this Monody the Author bewails a learned Friend, unfortunately drown'd in his Passage from Chester *on the* Irish Seas, *1637. And by occasion foretels the ruine of our corrupted Clergy then in their height.*

Yet once more, O ye Laurels, and once more
Ye Myrtles brown, with Ivy never-sear,
I com to pluck your Berries harsh and crude,
And with forc'd fingers rude,
Shatter your leaves before the mellowing year.
Bitter constraint, and sad occasion dear,
Compels me to disturb your season due:
For Lycidas is dead, dead ere his prime
Young Lycidas, and hath not left his peer:
Who would not sing for Lycidas? he knew   10

---

[1] Except for this title, and a few minor changes in the text, the essay is taken from "Essays in Analysis," in *Poems of Mr. John Milton*, by Cleanth Brooks and John Edward Hardy, pp. 169-186. The text of the poem, here as in the earlier volume, is from the 1645 edition. The headnote, "In this Monody . . . ," appeared with the poem in 1645.

Himself to sing, and build the lofty rhyme.
He must not flote upon his watry bear
Unwept, and welter to the parching wind,
Without the meed of som melodious tear.
  Begin then, Sisters of the sacred well,
That from beneath the seat of Jove doth spring,
Begin, and somwhat loudly sweep the string.
Hence with denial vain, and coy excuse,
So may som gentle Muse
With lucky words favour my destin'd Urn,   20
And as he passes turn,
And bid fair peace be to my sable shrowd.
For we were nurst upon the self-same hill,
Fed the same flock; by fountain, shade, and rill.
  Together both, ere the high Lawns appear'd
Under the opening eye-lids of the morn,
We drove a field, and both together heard
What time the Gray-fly winds her sultry horn,
Batt'ning our flocks with the fresh dews of night,
Oft till the Star that rose, at Ev'ning, bright   30
Toward Heav'ns descent had slop'd his westering wheel.
Mean while the Rural ditties were not mute,
Temper'd to th' Oaten Flute,
Rough Satyrs danc'd, and Fauns with clov'n heel,
From the glad sound would not be absent long,
And old Damœtas lov'd to hear our song.
  But O the heavy change, now thou art gon,
Now thou art gon, and never must return!
Thee Shepherd, thee the Woods, and desert Caves,
With wilde Thyme and the gadding Vine o'regrown,   40
And all their echoes mourn.
The Willows, and the Hazle Copses green,
Shall now no more be seen,
Fanning their joyous Leaves to thy soft layes.
As killing as the Canker to the Rose,
Or Taint-worm to the weanling Herds that graze,
Or Frost to Flowers, that their gay wardrop wear,
When first the White thorn blows;
Such, Lycidas, thy loss to Shepherds ear.
  Where were ye Nymphs when the remorseless deep   50

Clos'd o're the head of your lov'd Lycidas?
For neither were ye playing on the steep,
Where your old Bards, the famous Druids ly,
Nor on the shaggy top of Mona high,
Nor yet where Deva spreads her wisard stream:
Ay me, I fondly dream!
Had ye bin there — for what could that have don?
What could the Muse her self that Orpheus bore,
The Muse her self, for her inchanting son
Whom Universal nature did lament,   60
When by the rout that made the hideous roar,
His goary visage down the stream was sent,
Down the swift Hebrus to the Lesbian shore.
     Alas! What boots it with uncessant care
To tend the homely slighted Shepherds trade,
And strictly meditate the thankles Muse,
Were it not better don as others use,
To sport with Amaryllis in the shade,
Or with the tangles of Neæra's hair?
Fame is the spur that the clear spirit doth raise   70
(That last infirmity of Noble mind)
To scorn delights, and live laborious dayes;
But the fair Guerdon when we hope to find,
And think to burst out into sudden blaze,
Comes the blind Fury with th'abhorred shears,
And slits the thin-spun life. But not the praise,
Phœbus repli'd, and touch'd my trembling ears;
Fame is no plant that grows on mortal soil,
Nor in the glistering foil
Set off to th'world, nor in broad rumour lies,   80
But lives and spreds aloft by those pure eyes,
And perfet witnes of all judging Jove;
As he pronounces lastly on each deed,
Of so much fame in Heav'n expect thy meed.
     O Fountain Arethuse, and thou honour'd floud,
Smooth-sliding Mincius, crown'd with vocall reeds,
That strain I heard was of a higher mood:
But now my Oat proceeds,
And listens to the Herald of the Sea
That came in Neptune's plea,   90

He ask'd the Waves, and ask'd the Fellon winds,
What hard mishap hath doom'd this gentle swain?
And question'd every gust of rugged wings
That blows from off each beaked Promontory,
They knew not of his story,
And sage Hippotades their answer brings,
That not a blast was from his dungeon stray'd,
The Ayr was calm, and on the level brine,
Sleek Panope with all her sisters play'd.
It was that fatall and perfidious Bark   100
Built in th' eclipse, and rigged with curses dark,
That sunk so low that sacred head of thine.
    Next Camus, reverend Sire, went footing slow,
His Mantle hairy, and his Bonnet sedge,
Inwrought with figures dim, and on the edge
Like to that sanguine flower inscrib'd with woe.
Ah! Who hath reft (quoth he) my dearest pledge?
Last came, and last did go,
The Pilot of the Galilean lake,
Two massy Keyes he bore of metals twain,   110
(The Golden opes, the Iron shuts amain)
He shook his Miter'd locks, and stern bespake,
How well could I have spar'd for thee young swain,
Anow of such as for their bellies sake,
Creep and intrude, and climb into the fold?
Of other care they little reck'ning make,
Then how to scramble at the shearers feast,
And shove away the worthy bidden guest.
Blind mouthes! that scarce themselves know how to hold
A Sheep-hook, or have learn'd ought els the least   120
That to the faithfull Herdmans art belongs!
What recks it them? What need they? They are sped;
And when they list, their lean and flashy songs
Grate on their scrannel Pipes of wretched straw,
The hungry Sheep look up, and are not fed,
But swoln with wind, and the rank mist they draw,
Rot inwardly, and foul contagion spread:
Besides what the grim Woolf with privy paw
Daily devours apace, and nothing sed,
But that two-handed engine at the door,   130

Stands ready to smite once, and smite no more.
Return Alpheus, the dread voice is past,
That shrunk thy streams; Return Sicilian Muse,
And call the Vales, and bid them hither cast
Their Bels, and Flourets of a thousand hues.
Ye valleys low where the milde whispers use,
Of shades and wanton winds, and gushing brooks,
On whose fresh lap the swart Star sparely looks,
Throw hither all your quaint enameld eyes,
That on the green terf suck the honied showres,   140
And purple all the ground with vernal flowres.
Bring the rathe Primrose that forsaken dies.
The tufted Crow-toe, and pale Gessamine,
The white Pink, and the Pansie freakt with jeat,
The glowing Violet.
The Musk-rose, and the well attir'd Woodbine,
With Cowslips wan that hang the pensive hed,
And every flower that sad embroidery wears:
Bid Amaranthus all his beauty shed,
And Daffadillies fill their cups with tears,   150
To strew the Laureat Herse where Lycid lies.
For so to interpose a little ease,
Let our frail thoughts dally with false surmise.
Ay me! Whilst thee the shores, and sounding Seas
Wash far away, where ere thy bones are hurld,
Whether beyond the stormy Hebrides,
Where thou perhaps under the whelming tide
Visit'st the bottom of the monstrous world;
Or whether thou to our moist vows deny'd,
Sleep'st by the fable of Bellerus old,   160
Where the great vision of the guarded Mount
Looks toward Namancos and Bayona's hold;
Look homeward Angel now, and melt with ruth.
And, O ye Dolphins, waft the haples youth.
    Weep no more, woful Shepherds weep no more,
For Lycidas your sorrow is not dead,
Sunk though he be beneath the watry floar,
So sinks the day-star in the Ocean bed,
And yet anon repairs his drooping head,
And tricks his beams, and with new spangled Ore,   170

Flames in the forehead of the morning sky:
So Lycidas sunk low, but mounted high,
Through the dear might of him that walk'd the waves
Where other groves, and other streams along,
With Nectar *pure his oozy Lock's he laves,*
And hears the unexpressive nuptiall Song,
In the blest Kingdoms meek of joy and love.
There entertain him all the Saints above,
In solemn troops, and sweet Societies
That sing, and singing in their glory move,   180
And wipe the tears for ever from his eyes.
Now Lycidas *the Shepherds weep no more;*
Hence forth thou art the Genius of the shore,
In thy large recompense, and shalt be good
To all that wander in that perilous flood.

  Thus sang the uncouth Swain to th'Okes and rills,
While the still morn went out with Sandals gray,
He touch'd the tender stops of various Quills,
With eager thought warbling his Dorick *lay:*
And now the Sun had stretch'd out all the hills,   190
And now was dropt into the Western bay;
At last he rose, and twitch'd his Mantle blew:
To morrow to fresh Woods, and Pastures new.

With "Lycidas," as so often elsewhere with Milton, Dr. Samuel Johnson's comments form an excellent point of departure. When Dr. Johnson castigates "Lycidas" for the mingling of pagan with Christian references, he puts his finger firmly on the matter of first importance for a reading of the poem, even though it is a finger of the left hand and the gesture is deprecatory. Here again Johnson in failing to appreciate the poem has given us a valuable clue for our own understanding.

The problem of the pagan-Christian conflict has to be faced: the mingling either is turned to account in a rich synthesis, or it is not, and it disfigures the poem as a clumsy confusion. It will not do to write off the discrepancies as due to an improper attention to what Milton meant only as "conventional ornament." We had better side with Johnson in taking the poem seriously, in reading narrowly and precisely, in assuming that the pattern of statement is important, than try to save the poem by ignoring the implications of the pattern.

If the poem cannot survive a serious and close reading, we can be sure that Milton least of all would have wished it to survive.

It can, of course, survive the most rigorous reading. It can be closely read, for it has been closely written. We shall certainly need to take certain conventions into account as we read, but it will become clear that the poem does not lean unduly upon them: rather it reinvigorates and justifies them. The first lines will illustrate Milton's characteristic treatment of the conventions and the general tightness of the structure he employs. Milton's praise for Edward King[2] is that "he knew/ Himself to sing, and build the lofty rhyme." Milton's own poem in King's memory is *built* in every sense of the word, and, if we are to explore the poem, we must be prepared to become acquainted with its architecture, and an intricate and subtle architecture at that.

The laurel is a symbol of poetic fame. The poet comes to pluck the berries before they are ripe; that is, the poet apologizes for the fact that his own art is immature. The meaning of the conventional symbolism is plain. But Milton is not content to make a conventional *use* of the convention.

> *I com to pluck your Berries harsh and crude,*
> *And with forc'd fingers rude,*
> *Shatter your leaves before the mellowing year.*

Not only are the fingers which pluck the berries "forc'd"; the unripe berries are themselves "forc'd" from the stem. We have here a rich and meaningful ambiguity. And so with the whole passage: the fingers are "rude" not only in their brutal compulsion, but also in their unmannerliness and clumsiness. The poet is unripe, but Lycidas, "dead ere his prime," Lycidas for whom the berries are to be plucked, was also unripe, untimely dead; and there is therefore a kind of ironic justification in the poet's being compelled to sing thus prematurely.

We can see in the manner in which this idea is expressed yet another kind of unconventionality. The passage looks forward to the development of the pastoral mode in the poem — the plucking of the berries is "appropriate" to the shepherd — but the poet has taken care that it be sufficiently realistic. We have not, in the figure of the shepherd here, merely the often shadowy character of the conven-

---

2 The "learned Friend" of the headnote to the poem. He was a young poet and clergyman.

tional pastoral. It is, after all, Milton, the self-conscious young poet, speaking. Evidently this is not the first time he has come forward with an immature performance:

> *Yet once more, O ye Laurels, and once more*
> *Ye Myrtles brown, with Ivy never-sear,*
> *I com . . .*

He should know better; but even so,

> *Bitter constraint, and sad occasion dear,*[3]
> *Compels me . . .*

The point we are making here is not that the passage is difficult and cannot be understood but that it is rich; that the words are carefully chosen; that the network of connotations is important; that the "poetry" resides in the total structure of meanings. The opening lines, then, give us warning, if we care to heed it, that the various smaller items in the poem are mortised together most cunningly; and they offer the hint that we shall do well to expect, and look forward to, the same kind of careful articulation of the larger elements.

The shepherd imagery, simply as such, hardly calls for any special comment. It is pervasive, and it is important, particularly in helping to provide a basis for the fusion of the Christian-pagan elements: the "pastor" as pagan shepherd and as Christian "pastor." Further consideration of the pastoral machinery may await a discussion of some of the elements that are not ordinarily part of the pastoral convention — elements that we should not be able to predict merely from the assumption that this is a pastoral poem.

One of the most important of these elements — and one of the most startling, once it is seen — is the water imagery. Milton does not forget that King met his death by drowning. He makes much of the sea in this poem, and he makes much of water in general — the tear, the stream, the Galilean lake, etc.

---

[3] The word "dear" here means, of course, *heartfelt, profoundly affecting.* But it can also mean *dire* (see N.E.D.). The effect of the ambiguity is to emphasize the inescapable, fatal character of the poet's obligation to Lycidas.

The first instance of the water imagery occurs in the twelfth line:

> *He must not flote upon his watry bear*
> *Unwept, and welter to the parching wind,*
> *Without the meed of som melodious tear.*

The funeral couch is the tossing sea itself. *Welter* means "to roll" or "to toss" — but there was another *welter* in this period, a word which meant "to wither" or "to wilt"; and Milton's phrase, "welter to the parching wind," would seem to indicate that this latter meaning is present too.

Actually, one can make out a case for the double meaning in terms of the context — and thereby give some point to the otherwise rather pointless statement that Lycidas must not toss upon the waves without one more drop of moisture, the "melodious tear," which must be added to the ocean in which the drowned body is already immersed. The submerged metaphor at which the double meaning of "welter" hints is something like that of a shipwrecked man tossing on his raft, surrounded by water, and yet parching. "Water, water, everywhere/ Nor any drop to drink." Except, we should note, that it *is* "submerged" — that there is no "raft," nor even a "bier" (for Lycidas is dead, drowned, not just in danger of death, and therefore no longer in need of a raft) except the water itself; *and*, that, if we examine the figure more curiously still, a "tear" is also salt water, just like the ocean itself, and therefore of no help in refreshing the man who is simply *about* to die, of thirst. Whatever the efficacy of the tear, it will have something more precisely to do with its being a "*melodious* tear" rather than just a drop of moisture. The only possible refreshment that can now be offered to Lycidas must be spiritual, not physical.

The matter may seem of little importance at this point — how Milton has so contrived the figure as to suggest analogous meanings which, once entertained and then "rejected," direct us back the more surely to his precise intent. But as the poem develops, the apparently innocuous image is seen to have introduced a theme of great depth and complexity. In some sense, the "melodious tear" promises to overwhelm the "sounding Seas." If we can succeed in defining that sense, we shall have gone a long way toward defining the central theme of the poem, and what the theme does have to do with the pastoral *mode*.

It has been pointed out that Milton did not necessarily have any close friendship with King and that he therefore took the young man's death as a convenient peg on which to hang his elegy. The expression of grief is thus, we are inclined to say, conventional, and the elegy itself a *conventional* poem. But the term should not imply that Milton's feelings are not seriously engaged: the question is rather, what is the real subject? What theme does engage the poet's feelings? The answer can be found in the poem itself: Milton is at his most conventional in describing his personal association with King ("We drove a field, and both together heard . . ."); and he can afford to be conventional here, for what counts in the poem is not Edward King as an individual but rather what King stands for, the young poet and pastor. But if Milton is not deeply concerned with King as a person, he is deeply concerned, and as a young poet personally involved, with a theme — which is that of the place and meaning of poetry in a world which seems at many points inimical to it. In the dramatic development of this theme the "conventional" figure of King has, of course, the leading role. It is this theme that dominates the poem, and a variant of it — the relation of the poet to the forces of nature — which shapes the first paragraphs.

Immediately after the reference to the "melodious tear" the speaker invokes the "Sisters of the sacred well." Is the tear wept by the sorrowing speaker? Or since it is "melodious," is it drawn from the well of the Muses? Or is it wept by the Muses themselves? The ambiguity is not a meaningless one: the primary matter is the relation of the poet to the Muses; or, to put the question in other terms, whether the personal lament of the speaker can transcend the *merely* personal. The equivocation is meaningful and intended, for the speaker carries it further in the next lines. It is *he* in the first verse paragraph who apologizes for daring to write at this time; but it is the *Muses* to whom he says in line 18,

Hence with denial vain,[4] *and coy excuse . . .*

---

[4] "Vain" means "useless"; "Bitter constraint" forces the tribute. But it also means "desirous of admiration": the denial is an effect of vanity which asks for further urging.

And in the next line he makes it plain that the "gentle Muse" who he hopes will sing an elegy at his death is masculine — a poet like himself.

The relation of the poet to the Muse — even the question whether the Muse has any existence apart from the poet himself — is thus crucial for the theme of the poem, though Milton might be considered merely gracefully conventional in beginning his elegy by invoking the Muses and paying the usual tribute to the sacredness of the well with which they are associated. On this level the "sisters" are the nine Muses of Greek mythology, but Milton is careful to relate them to the island of Britain, and more intimately still to the scene of the disaster, to the Welsh coast itself. It is true that the beings whom he reproaches (l. 50) for failing to protect Lycidas are the "Nymphs." But as the phrase "your old *Bards*" suggests, these nymphs are not merely deities of field and stream; they have the poets under their care and are thus associated with the Muses. (If there is any doubt on this point, it is resolved by the very excuse which the speaker supplies for the nymphs: they are not to be blamed for failing to protect Lycidas since "the Muse her self that *Orpheus* bore" could not protect her son.)

There is a sense, of course, in which the nymphs are conventional nymphs. They might have been expected to be playing "on the steep/ Where . . . the famous *Druids* ly" or on the "top of *Mona* high" or by the stream of the Deva. They *are* the deities of hill and stream. However, since in this poem poethood is first identified with the pastoral, it is only proper that this should be so. The description of Lycidas's career as a poet has prepared for just this kind of association, for in his and the poet's earlier life together

> . . . the *Rural ditties were not mute,*
> *Temper'd to th'Oaten Flute,*
> *Rough Satyrs danc'd, and Fauns with clov'n heel.*

The pastoral is a poetry of wild innocence, close to nature, a part of the music of nature, and the nymphs are its natural muses and guardians. On the day of Lycidas's death the nymphs were not playing where one would have expected them to play. The speaker knows this — because, had they been there, they would surely have tried to save Lycidas. Calliope is mentioned simply to emphasize the deeper pessimism into which the elegist falls at this point — not only were the nymphs absent; even had they been present they would have been ineffectual, as the Muse herself (of a higher order, yet of the same kind) was powerless to save her son.

The point is that *all* the divine guardians of the classical tradition — from the highest and most remote, the Muse herself, to the lowest and most intimate, the nymphs — appear to be ineffectual. And one can see an implication of yet deeper despair. The exclamation, "Ay me, I fondly dream!," placed as it is *after* the statement that the nymphs were not present and *before* the statement that they would have been useless in any case, could mean either that the existence of the nymphs or their effectuality is a "fond dream." But the two propositions come to the same thing; to say nymphs are ineffectual is tantamount to denying their existence. The poet enjoys no special status. The old intimate relation between the poet and the forces of nature has lapsed — if it *ever* existed, save as a fable of some early and lost golden age.

To sum up: by hinting that the Muse cannot save her votaries, the poet has called in question the efficacy of the melodious tear, for which the poet has turned to the well of the Muses. Is the tear, after all, other than the waste salt water which it resembles and on the waves of which the body of the dead poet now welters? Is the sacred well really sacred? Does one not do better to turn to the flesh-and-blood Amaryllis than to this "thankles" shadowy being, who seems powerless, and who perhaps does not even exist? The poem at this point has moved dangerously close to a naturalism which divests nature of any special sanctity and the poet of any supernatural function.

The last statement may seem to read too much into the passage in question; and yet this is the general meaning up to which the whole of verse paragraph four leads. In lines 37-49, nature is represented as mourning. And, with regard solely to Lycidas himself, one might take the statement that the trees "Shall now no more be seen,/ Fanning their joyous Leaves to thy soft layes" to mean simply that the sympathetic emotion of nature has *changed* — from joy to sorrow. But for the elegist it would seem to be not merely a change, but a *loss* of the sense of nature's sympathy. Milton has been careful in this stanza *not* to give us personifications of nature. "Woods . . . desert Caves . . . And all their echoes mourn." The dancing satyrs and fauns of the preceding stanza are not represented here as weeping; neither they nor the nymphs are mentioned at all. When the nymphs are mentioned in the next stanza, they are referred to as absent. In this stanza, then, we are presented with an emptied nature, a nature which allows us to personify it only in the sense that its sounds seem mournful; and, finally, the interpretation that they *seem* mournful is justified by the concluding lines of the stanza:

> *Such,* Lycidas, *thy loss to Shepherds ear.*

It is the *ear* of the shepherd speaker that has been affected. He is not saying merely that he can no longer hear the song of Lycidas. The music of nature which accompanied that song, and (it is implied) which prompted the song, has also been stilled. But the voice of nature is not silenced by her own grief. The change which the death of Lycidas has brought is not actually a change in nature herself; the death is not a loss to nature, but a numbing of the poet's sensitivity to nature. What has happened to the ear is particularized quite explicitly: it is the same sort of thing that happens to the sheep when the taint-worm attacks them or that happens to early flowers cut off by a late frost. It is as though the shepherd in his grief, though he still calls himself "Shepherd," sees himself reduced to the level of his charges, the sheep themselves, in his relation to the forces of nature. In the elegist's compliment, Lycidas is made a kind of shepherd to him, without whom now he is abandoned and helpless. Nature is no more sympathetic with him in his sorrow than it would be with the sheep if their keeper should die and leave them to fend for themselves. Nature has no apparent respect for the memory of Lycidas. And it is questionable whether she had any for him alive. For Lycidas too, beyond the terms of the present compliment, is just such a shepherd as the speaker himself — as much as he, one of the helpless sheep.

The entire passage *can* be read simply as a compliment to the music of Lycidas; and the next stanza, with its implied comparison of Lycidas to Orpheus, whom "Universal nature" also lamented, carries the compliment further. But the passage, including again its reference to the fate of Orpheus, also reads as a dark commentary on any hopeful view of the relation of the poet to nature. The poet enjoys no special status. To judge by the fate of either Lycidas or Orpheus, the poet's name is literally written in water.

The poet is shrewd enough not to appeal to the justification of fame. That, too, is an effect of pride, "That last infirmity of Noble mind." Men live laboriously and stringently in the hope of fame; they endure a life of hardship, only to have that life extinguished by the "Blind *Fury*" — "blind" in the sense that she cannot see they are about to burst into a blaze of light, and could not see the blaze even if it had already flared forth. Better to eschew the light altogether, therefore, and "sport with *Amaryllis* in the shade."

It is here that the pastoral tone is first broken by a "strain . . . of a higher mood," by the voice of Apollo himself, who, touching the poet's deadened ears,[5] points out that true fame transcends this world. (True fame here is distinguished from "broad rumour" or "report," the sense in which the term is first used in the passage. The fame of which Phœbus speaks has taken on something of the meaning of "praise" — "But not the praise,/ Phœbus repli'd" — a word retaining from its Latin root a much stronger sense of evaluation and judgment than *fame* usually carries. The effect of *pronounce* may also be noted — "*Jove* . . . pronounces lastly on each deed" — with its sense of an authoritative judgment behind the "speaking" which, again, *fame* does not ordinarily have.) True fame is immortal, and does not grow on mortal soil.

This passage makes a distinction between the pagan deities of wood and field and stream — the genii of the place — and the higher deities — the gods of "heaven" — and therefore seems an anticipation of the specifically Christian doctrine with which the poem is to end. But we should be careful to remember that Apollo and Jove, even so, are *pagan* deities. The shock of transition from pagan to Christian is being cushioned by the poet's having one of the classic gods proclaim in effect that his "Kingdom is not of this world." But "cushioned" really overstates the case. Milton obviously wants us to feel some kind of clash in all three places: between the high utterance of Apollo here and the pastoral world of the poem;[6] between St. Peter's words and that same pastoral mood; and between, in the largest terms, Christian and pagan, at the moment of St. Peter's entrance.

By addressing the "fountain *Arethuse*" and the river Mincius (ll.85-86) he calls attention to the interruption of the pastoral, before proceeding again in that mode:

---

[5] See footnote 7, below.
[6] See footnote 7, below.

But now my Oat proceeds
And listens to the Herald of the Sea . . .

The transition is not one to a more hopeful mood. Nature cannot
protect the poet, as the section reproaching the nymphs has indicated. But the sea is a part of nature too, and as the next section
shows, if nature does not protect man, it is at least neutral: there is
no culprit to be found among the sea deities. The disaster must be
attributed to something outside nature, something supernatural, as
is hinted by the sinister reference to —

. . . that fatall and perfidious Bark
Built in th' eclipse, and rigg'd with curses dark.

But, again, if the sea deities are not actively hostile to man, the sea
over which they preside is consistently presented in the poem as
unfriendly and alien. It covers the "monstrous world." Its waters are
presented several times as something which is sterile and meaningless:
the first picture of the drowned man "welter[ing] to the parching
wind"; the second, of the "sounding Seas" which "hurl" the drowned
man's bones; the third, of "that perilous flood."

In this poem, for obvious reasons, the sea is associated with death —
the death of King, and also with the death of Orpheus. But, in relation to the theme of fate as announced in the earlier sections of the
poem, it is associated with a kind of aimless confusion, a type of
nameless oblivion in which the known and familiar human world is
swallowed up. The streams and fountains which run throughout the
poem flow with life-giving water: they are "crown'd with vocall
reeds," or flowers. They flow to some purpose — they go somewhere
— whereas the seas flow chaotically without pattern — mere tumbling
water. (It is ironical, of course, that the streams all have for their
destination the sea, and seem to lose themselves in its purposeless
waste: but this is the very point of the analogy: the lives of men, too,
with their purposes and meanings, spill themselves finally into the
sea of oblivion.)

But whatever the precise meaning of the sea symbol, it can hardly
be an accident that all the "resurrection images" have to do with a
circumvention of the sea, or a rising out of the sea: Alpheus, in his
love for Arethusa, flowing under the sea to come up again in Sicily

and mingle his waters, still fresh and life-giving, with hers; the day-star rising from the sea; "the dear might of him that walk'd the waves." On the purely naturalistic level, all life eventually ends in the sea, and thus far in the poem we have had a naturalistic account of the state of affairs. Devotion to nature — devotion to the muses, in Milton's deliberate confusion of these figures with the nymphs — cannot save the poet. Nature is neutral: it is not positively malignant, but neither is it beneficent. The only answer that can suffice to justify "the homely slighted Shepherds trade" is an answer that does not fall properly to the rural deities at all. It has had to come from the lips of Apollo, and it has had to consist of an affirmation of value that transcends this world.[7]

The pastoral mode, restored so briefly, is, of course, soon broken again — this time, more decisively, by a voice that transcends not only those of the deities of stream and field, but those of the whole classic order. But Milton attempts to bring St. Peter on the scene in accordance with the forms of the occasion. The "Oat proceeds," as

---

[7] Even Phoebus's words, to speak very strictly, do not really "suffice." This is perfectly apparent from the mere fact that the elegy continues from this point. And one insufficiency of the pronouncement is immediately clear, that which is remedied by St. Peter. But something still more complex is involved in the allusion to the traditional conflict of Apollo and Pan implied in the words, "and touched my trembling ears." (Pan with his flute and Apollo with his lyre were fabled to have engaged in a musical contest in which Apollo was the victor. But Midas dissented from the decision, preferring the music of Pan, and Apollo turned his ears into ass's ears as a sign of his inferior taste.) In the passage of *The Shepherd's Calendar* ("June," ll. 65 ff.) in which Spenser makes a similar allusion the influence of the Muses is dissociated entirely from the pastoral. The Muses are allied with Apollo in *disdaining* the inferior mode of the pastoral. It is important to note that Milton does *not* so dissociate them. In "Lycidas," the pastoral is true poetry, and its guardians, effectual or ineffectual, are ultimately the same as those of the higher modes of the classical tradition. It is precisely the failure of Apollo here that he speaks from his conventional attitude of *disdain* for the "earth" of the pastoral, its earthly values and earthly concerns. Something different, therefore, is required to satisfy the elegist, an affirmation which transcends but does not disdain the natural world — such consolation in short as that presented in the figure of Christ Himself, heroic and yet pastoral, the divine shepherd. We may see Milton, in his resolution of this problem, exploring again that favorite theme — the relation of heroic and pastoral ideals, and the paradox of the pastoral-heroic — and finding, as usual, the solution of the difficulties of the pagan tradition in the truth of Christian revelation. For further discussion of these questions, see the chapter on Marvell's "The Coronet," in this volume; and, in *Poems of Mr. John Milton* (Brooks and Hardy), the final essay, "The Progress and Form of the Early Career."

it must, since the conventions required by the pastoral form of the poem cannot be abandoned. Neptune has called up Æolus to make his report. Next comes Camus, attired as a river god, "His Mantle hairy, and his Bonnet sedge." (Whether he comes also in answer to "Neptune's plea" is left ambiguous. Presumably he does not, but he is presented as a river god just as St. Peter is introduced as the "Pilot of the *Galilean* lake.")

Yet, though Milton has thus accommodated the Christian figure to the classical procession, he does not attempt to conceal his Christian character. St. Peter's locks are "mitred"; he carries his keys. Moreover, if the University under the guise of Camus utters a plaint which can easily be called a conventional pastoral lament, St. Peter emphatically does not. He is talking about "pastors," it is true, but not the *pastores* of Virgil.

By Dr. Johnson's time, the two meanings of *pastor* had, for a serious mind, become so far divorced that Johnson must have thought Milton was taking advantage of a connection as frivolous as that which joins the discrepant meanings in a pun. But we must try to avoid prejudging what Milton is doing. Milton's age felt, and Milton himself felt, that the classic ages and Christianity could be united — that classic thought foreshadowed what Christianity had revealed, and that the men of the Renaissance were the heirs of both traditions, as indeed they were.

Actually, we beg the question if we assume that St. Peter can *a priori* have nothing to do with the pastoral tradition. He qualifies it, to be sure, by his very presence. And Milton, as lines 132-33 indicate, expects us to feel a shock. (Milton is simply more keenly aware of the implications — for both the conflict and the larger synthesis — of what he is doing than were his pastoral predecessors who introduced references to the corrupted clergy. The evidence, again of lines 132-33 especially, is that he is one step ahead of Johnson in awareness of the "pun.") But what St. Peter does is to bring in a note not so much completely alien as realistic. The shepherd's life, he reminds us, is not merely one of singing and meditating the muse, though he mentions singing. After all, there are the sheep to be fed and protected. It is a life of some difficulties and dangers: it requires knowledge and diligence. There are worthless shepherds who have their pipes too, oaten pipes like those on which Lycidas played and on which the protagonist now plays, but in St. Peter's angry description they are called "scrannel Pipes of wretched straw."

The worthless shepherds are "blind mouthes"; and the boldness of Milton's metaphor has caused some comment. How can a mouth be blind! Everything that is not specifically an eye is blind, and this is so obvious that some critics have wondered why Milton felt it necessary to imply the eye at all. Yet, even on the literal level, the yawning mouth resembles an eye, a monstrous sightless eye. And when we remember the shepherd's function (much more when we remember the Christian shepherd's function), the shepherds whose watchfulness has become simply a gluttonous and selfish desire are rightly "blind mouthes." Incidentally, the figure is balanced by an equally bold one which occurs a few lines below, but which has not excited critical comment. The poet asks the valleys to throw hither "all your quaint enameld eyes,/ That on the green terf suck the honied showres." The "blind mouthes" are thus balanced by "sucking eyes." We shall not claim that Milton has consciously worked out the contrast: such a claim would be difficult to prove. But the patterning, whether it has been arrived at consciously or unconsciously, by design or by chance, confronts us in the poem. And the reader does not have to dismiss either passage as a mere strained conceit. The poet seems to be saying that even the flowers, nature's nurslings, which one expects to do nothing more than "suck the honied showres," by contrast with the worthless shepherds who have failed in the responsibilities of their high office, have the kind of spiritual life and awareness we attribute to a seeing eye.

But to argue this is to anticipate, and we must say a final word on St. Peter's speech before taking up the function of the flower passage. St. Peter, as we have said, brings in a grim and realistic note. Lycidas was a good shepherd in a world in which there are too many bad shepherds. But though the speech as a whole praises Lycidas, in terms of the larger theme it makes his death even more meaningless. The good shepherd has been taken; the wicked remain. And even the warning to the wicked shepherds hardly helps Lycidas's case or that of those who mourn for him. Thus, if St. Peter's speech, like Apollo's, transcends the pastoral mode, it carries us away from the hope that Apollo's words had suggested. For the speech, taken literally, indicates that Lycidas was needed and should have lived: many others could better have been taken. The theme has moved simply from Apollo's hint of individual reward to that of general retribution.

The poet recognizes the disruption the speech has brought. He tries once more to establish the pastoral mood. Just as he invokes the "Fountain *Arethuse*" after the Apollo speech, in line 132, he here invokes the river Alpheus.

> *Return* Alpheus, *the dread voice is past,*
> *That shrunk thy streams . . .*

The dread voice has been endowed with something of the effect of blazing light — a hot sun inimical to the cool shadows of mythology and the flowers of pastoral poetry. The voice has shrunk the pastoral stream. In trying to re-establish the conventional mood, the poet attempts to conjure up a cool scene of secluded beauty —

> *Of shades and wanton winds, and gushing brooks,*
> *On whose fresh lap the swart Star sparely looks.*

He lavishes upon it all the resources of floral decoration. It is almost as if the poet said: Very well. I admit that with the intrusion of St. Peter, I have deserted the pastoral. But I'll try to make it up. I'll pick up all your scattered flowers — even the pathetic fallacies.

The flower passage is beautiful, granted. But we mistake its function in the poem if we think that it is merely to add a touch of decorative beauty. Actually, its function in the full context of the poem is ironic. The poet improvises beautifully as he attempts to recapture the pastoral spirit, but the "*Sicilian* Muse" will not return — does not return. Indeed, the poet himself gives over the attempt with lines 152-53:

> *For so to interpose a little ease,*
> *Let our frail thoughts dally with false surmise.*

With these words he cuts the ground from under the whole elaborate and beautiful structure. The flowers are not really wearing "sad embroidery" for Lycidas; the cups of the daffadillies are not filled with tears for him. Nature is neutral: it does not participate in grief for the dead man. And since it is a "false surmise" to assume that it does, the surmise can give no real comfort. There is, perhaps, some source of comfort yet remaining — St. Peter's speech has no more finally resolved the problem than has Apollo's — but it is not to be found in this wishful return to the conventional pastoral.

It is entirely proper, therefore, that the flower passage should be followed immediately by a realistic picture of the dead body:

> Ay me! Whilst thee the shores, and sounding Seas
> Wash far away . . .

On the literal level, of course, the very physically real absence of Lycidas, of his body, makes the "surmise" of comfort in the funeral ceremony, the strewing of flowers[8] on the bier, a "false" surmise — the "hearse" is empty. And though the absence and the falseness of comfort are, as we have seen, of a significance far larger than the merely physical and accidental, yet this literal "realism" of the passage gives it much of its strength. This is a realistic passage even in its geography — always a point to which Milton gave careful attention. Since King was drowned in the Irish sea, his bones may have been washed out through the northern passage into the Atlantic beyond "the stormy Hebrides," or perhaps through the southern channel out beyond Land's End. The poet appeals to the dolphins to "waft the haples youth" as one of them once in Greek fable carried the body of the drowned Palæmon to the shore.[9] The poet does not ask the angel Michael to lift the drowned body from the sea: his petition goes no further than to ask him to feel pity for Lycidas and his sorrowing friends:

> Look homeward Angel now, and melt with ruth.

---

8 And poems — the verse "posies" of the convention.

9 The reference, as T. O. Mabbott has shown in a note in *The Explicator*, is to Palæmon, not to Arion as most editors have interpreted it. When the poet Arion was cast overboard by the sailors, the dolphins, who loved his music, brought him safe to shore. But Lycidas, like Palæmon, is dead: There is no question of his being saved from the sea.

We would seem to be at this point at the nadir of despair. Even if we can, by looking ahead in the poem, read "homeward" as "heavenward" and see the gaze of the angel as guiding Lycidas thither, an unyielding irony remains in the very character of the spirit to whom the appeal for "ruth" is addressed — Michael the warrior prince.

The recovery begins with the next lines. With the command,

> *Weep no more, woful Shepherds weep no more*

the poet makes the first direct appeal to the Christian supernatural. With all false comforts rejected, the true hope may at last be entertained. Lycidas is not dead. The sun too sinks into the sea, only to rise again, and

> *Flames in the forehead of the morning sky,*

and this flaming is not the "sudden blaze" to be ended ignominiously by the "blind *Fury* with th' abhorred shears." Other symbols of the poem find a restatement here too. The day-star that flames in the forehead of the morning sky is after all the same sun which in the season of the "swart *star*" shrinks the pastoral stream. It is the full blaze of truth in which the poetic fancies seem to shrivel. In this final passage, however, it is not a sultry and parching light, but cool and brilliant as the morning. And even the sea participates in the resurrection image — it is the "bed" in which the sun repairs its strength for the new day's journey.

Indeed, Lycidas moves through a pastoral scene as the elegy closes, a scene where there are

> *. . . other groves, and other streams along*

which Lycidas walks, surrounded by the flock of his fellows,

> *In solemn troops, and sweet Societies.*

The Shepherds, under the Good Shepherd, have become the sheep. And since much has been made in the poem of the shepherd as poet and of the shepherd's song, the final passage is pastoral too in that the "sweet Societies"

> . . . sing, and singing in their glory move.

To sum up: the scene is pastoral in that the world of competition and distraction is done away with. It is "simple" in that it is quiet, peaceful, undisturbed, harmonious. But there is the suggestion — if we have attended the earlier sections of the poem — that only here can the true pastoral life exist; only here do the sheep feed perpetually by the still waters in an ideal and beautiful shepherd's world. This is the world which the ancient, pagan pastorals faintly adumbrate. The synthesis which is finally accomplished in "Lycidas" is a typically baroque mingling of Christian and pagan materials: the latter are not made completely false — they remain true insofar as they suggest the final truth of Christian revelation.

But Milton is unwilling to end the poem on just this note. And there follows, consequently, the curious last paragraph of eight lines. There is no third-person section at the beginning of the poem in which the "uncouth Swain" is introduced, and to which this last section recurs. The poem begins with the uncouth swain speaking. It is something of a surprise, therefore, to have this asymmetrical bit at the end.

The anomalous ending has been pointed out before, but we do not believe that its function has ever been adequately commented upon. Actually, it has a most important function: its effect is to throw the whole poem back into perspective. After all, the poem is the utterance of an "uncouth Swain," an unknown poet, and perhaps an awkward and unpolished one. His thought is "eager" — ambitious, ardent, even enthusiastic, it is suggested — but the instrument is rustic, and the mode is the countrified and old-fashioned Doric, the limitations of which the poet has been defining throughout the performance. If the "uncouth Swain" who speaks up to this point is carried away by his own utterance, Milton is not. He has not submerged his total personality as a poet in the character of the "Swain."

The last bit of natural description participates in the general qualification. Only a few lines earlier, the day-star, rising out of the sea, tricking "his beams . . . with new-spangled Ore," had become the sign of Lycidas's own resurrection. But now, as the Swain prepares to leave, it has

> *. . . dropt into the Western bay*

and is, along with the bones of the drowned poet,

> *Sunk . . . beneath the watry floar.*

The effect is not to deny the radiant vision of promise with which the elegy concludes, but only to place it definitely in that perspective which must be an essential part of its truth. Actually it is a perspective of realism, as we have already seen if we have read carefully, but here it is defined precisely and finally. We are simply *reminded* that the vision is one of hope, not yet fulfilled, that the elegy has been composed and delivered in a real world in which suns rise and set, day follows day, the flood remains perilous to all those whom Lycidas has left behind, and the young shepherd has to bethink himself of the duties of the new day. It is realism, but not a narrowing realism —"To morrow to fresh Woods, and Pastures new."

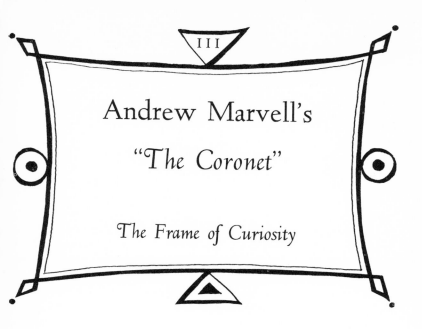

Andrew Marvell's "The Coronet"

The Frame of Curiosity

When for the thorns with which I long, too long,
    With many a piercing wound,
    My Saviour's head have crown'd,
I seek with Garlands to redress that wrong;
    Through every Garden, every Mead,   5
I gather flow'rs (my fruits are only flow'rs),
    Dismantling all the fragrant Towers
That once adorned my Shepherdesse's head:
And now, when I have summ'd up all my store,
    Thinking (so I my self deceive)
    So rich a Chaplet thence to weave   10
As never yet the King of Glory wore,
    Alas! I find the Serpent old,
    That, twining in his speckl'd breast
    About the flowers disguis'd, does fold,
    With wreaths of Fame and Interest.   15
Ah, foolish Man, that would'st debase with them
And mortal Glory, Heaven's Diadem!
But Thou who only could'st the Serpent tame,
    Either his slipp'ry knots at once untie,
    And disintangle all his winding snare;   20

> *Or shatter too with him my curious frame,*
> *And let these wither — so that he may die —*
> *Though set with Skill, and chosen out with Care;*
> *That they, while Thou on both their spoils dost tread,*
> *May crown thy Feet, that could not crown thy Head.*   25

This short poem of Andrew Marvell's has much thematically in common with "Lycidas," the work of his great contemporary Milton. It is in many respects, other than its length, a smaller poem than "Lycidas." And yet, in some sense by virtue of its very compactness, it finally achieves on at least one theme a largeness of implication that is denied to the longer poem. But it will be best to leave until the end of the essay any attempt explicitly to define that theme.

Marvell expresses here the basic paradox of all religious poetry, that the honor paid to God by the mortal poet, the "crown," or "garland," of the poem which celebrates Him, can never add anything to His immortal glory. Indeed, the love of Him enjoining first of all humility, the more carefully the poet works at constructing his tribute, the more "pride" he takes in his work, the more must it seem worthless to adorn Christ. Thus, in the final resolution of his conceit, Marvell pictures the flowers — the beauties of poetic expression — with which he had first intended to crown the Saviour's head, as worthy now only to be crushed under His feet.

But the "frame" of line 22, at least in one respect, is the poem itself — with its winding together of various images, various rhetorical and rhythmic effects, upon the one central theme, like so many flowers in the banded circle of a garland. It is a "curious" frame, in that it is intricately, cunningly wrought, and also, as its composition is a species of inquiry, in that it embodies intellectual "curiosity," about which there is inevitably a sense of overweening pride, when the object of the inquiry is as here a religious mystery. And, in order that the poet's final humility, his offering the frame to be "shattered," may be really effective — since the greater the apparent reason for pride the greater is humility's virtue — we must examine the structure of the poem to see just *how* curiously it is contrived.

The poet symbolizes his own sins, his offense against Christ, as adding more "thorns" to that crown which was put upon His head before the crucifixion — His acceptance of that original mockery, of course, having signified His assumption of the guilt of mankind.

Marvell proposes now to replace the thorns, at least the ones that he has contributed, with flowers. He would make up for, "redress" the wrong he has done to Christ, with a tribute of poetic praise. But we have to go no further than this before encountering the first "curious" construction — the ambiguity of the word "redress."

Its primary meaning — or what, so to speak, the poet first intends or hopes it should mean — is as we have observed "to make up for," offset, the wrong of his sins. But the *wrong*, "*that* wrong," is, in the metaphoric context, either the thorns themselves, or the wounds they make. And in this connection, "*redress*" carries suggestions of more literal significance. Again hopefully, the poet may seem to propose that the wounds will be "dressed" with the flowers, bandaged, with a view to healing them. But on the other hand, perhaps the garlands will only re-dress the thorns, in the sense of covering them up, to conceal and disguise their still remaining hurtfulness. In a sense, the garlands themselves threaten to become a kind of thorns, a further offense against Christ — of presumption.

And if we examine closely, we can see, well before his dismay is embodied in the image of the discovery of the serpent, the grounds for the poet's misgivings. In the passage (lines 5 through 8) that describes his going out to gather the materials for his handiwork, we begin to suspect how the garland might be taken as an insult to Christ. He says, parenthetically, "(my fruits are only flow'rs)"; and, recalling as it does the symbolism of Christ's parables, His warning of what happens to those who are barren branches of the mystical Vine, who do not "bear fruit," this phrase betrays a latent anxiety, a fear that the gift is necessarily unworthy. But, through line 7, it would seem that the flowers, although they are "*only* flowers," will at least be fresh ones. He seeks them in the "garden," and the "mead." And, the sense of this clause being grammatically complete before the "that . . ." modifier of line 8, the "fragrant Towers" could be taken simply as a striking, visual image of tall, flowering plants which he "dismantles," strips of their covering, in the sense of picking the blossoms off them. Indeed, the phrase, "that once adorn'd my Shepherdesse's head" could be interpreted as only continuing this meaning — the "towers," the plants, 'once furnished adornment (flowers), for my Shepherdesse's head.'

But then, if we learn that "tower" had in the 17th century the specific meaning of a kind of high, elaborate headdress for women, constructed sometimes of wire and pasteboard heavily covered with flowers, we realize that the "Towers" here must be, not living plants, but just this flowered millinery. The "garden," after all, is only the dusty properties room of pastoral poetry. The poet is proposing to "honor" Christ with a garland made up of whatever faded blossoms he can salvage from the discarded costumes of some Phyllis or Chloe whose wardrobe he has formerly furnished.

The proposal is an insult, not because the poetic convention represented by this frumpery derives from the pagan, classical tradition. The practice of merging Christian and classical themes is well established by Marvell's time, and often serves as a way distinctly of glorifying the Christian figures, with Christ Himself becoming, for example, a kind of superior Hercules, whom the classical hero only dimly foreshadows. Nor is it, unqualifiedly, insulting that the particular, derivative mode here should be the pastoral, which from the first was regarded by the classical writers as an inferior mode. For, regardless of this ancient opinion, the pastoral is inevitably a major Christian mode, from the clear dictate of Biblical usage. From *Genesis* on into the New Testament, the basic metaphorical materials, of fruits and flowers, the serpent, for that matter, among the flowers, the teacher as shepherd, with Christ Himself pre-eminent in that role, simply are as much the properties of the basic Hebrew-Christian writings as they are of Virgil and his Greek predecessors. Moreover, the Biblical writings may be taken (as they are by Milton, for example) essentially to dignify, on their own independent authority, the pastoral mode, and, combining it as they do with an heroic mode, ultimately to disqualify the harsh judgment that was imposed upon Midas and to reconcile, again pre-eminently in the figure of Christ, the conflicting claims of Pan and Apollo. This attitude once established, its grace can be secondarily extended to the classical pastoralists themselves, somewhat to redeem their apparent follies.

But the trouble with Marvell's usage here, at least temporarily, is that no such attitude, whereby the dignity of the classical mode is *dependent* upon the grace of Christ, has been established. At the moment, he is not saying in effect that some things in the classical tradition of pastoral faintly foreshadow the Christian truth, but rather that there is something about the Christian which, as it were, reminds him of the classical. Or, actually, it is not even classical, except in the most remotely derivative sense. This garden-party

Shepherdess with her fantastic headdress represents the all too modern, now merely non-Christian and faddish pastoral, in no sense genuinely mythic, at the stage of its final decadence. And to trick Christ out, not even as a secondhand Pan, not even as male, but in ornaments borrowed from the finery of this recherché bawd, is indeed the crowning insult.

But we have already observed that this is only a momentary effect. The assumption of the mask of pastoral decadence is only a part of the larger, dramatic design of the poem. The very ingenuity of the design — the compressed richness of this particular passage in itself, as well as the way it is integrated in the poem as a whole, just the degree of the poet's *awareness* of the shameful decline of the pastoral — redeems to a great extent the tawdriness of that to which he alludes. The faded flowers are, after all, freshened and revived in the replanting.

To the extent that the parenthesis "(my fruits are only flow'rs)" is an expression of modesty, like that of the "forc'd fingers rude" passage in Milton's "Lycidas," it is an apology only for the immaturity of this and the poet's former work, which has so far produced only blossoms and not yet anything more substantial, any fruit. Good or bad — and there is no implication that he does consider them, as flowers go, in any way inferior — they are finally at least *his* flowers, although taken from the convention yet growing anew in the ground of the poem's own context. And if the apology does, for a moment, seem to extend to the whole flower-kind of poetry, the pastoral — an identification which, in fact, it would be difficult to make, since the "fruit" is pastoral too — it can be only for a moment, in view of the status which the mode has in the Christian tradition.

In other words, what the poet ultimately fears, in his anxiety about fashioning a proper tribute to Christ, is not that there is anything wrong with gathering one's materials from garden or mead, nor yet that he has, in a sense, left the garden altogether now and is picking his flowers off old costumes. Even these did at first come from the garden, and as we have seen can be revived. Rather, what he fears is that the whole world of poetry, of all modes, is a ruined garden. Or is it not, indeed, the whole world, not simply of poetry but of man's work in general? Marvell does not suggest that the poet, in his special offices, offends Christ, but that he does so as spokesman for all men. In line 17, it is not "Ah, foolish Poet," but "Ah, foolish Man." It is still here, in the midst of this garden — ultimately, the world as one great, spoiled Eden — still in the pastoral scene, and making a battleground *of* the garden, that Marvell finally shows us Christ in a version of that traditional characterization which I have mentioned, as a superior Hercules — in His heroic role, subduing the serpent.

Marvell, then, is sufficiently proud of his own role as poet, and of his performance in the part. To pick up the argument now in the third section (lines 9 through 16), it is clear that the "sum" of his "store" is considerable. All this that he has set aside and now sorts and counts up, to see with what he may weave the chaplet — the total of all his knowledge of poetic conventions, and of Biblical lore, his skill in forming images, and intricate conceits out of the various meanings of words, everything that he has gathered from other sources and also built out of his own imagination — he values highly. The word "store" itself, in addition to the other meanings, has an evaluative sense. He will weave a "rich" fabric with it. His thinking that the chaplet will be, however rich, the finest that Christ ever had — such "as never yet the King of Glory wore" — is, of course, a delusion; "(so I my self deceive)." And his calling Christ "King of Glory" incidentally enforces the ironic disparagement of the chaplet's beauty also in a visual way. A "glory" is a nimbus, or halo; the projected light of Christ's own grace, such is the implication, provides for Him the perfect "chaplet," or crown, which the poet's can only obscure. But that the construction of the tribute can advance Marvell's own "Fame and Interest" as an artist, there is no doubt.

For, if he were convinced from the start that his work was merely trifling, if he had not so high an opinion of his prowess, and hence some real hope of making his reputation and fortune, then the problem which is the theme of the poem could not exist; there would be no serpent among the flowers. His pride *is* the serpent. The serpent's coils, in line 16, are precisely "wreaths of Fame and Interest."

And yet it is "the Serpent old" that he discovers. The problem as such, of man's noblest enterprise being mocked and betrayed by his pride in it, of his finding the aspiration to do the work apparently hopelessly entangled with the temptation to turn it to his personal glory and advantage, is not a problem that Marvell is the first to face. It is as old as man himself. Further, the serpent is "old," of course, in being identified with that one, Satan, who tempted Eve — which is just another way of stating what I have said about the antiquity of the problem itself that he represents, but which does define it as a more specifically religious problem, as that of the *sin* of intellectual pride.

And it is in this sense of the extreme age, the universality of it, that we with Marvell at once detect the true dimensions of his theme, the "problem" of it, and first catch sight of a possible way out. In the first place, merely the recognition that the danger is not entirely to oneself, but is shared with all men, is in itself humbling, and so begins to defeat pride. And further, in the specifically religious context, one is reminded by the age of the serpent as identifying him with Satan, the original tempter, that he is therefore the adversary of Christ, whose redemption is also universal. "As old as man himself," we have said; but Satan is even older than that. Just by identifying his own sin with original, universal sin, as he is implicitly doing here, Marvell has started already to shift the burden of it to Christ, to Him "who only could'st the Serpent tame."

But before we leave this third section of the poem, the point I have been trying to make — that the dismay of the "Alas!" is not despair, that almost from the very moment of this exclamation, when he discovers the serpent among the flowers and shrinks back from his work, the poet is beginning to see the way out of his self-deception — is a point which can be reinforced by consideration of the imagery of these lines. The image of the snake coiled hidden among the flowers, who is "twining," insinuating, his breast both "in" and at the same time, his "breast" being of course the whole under-length of his sinuous body, "about" the "flowers disguised" — the imitative cunning of the lines' movement is secured principally in the use of the verbals and prepositions — is a figure that picks up again the motif of masking, concealment, which we saw briefly stated in the implications of the word "redress" in the fourth line. Further, although the snake's breast is "speckled" in the sense of its representing sinfulness, the condition of being spotted, maculate — 'not-innocent,' ' touched' — there is also here a literal representation of the protective coloring which enables him so easily to merge his "wreaths" with the wreathed blossoms. Not only is it hard to distinguish his twisted shape from that of the thickly braided garland itself, but his mottled skin closely resembles the parti-colored petals of the flowers among which he hides. And yet, the point is that despite all the ingenuity of his "disguise" (the syntax of the lines permits "disguis'd" to be taken as modifying both "flowers" and "breast"), the serpent has now been "found" — "Alas! I find the Serpent old." If the disguise has not been quite penetrated, cannot be immediately stripped away, at least it has been recognized *as* a disguise. What was only a possible implication in the ambiguities of the word "redress," a sense of misgiving in the apologetic tone of the second section, where the poet is gathering his flowers, is now beyond question. Now he knows that the serpent is there; he has seen him. And once the problem has been recognized, the repressed anxiety openly admitted, the weight of sin consciously felt, he has already begun to relieve his perplexity.

Thus, there is a certain calmness of disillusionment about the quieter exclamation that opens the final section of the poem. The "Ah" expresses now a kind of sadly chastened *acceptance*, of the truth which in the first shock of discovery had provoked the dismayed "Alas!." And after, in these two lines — "Ah, foolish Man, that would'st debase with them/ And mortal glory, Heaven's Diadem!" — making full admission of the folly of his efforts, the poet proceeds without further hesitation through firmly balanced verses to the end, wholly resigning to the discretion of Christ's will the question of what is to be done about the serpent. But if there is no continuation of the mood of perplexity — the tone, reflecting the emotional attitude of the speaker, remains fairly constant, or at any rate is steadily intensified toward the climactic resignation, with no more uncertain shiftings — still there are in the statement many curious involvements, of diction, syntax, and imagery, which we shall have to explore more fully.

"Diadem" here is the last of a series of words, beginning with "coronet" in the title, which Marvell has used in referring to ornaments for the head, and which in their variety express something of the essential irony of his attitude in the poem. Now, the nearest referent for "them," in the preceding line, is "wreaths of Fame and Interest," or just "Fame and Interest"; but these being, as we have seen, inextricable from the other elements of the work, "them" must refer also to the "flowers." It is the entire structure — the interwoven wreaths, of flowers, *and* of Fame and Interest — that would "debase" the "Diadem." And it is, in this connection, easy enough to see one significance of the fact that all the words used specifically for the ornament which the poet would present to Christ — *coronet*, or "little crown," *garland, chaplet* — carry a sense of the diminutive, of something light and insubstantial. By comparison to the great crown, the Diadem of the eternal kingdom (the word "diadem" is normally reserved for the emblem of absolute sovereignty), anything made of corruptible, earthly substances is of small value and significance. It is, therefore, quite appropriate that the crown composed of the ephemeral flowers, even before the serpent is found among them, should be named as it is — and foolish, indeed, that the poet should ever have thought it could in any way please or honor Christ to have this flimsy contrivance as it were flung over the crown of His own glory, only to obscure that radiance.

And yet, while all along using the diminutive to name it, he *has* for a time thought it might be acceptable. And, curiously enough, the very smallness of the thing might be seen as the quality that seemed so to recommend it. For, what is merely the *biggest* piece of headgear mentioned in the poem is the "Tower" of the Shepherdesse's costume, the very outlandish size of which is the principal mark of decadence in the usages the Shepherdesse represents, the gross and corrupted elegance which it is offensive to have associated in any way with the poet's purpose of expressing his love of Christ. Thus, although as we have seen he is not able finally to purge his work entirely of the taint of decay that the borrowed flowers bear, yet the poet's tearing down the "Towers,"[1] and making the smaller, less pretentious chaplet from the remnants, tends as far as it goes in the proper direction of compliment to Christ.

That is, the use of the flowers in this way has, first, a certain basic artistic honesty about it; the work does not deny the nature of the materials. The structure is not so elaborate; but it is, unlike the "Tower" with its hidden framework of wire and pasteboard, self-supporting. Further, the chaplet does, in its comparative weightlessness and fragility, actually in a way imitate the "Diadem." For, of course, the value of the sovereign crown is not in its superior size or heaviness, but in what it signifies — precisely, the sovereignty. And

---

[1] Perhaps it is not too curious to see Marvell's Shepherdesse as a mock-heroic version of "towered Cybele," the goddess of cities and fortifications, who is commonly represented in art with the attribute of an immense head-dress designed to show the character of her patronage. "Dismantling" would reinforce this literal reading of "towers." And the usage would serve ironically to justify the true heroic mode of the final section.

the point can be put in still another way. We might at first think of the "diadem" as being a large, heavy crown of gold, made of enduring metal as opposed to the fragile substance of the flowers — having that genuine magnificence of which the exaggerated artificiality of the "Towers" is a mockery — and perhaps see in "debase" an implicit metaphor of the *debasement* of metals. Actually, however, "diadem" will support a quite different interpretation. The word has the literal meaning of something "bound over, or around," the head. It originally referred to the kind of simple crown, a headband, or fillet, that was so worn, rather than to the larger, more hatlike contrivances that sit upon and cover the top of the head. Its shape and size, then, and the manner in which the original "diadem" is worn, make it in fact very similar to the garland. Moreover, the first "diadems" were not made of metal, but of cloth.

What the usage finally tends to suggest, is that to represent the majesty of Christ, that most assured sovereignty, what one needs is the nearest thing to no crown at all. Recalling the previous reference to Christ as "King of Glory," and the significance of the word "glory" as "halo," we see "Heaven's Diadem," if it can be visually represented at all, just as this weightless radiance of inner sanctity. And in the way of "mortal Glory," the near-weightless crown of "flowers," the wreath of poetic praise, wreath of words, becomes the closest imitation of that circle of pure light.

Of course, the poet as "Man" is "foolish." But his foolishness is that of an over-subtle intelligence, overly fond of its own ingenuity; it is not simplemindedness. He knows, from the start, enough about the nature of Christ, and of man's proper relationship to Him, to realize that any conceivably acceptable gift must have some semblance of humility about it. What we have called the "basic artistic honesty" of his reducing the "Towers" to a "chaplet" is that initial semblance of humility; and in a measure, the measure of man's capacity for truth, which is the measure of his ability to own his foolishness, it is a semblance that holds good, or rather is restored and renewed, even in the light of this comparison to "Heaven's Diadem."

For the poet's error, after all, has been just his forgetting, in his fascination with the work itself, that it *is* a semblance that he constructs, an image. And once he has corrected this error, remembered that the crown of thorns has long since, without the need of his assistance, been replaced by the heavenly glory, to which divine original he can merely compare his tribute — once he has, to put the matter another way, simply recalled the nature of humility, that it is a disposition of the mind *toward* something, or someone, and so must seek its perfection outside itself — then he has already to a great extent recovered that humility. He has, just in recognizing that the poem cannot *take the place* of "Heaven's Diadem," or alloy that purity with its unpurged grossness, realized for the first time how closely it can, in fact, *imitate* that glory.

Thus humbled, the poet aspires then no longer to any closer view of Heaven itself, but instead urgently implores Christ as it were to come down again to his assistance. Since the serpent Satan appears here as "Fame and Interest," as pride, Christ is his supreme enemy, the one "who only could'st the Serpent tame," primarily by virtue of His perfect humility. In His grace, His own entire freedom from the motives of "Fame and Interest," He is the only one who can see through and follow up to untie them the intricate and ever-changing convolutions of the writhing serpent without risk of involving Himself, and being caught in their "winding snare." The knots, it should be observed, are "slipp'ry knots," constantly altering their position and configuration, rather than remaining hard and fast so as to make them easier to release. The poet, with the power of mere words, themselves "slipp'ry," unstable, their meaning changing always with time and syntax, can never wholly extricate the pure design, the pure formal intention, of his garland from the toils of his confused motives; but Christ, who is the Word, could if He so willed it "at once" set all aright.

But having once presumed upon his own strength, and seen his error in that, the poet is careful now not to presume still more foolishly upon God's grace. Christ could, *if* it were His will, disintangle the serpent, and leave the garland of flowers intact; but there can be no attempt to dictate His choice. As the final test of his humility, the poet must admit, and accept without complaint, the possibility that He will elect to destroy both garland and serpent together.

In other words, Marvell admits the possibility that man is utterly incapable of "framing" a pure intention of praise, that all his words, no matter with what care "chosen out" and with what skill "set" in context, are basically corrupt, from the corruption of his intelligence itself. In the complex system of reference among the pronouns — "these" in line 23 referring indefinitely to the flowers that make up the "frame" in the preceding line, but also serving as the antecedent of "they" in line 25, which in the possessive "their" obviously becomes inclusive of the serpent ("he" in the second half of line 23) as well as the flowers, so that ultimately "these" must refer back to "them" in line 17, which as we have noted primarily means the "wreaths" of "Fame and Interest," of the serpent — he suggests that the "frame" of the poem's formal statement of intention and the "serpent," prideful motives, have become almost entirely, almost "substantially," indistinguishable. It seems to me, further, that "my curious frame" clearly means not only the form of the poem but the form of his, man's, own being. It is the order or condition in which man's own parts physical and spiritual are joined in this life ("this mortal frame"), that image of Himself which God has made, and which Satan and man himself together have corrupted. Thus, the basic impurity of man's work, the poem, is implicitly attributed to the impurity of man's fallen nature, which would itself have to be changed if the work is to be purged and the wreaths of the serpent distinguished and separated from the wreath of flowers. So long as man remains what he is, corrupt and corruptible, destined for destruction, it cannot be otherwise with his work.

To the eye of God, of course, the serpent and the flowers are distinguishable. Christ, as we have observed, *could* untie them. He can, and it is promised that He will, redeem man's nature. But — if Marvell does not here dictate Christ's choice, between untying the knots at once ("at once" meaning both "all together" and "without delay") or crushing serpent and "frame" together, if in fact he does not demand anything, but only pleads that either be done — still, there is a distinct suggestion that the latter alternative is the more likely. The final redemption, according to the traditional interpretation of the promise, can come only after man in his present nature has suffered much pain of mind and body, and finally death.

And yet, is not the matter of ultimate importance just that the redemption is promised, and will be, whether soon or late? If as I see it "my curious frame" does mean both poem and man, Marvell is saying that he accepts the destruction of his work exactly on the same terms that, as a Christian, he accepts the necessity for his own death. And this is a considerable qualification of what might seem at first sight mere abandonment of the poem's purpose.

Christ's conflict with "the Serpent old" is prior even to the cause of man's salvation; the poet implicitly recognizes and accepts this. But what man purchases with his death in Christ, in willing submission to the exigencies of His mortal combat with Satan, is the renewal and perfection of life. And if man and his work are indeed inseparable, then the work shares in this compact, is also assured of immortality. As man images forth the mind of God, and in Christ's redemption is restored to perfect semblance of his original, so too the poem, that images man's mind, is perfected.

The poem seeks its own destruction. The image of His "shattering" the frame, and "treading" upon the "spoils"[2] of the mingled wreaths, of the dead serpent and the withered flowers — the tone here contrasting strongly with that of the opening sections, where the poet goes out in eager delight to gather his flowers — presents Christ in his role of martial hero. The garden, as we have put the matter before, is turned into a battlefield. In this connection, the implicit reference in the metaphor of the ruined wreaths' becoming a kind of "crown" for His feet, is to the practice of dressing the victorious warrior in the spoils, parts of the captured armour, of his fallen enemy. But the self-destruction, the "suicide," of the poem is that of martyrdom. It is as if the garland of flowers were used to *hold* the serpent for the blow of Christ's heel — "And let these wither/ So *that* he may die." The humility is more, after all, than mere submission to the cause of Christ's justice. It is active coöperation with that cause. The poem shares actively in the glory of the triumph over itself.

And if there is a tendency here to contradict what we observed earlier about the complex reference of the pronouns, if even to make such a distinction between the active and passive involvement of the flowers and the serpent in furnishing the sign of Christ's triumph is not quite possible — the two remaining grammatically still inseparable, the corruption of the image, the poem, remaining still unredeemed at the end — yet, it must be remembered that this entire passage is only a vision, of Christ's *final* triumph over Satan. What Marvell is suggesting, in a sense, is precisely that nothing in the complex problem of man's relationship to his work is resolved yet, nor can be, until that of his relationship to God is settled. And this gives

---

[2] There is, perhaps, some reference here to the "spoiling" (rotting, withering) of vegetable matter, appropriate to the flower imagery. But NED does not, in fact, give an instance of the use of the word, even as a verb, in this sense, before the end of the 17th century.

the poem (I think we have already sufficiently established the fact that Marvell considers this particular poem as worthy as any) claim at least to temporal "immortality." Although imperfect, it will last as long as man lasts, in the state of *his* imperfection.

Or, to come now at last to what is perhaps the central structural irony, this whole poem is in a way only a projection of intentions. The "chaplet" which the poet was *"thinking . . .* to weave" before he discovered the serpent among the flowers, seems never really to have been completed. The rest of the poem, beyond this point, becomes a kind of consideration of what *would* be the state of affairs ("Ah, foolish Man, that *would'st* debase with them . . ."), *if* such a project were attempted to completion. The poem has never actually committed itself to be judged as anything more than a statement, a declaration and rather hasty retraction, of ambitious intent. We can, therefore, make a distinction between this poem, finally, and that other, the "garland," "chaplet," etc., which so to speak it "imagines."

And in these terms — the terms of this poem's *imagery* — with the destruction of the chaplet's "frame," its being shattered and broken, knocked out of round and placed under Christ's feet, rather than upon His head, the frame of the poem proper is brought full circle, put into round. There is a curious suggestion, in these last lines, of an image of the uncompleted and broken garland — that "crowns," does not perhaps simply lie beneath, but again is bound over and around His feet — as a kind of snare for Christ: as if to say, that although He cannot be held by presumptions to honor Him, yet by humility, by man's admission that to add anything to the glory of which He is already possessed is impossible, He can be captured. And if the remaining entanglement of the flowers with the coils of the dead or dying serpent, as though *that* "snare" too still held His feet, makes such an interpretation of the metaphor finally intolerable — if there is no way yet perfected to catch Christ — assuredly the poem as a whole catches the reader. Its circle remains entire.

Once our interest is engaged, for whatever initial reason, there is no way out of the problems raised — as, for example, what devotion to Christ might have to do with compliments to a shepherdess — except farther in. There is no ultimately effective appeal to the history of poetic convention, or to mythography, or even to theology, as such. If an "answer" lies anywhere, not of course to how man is to know Christ, but simply to the meaning or "intent" of the poem, it is only in the total relationship between the image here, of the dismantled towers, and other images of *this* poem — or, further, between the imagery as a whole and the tonal structure, between these two together and the syntax, and so on. The critical emphasis must be, not upon what materials Marvell has used, and where he got them — out of what orders of knowledge and inquiry, what sciences, in which poet and critic both are inevitably amateurs (although the word may be taken to make them *lovers* of such studies) — but upon what he has, here, wrought with them. We bear down critically, not upon the admittedly flimsy structure of his intention to praise God, an effort in which man, whether poet or not, is always an amateur, but upon the vital structure only of his *statement* of that intention.

And yet, if this should seem after all to devalue the subject of the statement, to make it seem that the poem is merely rhetorical contrivance, I would insist finally that it *is* about man and Christ, that it has real reference to something outside itself. Perhaps the best way to put this point, of its meaningfulness, and at the same time the idea of how one finally "escapes" the poem only by going farther in, would be to pick up again the image of the "flowers."

In discussing the imagery, we have for the most part accepted it, so to speak, at face value. We *know* that there is no tangible wreath of flowers, no tangible snake among the flowers, etc. But we go along with the metaphor, and work out the details of its inner harmony, in some sense just because we know that the poet is not trying to deceive us with it.

Thus, the "flowers disguised" of line 14, as we have seen, are both disguised and disguising. Serpent and flowers disguise each other. But if we should at this point suddenly insist upon being literal-minded, and realize that the whole thing is a "disguise," that "serpent-and-flowers" as a unit must be a mask for still some other entity, we might ask what the *nearest* real referent for the imagery is. We should have to see, that it is language itself.

The matter has been mentioned, in passing, before. I have spoken of the "wreath of words," and of how words themselves are "slipp'ry," unstable, and of the corruptibility of language as reflective of the corruption of man's intelligence through sin. But language in itself is the true, central, "hidden" theme of the entire poem. It is the one, "external" frame of reference in which all elements of the metaphoric statement dependably cohere. (I should be careful to point out, in anticipation of remarks I shall make in the final chapter of this book, that I do *not* mean "poetic language." Once more, the speaker of the poem identifies himself as "Man," not "Poet.") Man's intelligence is corrupt, but we know this most specifically *as* the corruption of his language. It is when the Serpent *speaks* to Eve, speaks from the form of the dumb beast, and she answers, that the loss of innocence occurs.

It is then that man becomes "double-tongued," like the serpent, and can no longer keep clear the true distinctions between himself and God, himself and external nature (the plants and beasts), and hence can no longer truly commune with either. (Myths like that of Orpheus — see the chapter on Rilke's sonnet — express our desire to reverse this process, and to have the beasts and the trees "truly" speak to us.) There is no way in which he can express his thoughts except in speech; it is the medium in which he must frame all his intention and his "curiosity," his inquiring and communing intelligence; but it is also the curious frame that binds and represses him, that will not *let* him say ever exactly what he means. It is this fundamental duplicity of all language — not, as rational conceptualists would like to think, only "poetic language," but all language — its basic, ineradicable ambiguousness that defies all efforts at purification, which is exemplified by Marvell in the specific and deliberate ambiguities of the poem.

And it is thus, once we see it, in referring its own perplexity most immediately to the perplexity of language itself, that the little poem achieves in one sense the ultimate dimensions of poetry, and begins to break out of the frame in which it has trapped itself and us. Christ comes to the world as Logos, as the Word incarnate. Here, in admitting at last, at the very center of the "conceit" or formal preoccupation, the frailness of their own intentional order, of their contextual or syntactical frame — in willingly "falling apart," the words begin to move toward the Word, to seek that final unity which they cannot find in any of the sciences of man.

IV

Wordsworth's
"The Solitary Reaper"

A Music Within

Behold her, single in the field,
Yon solitary Highland lass!
Reaping and singing by herself;
Stop here, or gently pass!
Alone she cuts and binds the grain,
And sings a melancholy strain;
O listen! for the Vale profound
Is overflowing with the sound.

No Nightingale did ever chaunt
More welcome notes to weary bands
Of travellers in some shady haunt,
Among Arabian sands:
A voice so thrilling ne'er was heard
In spring-time from the Cuckoo-bird,
Breaking the silence of the seas
Among the farthest Hebrides.

Will no one tell me what she sings? —
Perhaps the plaintive numbers flow
For old, unhappy, far-off things,
And battles long ago:
Or is it some more humble lay,
Familiar matter of today?
Some natural sorrow, loss, or pain,
That has been, and may be again?

Whate'er the theme, the Maiden sang
As if her song could have no ending;
I saw her singing at her work,
And o'er the sickle bending: —
I listened, motionless and still;
And, as I mounted up the hill,
The music in my heart I bore,
Long after it was heard no more.

At least in so far as this is a "country" poem, written in praise of a life and art of rustic simplicity, it is a version of pastoral. But how different a pastoral from that older mode, with its cumbersome machinery of formal convention, in or against which the poems we have considered in the two preceding chapters were composed.

But, of course, with Milton and Marvell it was both "in" *and* "against." Chiefly "Lycidas," but on a smaller scale such a poem as "The Coronet" too, brought at the same time to an end what was brought to perfection. The religious realism in which these works of the 17th century resolved themselves was implicit in the pastoral tradition; but once made explicit, it shattered the conventional framework. And a concomitant of this realism was that of the poet's spiritual self-consciousness. "Or shatter too with him *my* curious frame." Or, more "professional," simply, Milton's backward look from the final verse-paragraph, skeptically doffing the modal mask. After that, there could be no further retreat to the pastoral shades, not even for Milton himself any "fresh Woods, and Pastures new" except precisely the oldest of all, and Eden a far cry from Arcady. And for the rest of English poetry, there started then the long road in the opposite direction, toward glorification of a nature, if any, completely "naturalized," toward a pastoral, if any, without benefit of nymphs, satyrs, and fauns, with none but comic fays, without deities local or general, and as often as not without even sheep and shepherds. This is not the place for a complete history of pastoral — and the plan of my selections excludes the 18th century altogether; but by the end of it, Wordsworth was asking for, and writing, a nature poetry which seemed to him totally realistic, and in which an essential part of the realism was an attitude at once acutely sympathetic and detached, observant, demanding that the poetic experience principally embody feelings appropriate to "real" experience, an attitude that we recognize as derivable, however remotely, from that of the final, third-person stanza of "Lycidas."

But, again "of course," it *was* a long road. If we see that the shift to the third-person, the "uncouth Swain," in the last stanza of "Lycidas" involved introduction of a new kind of "I" (which means "eye," observant and invisible, very couth indeed) who must be sharply distinguished from the masked "I" of the opening stanza — that one being the Swain himself — still, the self-consciousness was on Milton's part only an afterthought. The full-dress *persona*, uncouth, eager-thoughted, was still close at hand for the person to measure himself against. At most, the poem is "opened up," toward the abyss of self-awareness, only at one end. More than a hundred and fifty years later, the romantic Wordsworth's situation is much more acutely embarrassing. The same I, gross with self-awareness, awkwardly personal, grown again uncouth in its very couth-ness, is there both at the beginning and the end of the poem. The poem is open at both ends. Or, if somehow forcibly closed at the last, by the expedient of withholding actual use of "I" until then — exactly the reverse of Milton's maneuver, note — with what heart-wrenching effort; how exactly proportionate to the gain of self-awareness, the loss of self-*confidence*. Milton's postscript is much more graceful, so impersonal in its personalism, so confident of success in future performances, just because he is so sure the present *persona* has been established, the song of the "uncouth Swain" so beautifully and completely turned, brought whole, not *really* itself uncouth, "countrified" at all, except in the conventional character.

And perhaps all of this is only a way of saying that Milton had a more dependable tradition to work with, even simply a dependable

set of conventions.[1] But what I want to emphasize is the way Wordsworth tended to identify the "real" with the personal. The "universal"; yes. But the way to the universal truth was through the
intense, personal feeling of experience. In the *Lyrical Ballads*,
"humble and rustic life [pastoral] was generally chosen, because in
that condition the essential passions of the heart find a better soil . . .
and speak a plainer and more emphatic language," etc. The language
"really used by men," in which his poetry proposed to be written,
was presumably identifiable with this language of rustic passion; the
rustics, presumably, were "real men." But he liked the country (the
real country, in which he took real walks, and did not play pipes for
fauns and satyrs to dance, though he was no more a real farmer or
shepherd either than Milton himself, of course, but only did not
pretend to be) not just for this generalized, human reality it offered,
but for the opportunity of solitude. That, above all, was reality; the
chance to "present himself" to things, to store up incidents of direct,
personal, lonely experience which could then be meditated into
poetry.

   Not that he ever exactly *says* this — that the "emotion recollected
in tranquillity," which informs the poem, must in the first place
have been produced by an incident of personal experience, including
sights and sounds. At least the famous *Preface* pretty consistently

---

1 "The Solitary Reaper" itself has been much used by teachers of literature
as a kind of catalogue of so-called "Romantic Conventions" — the theme of
artless art, the admiration of life close to nature, the relative vagueness of
imagery, the personalism itself of which I have spoken, etc. But these are
not "conventions" in the same sense as the conventions of pastoral in the 17th
century. What we now think of as "conventions" in Wordsworth's poetry are
largely the category *inventions* of the literary historians, the same ones who
invented the concept of Romanticism. This is all "after the fact" of the poetry.
Such things were not conventions to Wordsworth, who of course had never
heard of such a thing as Romanticism. He was truly a revolutionary poet, trying precisely in consciousness of the *loss* of any dependable, received system of
poetic convention, anything answerable to his sense of reality, to construct for
himself a new language for poetry and a new "attitude" for the poet. When
we speak of the Pastoral Convention in the 17th century, we are referring to
something which it is obvious Milton himself really felt and thought of *as*
convention. But it is quite another thing to impose our own, belated historistic
conceptions on Wordsworth in this fashion. I shall attempt, after a bit, further
to distinguish another thing with which the pseudo-conventions invented by
modern literary historians must not be confused, and which I think really
served Wordsworth as a kind of substitute for the true conventionality of a
Milton, namely, the "occasion" of the poem.

skirts the issue, is chary of the "I." He says "I think . . .," but when he tells us *what* he thinks it is all rather warily generalized and abstract, universal. And one of the specific attributes of "the Poet" is his "disposition to be affected more than other men by absent things as if they were present, an ability of conjuring up in himself passions, which . . . resemble the passions produced by real events. . . ." But the context of this, a comparison of the poet to non-poets, obscures its relevance to the question I raise. And even if the personalism (the notion that poetry is to be produced only out of direct, personal, sensual-and-intellectual experiences — "recollection" identifiable with reminiscence) is not safely to be deduced from his critical writings, although I think it might be, in any event it haunts his poetic practice, a pervasive superstition if not a doctrine.

It is thus, indeed chiefly with Wordsworth, that the "occasion" of the poem took on so much importance, such as it had never assumed before in the history of English literature, at least for the lyric, and the ground was prepared for a whole new discipline of biographical scholarship which grew up after the Romantic movement.

Certainly, "The Solitary Reaper" has the appearance of being so "occasioned." It has the look, as much as any of Wordsworth's poems, of being based on an actual, single and intact, *incident* of his personal experience. It would be difficult to find any longer, I suppose, a critic inclined to talk about this aspect of the work as involving primarily a simple, "biographical" problem. Besides, the basic fact of the matter — that the poem does *not* recall an actual incident of Wordsworth's observation — is well known, and has been several times commented upon. So that, in going over as I shall do now the history of the poem's composition and early publication, I do not flatter myself that I invite a lively controversy. That part of the battle is won; the simple-minded biographical critics are long since driven from the field by my fellow explicationists. But what is, I think, still important, but obscured in the yet unsettled dust of our victory, is the fact that Wordsworth so plainly felt the need to make the poem *look* "real" in this way. If we had, with the text of the poem itself, only the one fact of its having been inspired by a sentence in Thomas Wilkinson's 'Tour' diary (see below), then the problem might be legitimately dismissed with such ease as Mark Van Doren, for example, uses when he takes the case to implement a distinction between poetry and prose.[2] But it would seem that Wordsworth was of somewhat hazier mind on the status of the piece, that in some sense he had himself fooled as to the relationship between its origin and its final integrity as work of art, even if he was not trying to fool anyone else.

The poem was one of a group appearing in the edition of 1807 under the title — *Poems written during a Tour in Scotland*. This same group, with some others, appeared again in the 1827 edition with the less apparently exclusive heading — *Memorials of a Tour in Scotland*.

It turns out that several of the poems even of the smaller 1807 group were not actually *written* during the Scottish tour of 1803. Wordsworth was often rather careless, when he came to the task of indicating the circumstances of his work, in his use of the terms "written" and "composed." His sister Dorothy's journal is usually more reliable, and mentions several of these poems with such an explanation as — "William wrote the following poem long afterward" (i.e., after the experience that ostensibly called it forth). And on the "Solitary Reaper," we have the evidence of a letter of Dorothy's which definitely fixes the date of composition as November 5, 1805.[3]

But the question of Wordsworth's reliability in dating his poems might seem not materially to affect the problem of their personalism. Considering his doctrine of "recollection" — and assuming, for the moment, that we can equate recollection with reminiscence — perhaps it would not matter just how long it was after the supposedly actual incident that the poem came to be written, so long as it could be shown that there *was* an actual incident. Perhaps the longer the memory the better. But, as we have already noted, there was for "The Solitary Reaper" no incident, no recollection.

Dorothy wrote, in *her* recollections of the events of September 13, 1803, "As we descended, the scene became more fertile, our way being pleasantly varied — through coppices or open fields, and passing farm houses, though always with an intermixture of cultivated ground. It was harvest-time, and the fields were quietly — might I be allowed to say pensively? — enlivened by small companies of reapers. It is not uncommon in the more lonely parts of the Highlands

---

2 Mark Van Doren, *Introduction to Poetry*, p. 51.

3 *Early Letters of William and Dorothy Wordsworth*, edited by Ernest de Selincourt. No. 232, p. 537 ff.

to see a single person so employed. The following poem [i.e., "The Solitary Reaper"] was suggested to William by a beautiful sentence in Thomas Wilkinson's 'Tour in Scotland.' "[4]

And Wordsworth, in the note he appended to the poem in the 1807 edition, "This poem was suggested by a beautiful sentence in a MS. 'Tour in Scotland,' written by a friend, the last line being taken from it *verbatim*."

The passage referred to in Wilkinson's account reads: "Passed a female who was reaping alone: she sung in Erse, as she bended over her sickle; the sweetest human voice I ever heard: her strains were tenderly melancholy, and felt delicious, long after they were heard no more."[5]

As a "source," this could hardly be clearer. At least five details of Wordsworth's poem are plainly foreshadowed in Mr. Wilkinson's quaint, if not exactly beautiful, sentence. But, for the moment, what seems to me more interesting than these details, is simply the fact that Wordsworth, as well as Dorothy, has admitted that the suggestion for the poem came, not from an actual, particular incident of the Scottish tour which these two took in the company of Coleridge in 1803, but from a sentence in another man's account of *his* tour. Dorothy, introducing the poem, speaks of groups of reapers that she and William saw, and of the fact that it is "not uncommon . . . to see a single person so employed." But she does not mention any particular girl reaping, and singing, or otherwise situated in any precise detail as the girl in the poem is.

"Admitted it," I say, but admitted it, I further say, with what at least on the poet's part, if not his sister's, is a curious diffidence. We should observe, at least, that Wordsworth himself, in the note he appended in 1807, did not think it worthwhile even to identify the "friend" whose manuscript he had read — much less to quote the sentence which had suggested the poem, and from which as he said his own last line was "taken . . . *verbatim*." And, although the question of "dating" the poem is not in itself critically important, still there is an irreducible sense of contradiction between the note on this particular piece and the group-title for the poems among which it appeared — *Poems written during a Tour in Scotland*. Nor is the later,

---

[4] *Journals of Dorothy Wordsworth*, edited by William Knight, p. 369.
[5] See the editor's notes — *Wordsworth, Poems Published in 1807*, edited by Helen Darbishire.

1827, title of much help. *Memorials of a Tour in Scotland* . . . but, we still have to ask, *whose* tour?

It is not too difficult to make out what probably happened. Wordsworth liked Wilkinson's sentence. He saw in the course of his own tour reapers enough, and perhaps some of them singly employed, to assure himself that something like Wilkinson's experience *could* occur. In short, he "read in" his particular, mental experience of Wilkinson's account upon his own, generalized, mental-and-physical experience of the ways of Highland reapers, and so produced a composite experience which becomes the poem.

And this is a perfectly legitimate procedure. It is not quite so simple a procedure as Van Doren makes it seem — "many great poems have come thus out of books." But so to insist, that it did not come just "out of the book" by Wilkinson, that the reading experience was undoubtedly combined with some concrete experience, is only to give Wordsworth more right to what I have called his "diffidence" in acknowledging the source. The total, composite experience *was* his, was it not? The poem proves it, does it not? By what right, then, do I continue to call it diffidence — that he did not provide Wilkinson's name or quote the sentence in his note, that he took the convenience of placing the poem with the others of the Scottish tour under a group-title? Has he not, in fact, leaned over backwards, in providing any note at all, to give due credit to his friend? Why can we not, now, dismiss all this pother of circumstances, and get on with reading the poem?

But I am not accusing Wordsworth of *dishonesty*. Rather, the implications of the diffidence are, if anything, evidence of his overscrupulosity. But I do insist that this, the overscrupulosity, the uneasiness of mind about the relationship of the poem to its experiential source, is an essential part of the circumstances. And I even insist that, peculiarly in Wordsworth's case, we cannot fully "read the poem" without consulting the circumstances. Here, the "circumstances" so defined, as that unease of mind, are truly a part of the poem.

We shall have, then, patience to take a few more notes. The probable procedure by which the poem was brought into being is a legitimate one, and often followed by other poets. But, if we are to take what he got from "the book" as at least the *primary* experience, it is for Wordsworth himself a highly unusual procedure. To restrict ourselves just now to the poems of the Scottish group, wherever

Dorothy and William provide an account of the origin of other pieces the situation indicated is quite different. The girl of "To a Highland Girl" is precisely identified in a charming passage of Dorothy's recollections. We are assured that another poem was suggested by the actual greeting of a Highland woman who encountered the poet and his sister as they set out on an evening walk — "What, are you stepping westward?" And so on. The notes on the occasion of "The Solitary Reaper," as we have seen, are not nearly so clear in their reference to actual events of the tour.

Now, when we realize just how "solitary" the poem of the reaper is in *this* respect, among the group — and realize it in connection with the fact that it is also far and away the *best* poem of the group — then, and only then, are we nearly prepared to start "reading the poem." (I should say, of course, that we are already reading the poem, and have been since the beginning of the chapter; but I will, in a moment, "get on with it" in what may seem to some readers the only plain sense.) I am not now about to pull a quick reversal on the popular notion of Wordsworthian "sincerity" — the idea that poems of the type of these "memorials" are dependent for their honesty of appeal, emotional conviction or whatever, upon that experiential "reality" of background of which I have spoken as the poet's superstition — and demonstrate that it is precisely the poem of "counterfeit" experience which seems most sincere. With the problem of sincerity in this sentimental sense I am not concerned. It is a pseudo-problem, largely foisted upon Wordsworth, and the other romantics, by misunderstanding readers whose opinions (so far as they are still current in print) are not worth refuting. But what I am concerned to explore is the connection between the peculiarly tentative circumstances of this poem's origin, the circumstances of what might be called its "immaculate conception," and the peculiar strength of its statement of that theme — of human solitude, and of the need of communion, of speech, song — which is the central theme of all Wordsworth's great poems, and the source strangely enough of that very superstition of the personal-as-real which the success of this work might seem to violate.

II

We are concerned, then, with the *truth* of the work, not its "sincerity." In saying that it is "open," even open-at-both-ends, as "Lycidas" for example is not, that its circumstances of composition are peculiarly a part of its meaning, as the personal circumstances of the composition of "Lycidas" (the dedication to Edward King) are not — I do not mean that the poem tends to collapse, or disappears into its background. I mean only that, to define its theme, we have at least as much critical right, or need, to know about Wilkinson's sentence as we have to know that the "scene" of the poem is the Scottish highlands. (And simply the phrase "Highland lass," *in* the poem, does not give us the latter information.)

The poem does not collapse. At the level of fictive conviction, dramatic unity, it creates a complete sense of reality. This, not "sincerity," is the purpose of certain *gestures* that the poet makes toward the reader and toward the girl of the poem.

It begins with an almost peremptory summons to the reader — as if Wordsworth had stopped him abruptly, with an arm across his chest, and facing him about, pointed his attention, with grave, long-levelled finger, to the distant scene. "Behold her . . .!" And the same little dramatic fiction, the poet's sketching out with rhetorical gestures at his side some shadowy companion, fellow-witness, with whom the reader is to identify himself, is continued throughout this stanza with repeated admonitions — "Stop here, or gently pass!"; "O listen!" — and is picked up again in the first line of the third stanza. The way the device works, is that the reader is not to think of questioning whether the scene, the incident, is real, is something that happened to the poet, because he himself is there with the poet, seeing it happen. He knows that he is there, quite simply, because the poet so confidently assumes that he is, proves it by talking to him. Indeed, since the very first phrase is an imperative, he must suppose that he was there even before a word was spoken. That first word comes whole out of silence, the silence in which only, perhaps, we are most really there, together with the poet.

It is plainly appropriate to the themes of the self-sufficiency of life close to Nature, and of "artless art," that the girl of the poem should be alone. But these, as I have suggested before, are sub-themes. It is good to walk in the country, for Wordsworth, principally for the opportunities of solitude itself.

Why does Wordsworth so *insist* upon the fact that the maiden is alone? I suggest that what he is carefully preparing for is the statement of the last stanza — the claim that he carries away with him the essence, the wordless music, of the song. For his sense of the reality of this mysterious communion, entirely unconscious on the part of the girl, is the whole value of the experience for the poet. If this should seem in any way implausible, the poem misses its climax. (For some, like Van Doren, it does miss its climax. Mr. Van Doren thinks all the rest of the poem, after the first stanza, superfluous and nearly worthless. But that is from failure to understand the paradoxical character of Wordsworth's love of solitude — the identification of solitude with communion.) And the point is simply that it would be impossible to suppose the girl *wholly* unconscious of the effect of her singing if there were any suggestion that she shared her labor with other reapers. Wordsworth, then, in emphasizing her solitude, is attending not simply to the requirements of the "praise of Nature," but to an essential dramatic, and psychological, condition of that subjective, necessarily entirely private, experience of his with which the poem concludes.

But, *"entirely* private" does not mean *"merely* private." The Wordsworthian intensification of privacy is the doorway to the universal. At the end of the first stanza, the poet invites the reader to listen, "for the *Vale profound* is *overflowing* with the sound" of the girl's song. Now, "Vale profound" is, from one point of view, simply a fancy way of saying "deep valley." But considered as furnishing one part of the image of overflow — as a receptacle for the outpouring song, and a receptacle which proves inadequate — "vale" is a good deal more than just "valley," and a "profound" vale more than simply a deep one. For *profound* is a word more often applied to mental, or emotional, or spiritual phenomena than to topographical features of landscape. And with this as an adjective, hinting strongly at something *figurative* afoot in the descriptive statement, "vale" carries suggestions of "vale of tears," "vale of sorrows" — the strain is *melancholy*, we have already been told — in short, "vale of the world, of human existence." The song pours out, mounts and spills over the rim of the Highland valley, and with the valley already becoming epitome of the world, eventually overflows in significance and beauty the bounds of all that the poet can remember (at least temporarily) of all song and its burden.

The second and third stanzas become, thus, an attempt to define more precisely — or rather, to extend or expand — the sense of the song's inherent catholicity that is introduced in the overflow metaphor of the last two lines preceding.

The device of expansion in the second stanza is simply that of far-sought comparison. The girl's singing is compared to two other, widely separated and widely famous songs. We may note that the two songs, of the nightingale and the cuckoo, belong to two fairly distinct traditions, one exotic and the other of folklore. But it should be observed that this distinction reinforces, or is reinforced by, actually is inseparable from, a pattern of balance in the stanza that can be stated also in geographical terms. Wordsworth looks first in one *direction*, toward Arabia, and then roughly in the opposite, if not so far away, toward the Hebrides. The two references have in common, of course, the theme of relief and rejuvenation which the songs bring to those who hear them, weary in the one instance from the long, hot journey through the desert and in the other from the long, frozen silence of the northern winter. But the *balance* is an essential part of the effectiveness of the two comparisons. Wordsworth has not merely gone extravagantly far afield for something comparable to the delight which the song of the girl gives him, but very far in two opposite directions, which is to say, implicitly, in all directions.

But while we are on the subject of balance, and control, it might be pointed out that the universalizing process never gets quite out of hand. A poorer poet (a Francis Mahoney, say) could well have made the mistake of comparing the reaper's song favorably to the performance of some world-famous concert artist, or the like. But Wordsworth, conscious both of the proprieties of *genre* and of the requirements of the particular situation of his poem, never forgets that what he is dealing with is unconscious art, "natural" song, never violates the principle of kind. What he does do, comparing human song to bird song, is perhaps ultimately even more outrageous than the comparison of folk-singer to concert artist would be. But it is outrage of the proper sort. It does not involve him, as the other would, in difficulties with the aesthetic sophistication which would protest that this kind of admiration of the "simple and natural" is mere vulgarity of taste, or even question him sharply whether he had not thereby made his own, conscious art in writing the poem superfluous.

To continue with stanza three — if the extension in stanza two is primarily in terms of space, in the third it is in terms of time. Having praised the song by comparison, and defined by analogy the kind of effect it has upon him, the poet then turns to question what its subject may be, and in so doing suggests that it may be something past

— "old, unhappy," etc.; or something present — "Familiar matter of today"; with the present becoming finally past and future too — "that has been, and may be again." Once more, then, he has turned in every "direction," without exhausting the possibilities of the song. The central purpose in the two stanzas is to say, and amplify the statement, that the present and immediate experience of the girl's singing contains in possibility both quality and substance of all like experience anywhere and any time. And it may be noted finally on the balance of the sections, that in each the second half brings us back very near to the present scene. The Hebrides are, to be sure, the "farthest" Hebrides, but that is not so far as Arabia; and the Cuckoo's song, and the delight it gives, suggests in every sense something "homelier" than the Nightingale's. The final phrase of the third stanza is "may be again," but (if I read rightly in seeing "natural sorrow, loss, or pain" as in apposition with the preceding) *what* may be again is the "familiar matter of today."

This pattern of return anticipates, then, that of the final stanza, in which a direct view of the scene is briefly restored before the poet moves away — up, of course, as well as out, the hill-climbing (a favorite device of Wordsworth's) vaguely symbolizing an ascent from one level of experience toward another, the particular toward the universal, the scene toward the vision — bearing the music in his heart. This is a delicate task, of course, this trying to hold the particular thing in focus, as particular, while insisting upon its essential, universal significance. It is difficult even when the poet has so convenient a circumstance to work with as the one here — i.e., that because the girl is singing in dialect, the specific subject cannot be known, while still the *music* (note how carefully Wordsworth has reserved the term "music"), as distinct from the words as such, can communicate much of its emotional and formal significance. If Wordsworth had given us only one first look at the "real," present scene, the poem might have vapored away quickly into the universal ether, which is to say, simply into banal generalization. On the other hand, the universal significance is, within the apparent purpose of the poem, essential — so that he could not risk so fascinating the reader with the concrete particulars of scene and situation that it would be impossible to tear him away. (Wordsworth, I might add in passing, seems to me always most successful at keeping his eye on the object when it is as here, even at the closest, a distant object. There is no poet in whose work the assumed, visual vantage point is more important — cf., the Westminster Bridge sonnet, the opening passage of the Tintern Abbey poem, etc.) The problem is at least partly solved in "The Solitary Reaper" by the way in which, as we have noted, the view is twice directed considerably away from the immediate scene, but both times brought *nearly* back, and then before the final leave-taking, all the way back — and yet again with a qualification that seems to me the most brilliant effect of the poem.

The tense is changed in the final stanza! He has been saying — "behold," and "she cuts and binds," and "what she sings," and "*is* it some more humble lay." But now it is "the Maiden *sang*," and "I listened." In other words, he has brought us back to the real scene, but before we could return it is no longer the present scene. We might almost have expected him to shift to the past tense for the last three lines. But to begin the change while the girl is still before us, and so to take poignantly the sense of the present's always becoming the past — this, in connection with that most artfully unpretentious phrase "as if her song could have no ending," meaning that the girl sings as if she never intended to stop, and that her song has an age-less, unending theme, and that as formless "folk art" it has no distinct beginning or end, and that it does not end, of course, just because the poet takes it away with him and makes it into his song — is a rightness beyond expectation, a stroke of genius.

Further, this device of shifting the tense is a final earnest of the experience's fictive reality. 'All of this could happen, because, you see, it *did* happen — I have simply been recalling it here.' And we are reminded also of the qualification that must be made when we say that the essence of any particular experience is for Wordsworth its universal implication. It *is* always *im*plication; the language of his intuition is always "the language of the sense." And if the experience must in a certain way be stripped of its sensory particulars in order that the "heart" may carry away its essence — still, for Wordsworth it is always the ability of the memory to restore those particulars upon demand that proves the worth of its currency. What he does here in recalling the scene, but recalling it as if present, and then when it is most again present at the end, in lively immediacy, reminding us again that it is past, is a smaller but essentially no less complicated version of what happens in the Tintern Abbey poem, say, when "the *picture* of the mind *revives* again."

Everything, always, "in connection" — and perhaps it would have been better to pull in somehow matters of versification with the discussion of other patterns. But that could hardly have been done without the discussion's becoming even more parenthetical than it has been. And at the risk of repeating now, or overlapping in some places, we may go back to fill in a few gaps in the analysis.

A complete prosodic analysis is not necessary. But sound and sense concur so neatly, or subtly, in a few instances we can choose, that the whole case for the integrity of the poem in this respect may rest on examination of those.

First, a note on the general stanzaic structure. The key numbers are two, and its multiples, four and eight. An opening stanza, of scene-setting, is opposed with certain complications we have already noted, by a closing stanza of scene-dispersal. This opposition buttresses the central section of two stanzas, in which the theme that is stated in the first stanza of the poem, and re-stated and resolved in the last, is augmented and elaborated.

Each of the stanzas contains eight lines, comprising two sections of four lines each, distinguished by a difference of rime-scheme, and by a shortening of the normal four-stress, basically iambic line, to a three-stress pattern in the final line of each section. The division between the two sections in each stanza marks, of course, a turn of thought. And I think we may generalize further on the effect to say that there is a tendency in all the stanzas for the statement to develop easily and expansively through the opening section, and then, with the tighter couplet rimes of the second introduced by the short line preceding, to narrow or become more intense, pointed, to the close. This is most apparent, I suppose, in the two middle stanzas, with the view being directed out from the present scene and then back. But something similar, if not identical, is going on in the other two stanzas as well — with, in the first, a heightened solemnity, and in the last the tone of finality, enforced by the insistent, measured beat of the couplets.

But the features of regularity also set up an opportunity for some striking variations. The rime scheme, we may say, is normally abab followed by ccdd. The first break in this pattern, coming before the pattern is really established, in lines one and three, is not perhaps very noticeable as a variation — although on a second reading it might be, and I cautiously venture the suggestion that the lack of a rime here does serve to emphasize the reaper's solitariness. But after three stanzas, the pattern is firmly established; and it can hardly escape notice that the first and third lines of stanza four also are not rimed.

I said before that the shift of tense at the beginning of the fourth stanza seemed to me the most brilliant effect of the poem. The effect is unquestionably secured, at least in part, by the emphasis which is thrown upon "sang" by its lack of a rime.

Probably also the feminine rime of "ending" — "bending" in the fourth stanza has some special significance. It is, of course, the only such rime in the poem — all other lines have masculine endings — and could, therefore, hardly fail to attract attention. Further, the present participial ending of the two rime words is reinforced by the same in "sing*ing*," in the third line of the stanza. As I see it, the effect is tied up here with the idea of the present-becoming-past, which we have previously noted. The irregular rime is not only achieved by the use of the present participial forms, but is I think calculated mainly to emphasize what might be called a present-participal *feeling* in the passage, a sense of a continuous motion *through* the rigid, static pattern created by the past forms "sang," "saw," "listened," "bore." Also, in spite of the full stops at these points, the feminine line endings have a tendency to permit a rhythmical overflow of one line into the next that very nicely reinforces, here, the sense of the phrase — "as if her song could have no ending."

Two other lines that seem to me among Wordsworth's best anywhere are — "Breaking the silence of the seas/ Among the farthest Hebrides." It is extremely difficult, perhaps impossible, fully to analyze the effect. But one part of it is something of a simple kind that Wordsworth was always very handy with. He has established a basic pattern of iambic (there are other variations earlier, but nothing fully to disrupt the set); he has now to develop a figure of something *breaking* something; and it is simply, and beautifully, logical that there is no better way of doing that than to use the *word* "breaking" as the first word of the line. Thus, it not only gets the normal emphasis of prime position in its phrase, but also, because the established metrical pattern does happen to be iambic, at the same time literally *breaks* that pattern, and reinforces its sense with what it is doing in the verse.

Finally, we might notice how the pattern of assonance and sibilance in the center of these lines — "the silence of the seas/ Among the farthest" — that might become too sonorous-soothing, rather than "thrilling," if unqualified, is shored up by the br-br consonance of "Breaking . . . Hebrides," with whatever hardness might still be lacking because of the relatively unaccented position of the sound in the latter word supplied by the sharp d of -des. The two words would ordinarily be too far apart for repetition of sounds to be effective, but the initial and terminal positioning in the phrase offsets the effect of separation. And the tone struck by the first syllable here is so strong, for the reasons already indicated, its resonance continuing easily through the softer sounds following, that a good ear might reasonably be expected to anticipate and pick up its recurrence.

In any event, I think I have demonstrated that the poem is at the very least a *tetra*chordon, "And wov'n close, both matter, form and stile." It is its own, multiple, but one thing. Perhaps, if I wanted to prove that the poem's "fictive unity" is all, that such an analysis as I have given gets us as close to its full meaning as we shall ever get to the significance of any poem (due allowance being made for the possibility simply of errors in application- of the analytic method), there would be no better way to conclude than with a further reference to its "source," in Mr. Wilkinson's sentence. Let us note that Wordsworth has *not*, despite his own statement, taken his last line *verbatim* from Wilkinson.

We have observed the importance, for exactly what Wordsworth is saying, of the fact that it is the "music" which he bears away, the single, central, formal essence refined from the girl's singing, the "plaintive numbers" — not the song itself, the *words*, with their multitude of possible but undeterminable, their 'numberless' significances. And the final effect of singularity, I might say, the difference of pronouns enforced by the use of the singular noun — Wordsworth's "*music* . . . long after *it* was heard no more," as against Wilkinson's "*strains* . . . long after *they* were heard no more" — is all the difference. I would say that it makes all the difference between a poem, with the prime responsibility of its own order, and a vacation reminiscence, quite beyond the question of whether it is William Wordsworth's or Thomas Wilkinson's.

III

And yet, whose *poem*? All of this is somehow too much about what the poem *says*. And, although it may be true to some extent of any poetry, yet there is some special sense in which romantic poetry and more strictly still Wordsworth's poems, always, are more significant for what they do not say, than for what they do say. It is *the* romantic effect, is it not — this lingering dissatisfaction? By lesser poets "contrived"; by Wordsworth, at his best, merely achieved.

I discover, for one thing, that I have been talking as if the poet *liked* not knowing the theme of the girl's song. I spoke of it as a "convenience" to him — in concentrating upon the wordless essence of the music, in drawing out the universal from the particular — that she sang in Erse (the Scottish dialect) and he could not understand. But surely we miss the whole point if we do not see that the music which he carries away within himself — the "universal" meaning — is a consolation for his loss in failing to understand the song.

Consolation; not a triumph over the loss. There is an inextinguishable regret in that cry — "Will no one tell me what she sings?" I will not at this point dwell upon the fact that, except for William's and Dorothy's notes on the sentence from Wilkinson, and the diligence of such scholars as Miss Darbishire in following up the references, we should not know that the girl "sang in Erse" — and that this is why the song is meaningless to the listener. But certainly it is no circumstance "accidental" to the poem that the song *is* meaningless. The meaninglessness of the girl's song — the song within Wordsworth's song — is the essential condition of whatever meaningfulness the latter may claim.

And this same anguish over the meaninglessness of things (the "romantic agony" which has flowered into our peculiarly modern agony) is everywhere the central motivation of Wordsworth's poetry. More specifically, it is an anguish over the disability of *language*. I have said that Wordsworth loved solitude, that this is why he liked to walk in the country. And solitude is another name for silence. But I also said "solitude . . . and the need for communion." And communion means human companionship, means speech. His solitude was most often, in the literal sense, a companioned solitude. A silent companion — but the value of the silence was its promise of giving forth the word, a new word of meaning to set against the mere noise of words that he heard in most of the literature of his time.

With Milton, for example, with any of the great 17th century poets, there was as yet no such radical anxiety as to the capacities of language. One might deplore specific degeneracies of usage. But there was a vast, dependable, public structure of verbal tradition. There were dependable, specific structures of literary convention — such, again, as the pastoral mode — the essential meaningfulness of which no one doubted, even when they poked fun at it. There had to be a meaning, for the joke to achieve its point. Even when one, as I have said of Milton and Marvell, "shattered" it, the framework was still there, the flowers and the thorns and the serpent still retaining their integrated symbolic values, words joined to the things, in a known and intelligible order. There were no such things as "mere" flowers, mere thorns and snakes. And the ironic truth is that the modern explicationist method of criticism, in its strictest application to the "internal" structure of the poem, the bare text, the "mere" verbal structure, works best with the older poetry precisely because the words there are *not* mere words, because the words pull the whole public structure of symbolic convention into the poem with them. It is all there, and we do not *have* to go outside for it.

But Wordsworth (how fatally ironic his name is!) was burdened with awareness of the loss of all this. He offered himself various consolation — "a sense sublime of something far more deeply inter-fused."[6] That is, the music within. But I insist once more that it was *only* consolation. His tone, at its most exalted, is never more than consolatory. The "sense sublime of something" was a poor substitute for the known, the believed and nameable, for the firm, verbal grasp of the invisible that would have made it possible for him really to get close to the visible, the physical things, and not be always shying away from them. (I have given him credit for using, in his own phrase, "the language of the sense," or as I put it, for "restoring the sensory particulars" — but, of course, it is always just as few as he can get by with. He is much better with "sense" in the other sense, the vague intuition.) The "presences" were a poor substitute for some-one, human, who might understand him if he should start to speak, to name the presences. And he knew it.

In other words, he was actually terrified of being alone — in a world

---

6 Earl R. Wasserman (Foreword to *The Finer Tone*) sees this as the key to the meaning of "The Solitary Reaper." In a sense, it is. But to speak of it as expressing a "pantheistic ontology" which informs Wordsworth's poetry is all too desperate an attempt to make a systematic "philosophy" of what was, only and better, a "sense." And Wasserman, in quoting the phrase, leaves out "a sense . . . of."

bereft of meaning. That is why he could never even look at a flower without trying to speak to it, humanizing it. Of course, he courted the fright, and called it endearing names, in the hope of mastering it. And "terror" may seem to some readers too strong a word for most of Wordsworth — though *terrifying* is exactly the effect his vision of daffodils dancing has always had on me, for all his distracted mumbling of "gay" and "jocund." But, "desperation" at least — that loose-jointed hysteria of language, repetitious piling up of words in despair of ever finding quite the right ones, which continues so to embarrass Mr. Brooks when he scans with his fine, ironical eye the texture of the great "Ode." That is why so many of the poems are "to" or "about" someone, if not, shall we say, *with* someone, whether the "dear, dear Sister," or only some past self of his own, whom he could objectify in remembrance.

And that is why, once again and finally, there was always an "occasion." The "meaning" of words is their inclination, a motion toward. We can only *mean*, when we intend to communicate, or commune. Now, when one has the dependable, public structure of tradition, a dependable convention of language, he does not necessarily require either the specific presence of a communicant (or fellow-communicant) or a specific occasion for speaking — i.e., writing a poem. His words are addressed and have meaning toward, a known world of men. But when he does not have this, then the companion and the occasion become all-important. And if, I think, one would be hard put to it to argue that the *presence* of Dorothy (the "dear, dear Sister") is not essential to the meaning of "Lines Composed a Few Miles Above Tintern Abbey," that she is not, and thoroughly, *in* the poem — then I fail to see how it is not equally essential that she is *absent* in "The Solitary Reaper."

This is the significance of the reference to Wilkinson, its inextricable tie to the poem. This is the peculiar strength, and the peculiar terror, of the poem — what *drives* it to a formal, rhetorical near-perfection the like of which Wordsworth seldom attained elsewhere. The "invisible companion" whom the poet sketches out at his side, commanding him to "Behold!" is for once really invisible, really and eternally silent, nonexistent, except as the product of the faithless words, the rhetorical gestures, not as the recipient of meaning. He, or she, is nonexistent, because so is the girl in the field. The girl never sang, and the poet never listened. There were no particulars, from which to draw the universal, no song, from which to extract the essential music, that should console him in the absence of singing. The specific meaninglessness of the girl's song, its unintelligible dialect, contains only a hint of the final, total absence of meaning.

In others of Wordsworth's poems, we strongly suspect this situation, of an eloquence, a command of language, that is dedicated to, or despairingly celebrates, the denial of meaning. But here it is pushed perilously close to a denial of the poet's own existence — to a yearning for speech, in its absence, so intense that it nearly identifies speaking with existence. The note to Wilkinson, the "acknowledgment" — earnest of confidence that at least it did happen to someone else, whom he could call "friend," that there had been, therefore, an occasion — is the faintest, frail guarantee (hardly more than a hope) of meaning.

This is not an appeal for return to "biographical criticism," the mongering of stale literary gossip. Thomas Wilkinson and his tour are of no importance to us. It is essential only for us to recognize that he *was* important to Wordsworth.

Whoever will, may continue to suppose that meaning, in such an instance, is equal to structure — and exclude the note from the poem, exclude the "friend," Wilkinson. I should only require him to understand that this means, unequivocally, the exclusion of Wordsworth as well.

Baudelaire's

"Rêve Parisien"

The Silent Babel

A Constantin Guys

I

De ce terrible paysage,
Tel que jamais mortel n'en vit,
Ce matin encore l'image,
Vague et lointaine, me ravit.

Le sommeil est plein de miracles!
Par un caprice singulier,
J'avais banni de ces spectacles
Le végétal irrégulier,

Et, peintre fier de mon génie,
Je savourais dans mon tableau
L'enivrante monotonie
Du métal, du marbre et de l'eau.

Babel d'escaliers et d'arcades,
C'était un palais infini,
Plein de bassins et de cascades
Tombant dans l'or mat ou bruni;

Et des cataractes pesantes,
Comme des rideaux de cristal,
Se suspendaient, éblouissantes,
A des murailles de métal.

Non d'arbres, mais de colonnades
Les étangs dormants s'entouraient,
Où de gigantesques naïades,
Comme des femmes, se miraient.

Des nappes d'eau s'épanchaient, bleues,
Entre des quais roses et verts,
Pendant des millions de lieues,
Vers les confins de l'univers;

C'étaient des pierres inouïes
Et des flots magiques; c'étaient
D'immenses glaces éblouies
Par tout ce qu'elles reflétaient!

Insouciants et taciturnes,
Des Ganges, dans le firmament,
Versaient le trésor de leurs urnes
Dans des gouffres de diamant.

Architecte de mes féeries,
Je faisais, à ma volonté,
Sous un tunnel de pierreries
Passer un océan dompté;

Et tout, même la couleur noire,
Semblait fourbi, clair, irisé;
Le liquide enchassait sa gloire
Dans le rayon cristallisé.

Nul astre d'ailleurs, nuls vestiges
De soleil, même au bas du ciel,
Pour illuminer ces prodiges,
Qui brillaient d'un feu personnel!

Et sur ces mouvantes merveilles
Planait (terrible nouveauté!
Tout pour l'œil, rien pour les oreilles!)
Un silence d'éternité.

II

En rouvrant mes yeux pleins de flamme
J'ai vu l'horreur de mon taudis,
Et senti, rentrant dans mon âme,
La pointe des soucis maudits;

La pendule aux accents funèbres
Sonnait brutalement midi,
Et le ciel versait des ténèbres
Sur le triste monde engourdi.

Baudelaire has been called the first of the anti-Romantics. In a sense he was, even in France. And it was to be a long time before his essential influence (*via* the later French symbolists) was felt among major English poets. Anything really resembling his cult of *artifice*, for example, not as "art-for-art's-sake" affectation but as profound revulsion from the disgust of mortality ("Rêve Parisien" is the basic poetic text), we are likely to recognize first in the later Yeats.

But anything *anti-* something else is usually a reversal or inversion of attitudes — a turning upside-down or a wringing inside-out — rather than direct departure. Even if we know only English romanticism, the preceding offering from Wordsworth is not the worst background for approaching Baudelaire. There is the fascination with silence, for one thing, with solitude and the incommunicable.

It is the famous French "rationality" — and the other side of it, French sensuality — that makes the difference. Baudelaire simply tried, more rationally, to push directly through the stench of fleshly corruption by sticking his nose in it. ("Une Charogne.") He tried to break through the senses (*not* the same thing as subduing them, so that the familiar analysis of the process as inverted asceticism is wrong) by exciting them to quicker satiety, as with opium.

But, to come then to the poem, the matter of first importance is not that it is an opium-dream, but simply that it is a dream. Baudelaire, so far as I know, was about the first poet (since the Renaissance) to handle the dream for its possibilities as a rival order of insight — opposed to that of waking rationality — rather than just as uncontrolled escape-fantasy. This was, of course, before the discoveries of modern psychology, indicating that the key to the dream-order lay precisely in the lack of control. So that the "rival" order in the poem — order of imagination, or whatever we are to call it — comes out here looking rather like a simple *super*-rationality, pseudo-divine rationality, more than anything non-rational; and the dreamwork something more on the plan of an old-fashioned dream-*vision*, the "sent" dream, than on that of our modern dreams, which simply come, without being either sent or sent for.[1] (Perhaps the fact that Baudelaire's is an induced dream, the dream of drugged sleep — sent for, at least, if not sent — does have something to do with this visionary quality of it.) But, in any event, the poem is prophetic of the modern temper in its central quest for order, to substitute for that lost in the waking world; and, most specifically, in its emphasis upon the suspension of *time*, in the dream-state, as the condition of order.

And, in this connection, the dedication of the poem has some significance. For that concern with time is entirely of a piece with Baudelaire's interest in painting. The *modernity* of the essay "Le Peintre de la Vie Moderne" is not, of course, mere contemporaneity. The point of final importance, surely, is that the work of "Monsieur G.," to the extent that it is *modern*, is really *timeless*.

But this means, also, that we need not over-particularize the reference. Constantin Guys, it has been many times observed, was honored as the subject even of the essay only because there was no one else painting at the time, no Degas, as someone has suggested,

---

[1] But see the curious "Freudian" analysis of "Rêve Parisien" offered by a character in Caroline Gordon's novel *The Malefactors*. The poet-hero of the novel rejects the interpretation as absurd.

in whose work Baudelaire could better have found what he was looking for — seen, what he envisaged. This one piece of Baudelaire's art
criticism has no especially compelling relevance to the problems of
the poem; and the paintings of Constantin Guys, so far as I know
them, have still less. But it is significant that the poem is dedicated
to a painter. *All* of Baudelaire's art criticism (the best of its time) is
basically concerned with the problems of comparative aesthetics; the
"Salon" studies are studies in the "poetry" of painting. And, a bit
later, I shall attempt to close in on the crucial problem of this poem's
"painterly" character — the fact that the dream, as the speaker recalls
it, is entirely a *visual* experience — and examine the relevance of this
to the *timelessness* of the scene, with its "silence d'éternité."

But this can wait until we have dealt more directly with those
themes of the poem which would present themselves to anyone on
first reading: the themes of the self, and of solitude.

In the dream, the mind is its own place. It is that "*terrible* paysage"
— and the terror, in part at least, is the terror of loneliness. The mind
wanders this landscape, of its own self-contained perfection, utterly
companionless.

The emotional attitude expressed in the word "terrible" — "terrible
paysage," and, in the last stanza of part one, "terrible nouveauté" —
is ambivalent, of course. It is not, in any unqualified sense, a feeling
of revulsion that is indicated. When the dreamer awakes, it is the
reality of his everyday world — the sight of his room, the sense of
waking cares — which is, rather than the memory of the dream,
"l'horreur." He wakes up with a sense not so much of relief, as of
regret, that the dream has ended.[2]

We might put it that the dream-vision is "terrible," principally
because it is insupportable. And the sense of its being so is not simply
read back into the reconstruction of the dream, from the fact of the
awakening. I shall attempt to show that the causes of its insupport-
ability, the flaws of the dream "architecture," are apparent in the
structure itself, as the speaker describes it. It is not clear whether
M. J.-D. Hubert, in his remarks on this poem, is speaking of the
dream-vision proper when he observes that "le surnaturalisme baude-
lairien est un conflit violent entre l'imagination poétique et le monde

---

[2] The psychological experience here is essentially the same as in the prose-
poem "La Chambre Double"; and the two works are strikingly similar in many
details of scene and phrasing.

réel où la poésie finit toujours par triompher."[3] If he is, the judgment requires some qualification. But, although the vision is inevitably to be defeated, there is a sense here not only of terror as fear, but also of a terrible *exultation* — perhaps the stronger *because* it is foredoomed to despair — in the mind's control of the perilously balanced structure.

In any event, we do not have, in the poem as a whole, an uncommunicative and irresponsible, narcissistic isolation. The poem is about the isolation of the self — the isolation of the mind in the province of its own perfection. But only, "about" it.

In the first place, the dream image is presented as past. The dream passage is buttressed by direct references, in the first two stanzas, and again the short section II, to the moments of waking, temporal reality, from the vantage point of which we look back with the speaker upon the dream. What is presented is precisely what the poet calls it — the "image" of that landscape. There is no sense of an effort to restore the fabulous palace, no effort presently to re-enter it.

Further, within the extended dream-image proper, the state of the mind's solitude is so perfected that it gets beyond isolation in the usual sense. The kinds of cultivated loneliness, for example, that are more typical at least of English romantic poetry — the scene of the poet's watching a natural waterfall or a grate-fire, or the state of mountain-top "splendid isolation" — are situations in which the sense of isolation depends upon the active memory of company, upon the feeling of temporary escape. In these situations, there is always a sense that the isolated self, although *in communion with* great things — the sky, the earth, all time past-present-and-future — is itself essentially small. The sense of the receptive smallness is altogether necessary to the sense of greatness in what is received. (At least this much is true even of Wordsworth's wholly "invented" situation in "The Solitary Reaper.") But in Baudelaire's dream, there is almost nothing of this. The artful mind has expanded itself until it has all but *become* the universe. And, of course, when this extreme is reached, self-assertion, the denying of the *limitations* of self, becomes hardly distinguishable from denial of the existence of a self.[4]

---

[3] J.-D. Hubert, *L'Esthétique des "Fleurs du Mal,"* p. 105.

[4] I am talking here about the "self," and the denial of its existence, in the abstract. I trust it will be apparent that this is a problem different from, though related to, that dealt with in the closing paragraphs of the chapter on Wordsworth.

Although the speaker is still full of it, enraptured, carried out of himself toward the remembered scene — the pleasurable meaning of the word "ravit" might be noted, incidentally, as reinforcing the ambiguity of which we have spoken in reference to "terrible" — the image of the dream landscape is presented at the outset as "vague et lointaine." And it is, in fact, difficult to visualize very distinctly the different features of the dream composition. There is some sense of progression: outward — from something like the rooms of a building, to the palace gardens, the colonnade and the pool, and then to a surrounding, mountained parkland; thence upward — to the arch of a kind of sky; and finally downward — to the captive ocean, somewhere beneath the whole. But in other senses — that of the imitation of dream, in which we lose awareness of location in time and space, and the imitation of painting, in which all planes are one—it is all palace, the gardens and parkland, the very firmament and underlying depths themselves, a part of the totally contrived structure. And this, of course, is just the point. Nature, "le végétal irrégulier," has been absolutely banished. The immense artifice — "l'enivrante monotonie/ Du métal, du marbre et de l'eau" — crowds against "les confins de l'univers."

Whereas some of the other romantic attitudes of self-isolation, which we have recalled by contrast, involve only a retreat — merely from human society *into* external nature — here all nature is excluded. From the title, we may take the suggestion that the vision is of a world become ultimate city, a fantastic and terrible perfection of the artificiality of the urban scene. So. M. Hubert sees it, as "une idéalisation extrême de la cité dont les irrégularités végétales ou autres auraient été supprimées."[5] He then goes on to suggest identification of certain scenes as reflections of scenes in Paris; that in the seventh stanza, for example, might recall the quays of the Seine.

The general theme, in any event, is that of the familiar "palace of art." In the metaphor of *sovereignty* which this involves, one would ordinarily think of the sovereign, art, as ruling over the "realm" of nature. Here, however, the sovereignty insisted upon is so strict, a despotism so insatiable, that in effect it swallows up its territories. The realm, as distinct from the ruling power, ceases to exist; the palace encompasses the realm. "Le végétal irrégulier" — nature, the

---

[5] J.-D. Hubert, *op. cit.*, p. 104.

nonvolitional, and the merely instinctive, nonrational life processes, of growth, reproduction, and decomposition, the irregularity in the shapes of things produced by nature — is "banished." (The word "banni" itself has, of course, political connotations.) And the victory of art is the more ironically complete for the fact that, while nature as ruling power or principle has been excluded, her properties have been seized and exploited. For its own purposes, art has taken over, and "unnaturally" idealized, the forms of natural objects.

This notion is developed, for example, in the description of the pools, which are surrounded "non d'arbes, mais de colonnades" — i.e., by an artful perfection of tree forms. Everywhere, there is restriction and confinement of natural movement. The use of water images through much of the poem is especially significant. What sense of life and motion there is in the scene is carried principally, in fact entirely, by the references to water. And yet, in each instance, the normal suggestions of restlessness, of ceaseless flow and change of form, are ironically contradicted.

The cascades in the palace fall into golden vessels, are caught and contained. The cataracts are imaged as "hanging suspended" — "like curtains." The pools surrounded by the colonnades are "sleeping" — a figure that at once attributes to the water a vitality beyond its nature, and denies the implications. Just as in the palace proper, if we can make such divisions of the scene, so also in what I have called the surrounding parkland, the sheets of water that fall between the rose and green banks (it is worth noting that here "vegetal" colors are cunningly applied to what must be thought of as rock formations) are suspended, hanging. The streams of the Ganges pour from vessels, urns, and are caught in "diamond" gulfs. (The adjective is "insouciants," and although it is specifically applied to the Ganges, it characterizes something of the dream architect's own attitude throughout — a fine, assured "carelessness," of dreamlike detachment, bemusement in "l'enivrante monotonie" of the work.) And, finally, there is the captive ocean, made to flow in a tunnel.[6]

The water in the sleeping pools is so still, its surface so unruffled, that it serves as a mirror. But in one of the most brilliant effects of the poem, beyond the merely visual images of reflection, Baud-

---

[6] Cf. Coleridge's "Kubla Khan."

elaire "mirrors" in his description of the gigantic naïades the same ambiguity of intent that we noted in the implications of "dormants" as applied to the water. The naïades — statues, presumably — are "like women" as they stand beside the pool, looking into its polished surface. In the first place, of course, naïades as such are not real women, but demi-goddesses. If an image of any living "person" were to be introduced into this scene, it would have to be something only idealistically "like" the human. But, further, the irony is just that these figures are *not* living, either naturally, or, in idealized but lively fancy, "supernaturally." And it is strangely startling — an effect that makes the dehumanization of the scene only the more complete — to be reminded in that at first seemingly innocent phrase of comparison, "comme des femmes," that there is any recognizable semblance of the attitudes of living creatures in the posture of eternally fixed, stony vanity with which these effigies regard themselves in the polished surface of the water. But lest to speak merely of the "human" and of "dehumanization" obscure the fact, it is most important that the figures are a mocking image of *women*. For in the conventional picture of despotism, sexuality, even in the most sadistic or otherwise depraved form, is likely to provide the final saving measure of the human. Here, it most chills the blood to realize, our artist-despot is beyond even that. In the image of the "gigantesques naïades," sexuality itself is made his captive giant.

But further, the entire composition is surrounded at its outer limits, above and beyond the sheets of water apparently, by mirroring sheets of ice. This is the ultimate fixedness of the flow of water that is everywhere rigidly controlled. The ice-mirror fences the whole in the confinement of countless dazzling repetitions of its own image — the vision ever expanding, repeating itself, ever thrown back upon itself.

Moreover, the water is "unnatural" just in the fact that it does not nourish the growth of anything. I have spoken, in analogy, of palace "gardens" and of a "parkland." But the significant fact is, of course, that there are no trees, no flowers, no grass or shrubs in this garden and this park. (No doubt, the actual, background image is of the traditional "French garden," with its geometric regularity of form. But, in the dream-vision, not even so much "nature" as of that is left, much less, might we say, as of the "English" garden!) "Le végétal irrégulier" has all the other meanings, but there is a basic reference to the absolute exclusion of plant life.

The hardness, the coldness and sterility of the scene, of the artful ingenuity which has produced this extravaganza of stone and metal, has its "human" image in the great statues of the naïades, the forbidding indifference of their gigantic loveliness. But this image, and its ironic significance, is immediately anticipated by that of the lifeless columns (as we have noted before, the perfection merely of tree *forms*) which also stand by the pool, where, as the wording of the line indicates, one would ordinarily expect to find real, growing trees. It is in this denial of the primary life-giving function of the water, more perhaps than in anything else, that the sense of the dream artist's triumph over nature, and over the "natural" symbolic usages of traditional art, is secured.

But despite the "architect's" delight in its self-contained perfection, the scene *is* terrible. A sense of depression and dismay threatens throughout to undercut the exulting sense of control. And the aspect of loneliness and of desolation in the scene — something beyond even its sterility, in the basic sense of the word — can be precisely accounted for. The perfection of the structure is managed only at the cost of a certain deprivation of the faculties.

It is defined in the parenthesis of the final stanza of Part I — "(terrible nouveauté!/ Tout pour l'œil, rien pour les oreilles!)." "Un silence d'éternité," there is motion, the semblance of life, but no sound: not only no human voice, nor those of other creatures, but none of any of the motions of nature. No leaves rustle. Even the water, it seems, moves noiselessly. And it is true that from the area of the entire dream image, all but one of the senses is rigidly excluded.

According to the traditional (originally Platonic) doctrine, the sense of sight is the intellectual sense — and that which chiefly regards the beautiful, because it is most cognitive. Baudelaire's dream is of a thoroughly intellectualized art, luxuriant, but exactly calculated, with "le végétal irrégulier" banished, the creation of a triumphantly *regular* beauty, of "pure," visual and essentially static forms. Within the range of nonabstract statement, image, the vision of such an art has here its extreme expression. And, as image, there is something inevitably terrifying about this ultimate refinement of the aesthetic to the purely visual — about the picture of a mind, for which the sight stands here, wandering or surveying its provinces entirely deprived of the familiar companionship of the lower senses. For no mortal eye ever before saw this "terrible paysage" — and for an "immortal eye," perhaps, there would be no terror, but all delight in it. But the effect here clearly depends upon the implication that the eye with which the poet has now looked into that region has retained something of its mortality, and its mortal frailty. (There are, after all, as in the image of the naïades, disturbing although faint reminders of mortal life.) And it fears its own instinct of immortality, fears the risk it takes of actualizing all the possibilities of that sovereign, intellectual detachment which it conceives as the symbolic perfection of its function.

It is repeatedly emphasized — "caprice singulier," "architecte de mes féeries," "à ma volonté," "feu personnel" — that the attainment of this detachment, the re-building of Paris and the world into this cold, statically ordered perfection of metal, stone, and glassy water, is the result of a defiant, all-daring, single act of individual will. For all that it is an image of the perfection of rational control, it is the creation of *caprice*. And there is a suggestion of the fear that such daring, the quest for total rationality, may after all take the creaturely mind beyond its capabilities. It may be "capricious," finally, in the sense of *ir*rationality, a foolhardy wilfulness and reckless pursuit of mere whim.

But, to recall now some observations we made at the outset, the dream as such is only a part of the poem, not the whole. The dreamer, *in* the dream, is not precisely identifiable with him who now *remembers* the dream. Something, unquestionably, of the original dream-feeling is retained. But there is little here, say, of a Kafka-esque attempt to recapture or re-enter the dream state — the realistic, un-marvelling state of mind the dreamer is in at the time he experiences the marvels.

What we are given is rather an image *of* the dream, consciously re-ordered, the speaker himself openly "interpreting" what he has seen. The basic, concretely representational language is here and there relieved with abstractly qualitative adjectives — "insouciants," "taciturnes," "terrible"; and more or less abstract nouns — "spectacles" and "nouveauté." The visual image of the naïades at the pool, and what tacit symbolic significance might be read from that, is overlaid with the directly comparative figure, "comme des femmes." And the speaker metaphorically *characterizes* his dream-self — as "peintre," "architecte." Further (what is, I think, of great importance for our task of defining how the poem *uses* the dream), the properties of the dream vision are involved in more or less direct *allusions;* they take on the significance of belonging to a *tradition,* of conscious poetic usage.

We may take the use of two proper names as the most obvious examples of such relevance. The palace is a "Babel" of stairs and arcades. The significance of this reference is rather complex. In the first place, there is the ironic fact that the scene here is entirely silent. But this is further complicated, when we consider that the great noise at Babel was after all a kind of silence, since everyone was speaking a tongue which was unintelligible to everyone else. And still further, Baudelaire transfers the notion of the confusion of voices among the workmen in the Biblical story to the architectural structure itself — representing that confusion here, in the image of his "tower," as an intricate profusion of visual forms. And there is then the question of whether the profusion here *is* confusion, or an incredibly subtle order — that is, whether the present structure is "destroyed," its beauty defeated, as the result of the very overambitiousness and oversubtlety of its own design, as in a sense the original Tower of Babel was self-destroyed.

Moreover, the idea of the Tower of Babel as an affront to God, the effort of man to ascend to the heavens — the pride which was the reason, of course, for the punishment of the division of tongues — becomes one of the principal means of establishing a certain character of the whole vision here. But we will come back to that in a moment.

The significance of the reference to the Ganges is more difficult to define precisely, and perhaps is left purposely vague, or mysterious. Generally, it is a sacred river, of course, and an oriental one at that, so that as it is made a part of the artist's composition here, forced like the other waters to flow according to the order of his caprice, it emphasizes again the absolute sovereignty of his imagination, his control of all mysteries. (As we have observed before, the "insouciance" attributed to the Ganges actually characterizes, in part, the dream artist's own attitude.) There may be some allusion also to the position of the mouth of the Ganges, in Dante's cosmogony, as defining one extremity of the hemisphere of earth. Here, the mouth defines the uppermost limit of the enchanted world, and from there, the arch of the firmament, the streams pour down into the gulf that is perhaps to be thought of as the lowermost depth. Or, there is the Indian legend that the Ganges rises from a lake among the highest mountains of Tibet, the "roof of the world" or "basement of the firmament"; and Baudelaire's placing his Ganges *in* the firmament — the dream artifice having, or aspiring to have, no definable limits, being an effort to construct an independent universe — would be a thoroughly appropriate exaggeration of this conception, as of Dante's.

At any rate, the general irony is that these names, Babel and Ganges, do furnish some kind of traditional framework for the vision. And there are several other details of imagery that, in most emphasizing the *formal* idea of self-containment, at the same time involve clearly allusive *references*. There is, for example, the "feu personnel" with which the marvellous things of the scene burn.

The fact that the scene is lighted from within, without benefit of rays from sun or stars, defines its self-sustaining character. The sun is the light of natural generation, of course, that which nourishes the growth of "le végétal irrégulier." And the stars, I take it, are symbolic here, as customarily, of the light of divine influence. Both, we are told, are missing from this triumph of the self-sufficient imagination. And yet we recognize in this very imagery of illumination from some hidden and inner power of the objects themselves (the water, the stones, etc.) something familiar from the tradition, a suggestion of the light of infernal flames. One recalls the fires, the lights of Hell, in Dante, where also there is a reiterated emphasis upon the absence of sunlight. And perhaps a still closer reminiscence is that of Milton's "darkness visible," in the Hell of *Paradise Lost* — especially in Baudelaire's reference to the fact that "tout, *même la couleur noire,/* Semblait fourbi, clair, irisé." (*Comus*, too, is shot through with imagery of this kind — the Lady's song "smoothing the Raven doune/ Of darkness till it smil'd"; or, more relevant to the present intent, the argument of Comus that if the earth's stores are not tapped, " . . . th'unsought diamonds/ Would so emblaze the forhead of the Deep/ And so bestudd with Stars, that they below/ Would grow inur'd to light, and com at last/ To gaze upon the Sun with shameless brows.")

The point is not that the "terrible paysage" of Baudelaire's vision is, in any precise and orthodox sense, Hell. But the point *is* — that the central ambiguity of attitude in the poem, the balance of repulsion and attraction, of dismay in the desolation of the scene and of exultation in the perfection of imaginative control, can be translated as a question of whether the vision is, so to speak, a heaven *or* a hell. And the point is that Baudelaire, in "stating" this question, has quite obviously drawn upon the material of attitudes and imagery familiar in the poetic tradition of diabolism.

Not only is the state of supreme self-sufficiency itself traditionally associated with the diabolic — see Milton's characterization of Satan, whose ultimate torture, and ultimate glory, is just in this fact of his supreme self-containment — but so, of course, is the idea of the emulation of heaven. Nimrod, the chief architect of Babel, ends up in Dante's hell looking like a tower himself; and it is this appearance, reminiscent of his aspirations to build a way to heaven, that precisely defines his infernal character. So also, Milton pokes his sharpest fun at the angel-demons in the scene in which they build Pandemonium in imitation of the palace of heaven (a passage, incidentally, in which the comparison to the Tower of Babel is directly made): the hopelessness of their condemnation is most apparent in this most magnificent display of their art and power. Dante and Milton keep very clearly in mind the difference between heaven and hell, are in no doubt where they stand at any point. In Baudelaire's poem, there is nothing of such doctrinal certainty, of course. Nor emotional certainty either, for that matter. Whatever other differences there are between *these* two poets and their total attitudes, the very fact that Dante, in his picture of Nimrod in Hell, and Milton, in his treatment of the tower-building fallen angels, are able to handle the condemned spirits with scathingly conscious *humor* defines more clearly than anything else the essential difference of Baudelaire's concern, deadly serious throughout, from theirs with somewhat the same problem. But there *is* the similarity, as well as the difference — evidence of Baudelaire's dependence upon the terms, the frame of reference, of an available tradition.

And the poem contains another, extended allusion that is still more definite and striking than these we have observed. In the same year, 1860, in which "Rêve Parisien" first appeared, Baudelaire published his adaptation (*Un Mangeur d'Opium*) of De Quincey's *Confessions of an English Opium-Eater*. And much of the fabulous architecture of the vision recorded in the poem is unmistakably a reminiscence of De Quincey's description of his dream in the section

"The Pains of Opium" — the terrible beauty of which he compares to certain plates of Piranesi (the prison studies, evidently) that Coleridge had once shown him, and to an unidentified passage of Wordsworth (Book II of *The Excursion*) describing a fantastic palace in the clouds.[7]

Now, the question is not whether Baudelaire had his own, actual dream, in opium-induced sleep, that paralleled De Quincey's dream. Perhaps he had. Reading can influence dreams, as well as poems. And perhaps there is something in the effects of opium itself which sets up strikingly similar psychic disturbances in different persons. All of the "opium-dream" poems with which I am familiar do have remarkable similarities of structure, which perhaps cannot be entirely accounted for as literary convention. (Cf., again, Coleridge's "Kubla Khan.") I imagine there is a good deal of complicated interaction, in such experiences, between the literary and the narcotic habituations of the subject. In any event, the "personal" validity of the poem's experiential base seems to me never to have the same kind of importance in Baudelaire's case that it has, for example, in Wordsworth's.[8] (For all sorts of reasons — that Baudelaire was a Frenchman, for that cause alone more likely to be *intellectually,* if not politically, morally, and socially conscious at least of the shattered forms of tradition; that he was, in himself, more "literary-minded," aesthetical; and that, simply, he was so protean a person, slipping himself so easily in and out of the personalities of others, like Poe.) And, in this particular instance, quite apart from the question of his personal experiences as member of an international confraternity of opium-eaters, the point is that the proceedings of that confraternity exist in a *published* tradition, and that the *poem* "Rêve Parisien" refers to one of the other publication.[9]

The "caprice," then, of Baudelaire's vision is not so "singular" after all, the "fire" not so "personal." We have been here before. The

---

[7] See G.-T. Clapton, *Baudelaire et de Quincey,* pp. 64-65.

[8] I realize that precisely that cloud-castle of *The Excursion,* Book II, may be an example of well-nigh pure, literary conventionality in Wordsworth — and that this may seem to contradict what I have said about him in the preceding chapter. But this is only one part of a long poem. *The Excursion* as a whole has the same kind of personalism that the short poems have.

[9] See Enid Starkie, *Baudelaire,* p. 373 ff., for an intelligent discussion of Baudelaire's contributions to the literature of opium addiction, and of his debt to De Quincey and others. Miss Starkie seems to doubt that "Rêve Parisien" represents a real opium dream at all.

dream cannot be recalled, or the recollection expressed, verbally, in such a way as to leave it whole. In the verbal presentation, it cannot remain only internally lighted. For, all words having a history, a verbal conception is a conception in time; and as soon as the vision is put into a structure of words, the tradition inevitably lights it from the outside.

And there is a hint here, as in much of Baudelaire's poetry, of a radical despair, a fear of the inadequacy of words ever to contain the unique experience of vision. But if this explains, to a great extent, the fascination which the art of painting held for the poet, suggesting that he saw in the purely visual representation a way of capturing the eternality of the moment of vision that is forever closed to the verbal artist — since even the *real* painting, not the dream-painting, occupies primarily space and not time — still, the despair is not permitted to destroy the poem as poem. We have some further discriminations to make.

To repeat, the dream image is not the entire poem. The short second section is, in a formal sense, very important. It is here that the dream structure collapses; but this fading out of the dream-vision is, in a way, essential precisely to the poem's coming whole. The order of the dream, based on an impossibly severe limitation of sensibility, cannot sustain itself; but the poem stands, finally, on the establishment of another balance. Against the rigid, silent and timeless scene of the dream — the silence, we have noted, is the silence *of eternity* ("silence d'éternité") — there is balanced immediately a rush of sensation upon the dreamer's awakening. He *hears* the clock. He *feels* (the figure, at least, is one of the sensation of touch) the "point" of care enter his soul. He *sees* the shadows pour out over the torpid world; and "seeing" now is only seeing, only one among the other sensations, not the visionary power of the dream. (We may observe, in this figure of the sky pouring shadows, a reminiscence of the earlier image of the Ganges pouring from the firmament, with the mockingly significant difference that here there is no sense of the former *control* of the flow, from the "urns" into the "diamond gulf.") He lies now passive and will-less before the rush of time and decay (time, the clock, speaks in "accents funèbres"), himself in a rather "vegetal" lassitude that contrasts directly and violently with the illusion of complete self-mastery and self-sufficiency that he had as architect of the dream palace.

And perhaps the final irony of the Babel reference is simply that poetry is *not* architecture, or painting, not a visual and static art. Merely having to use words, as we have observed, precludes attainment to that kind of perfection of formal control which the poet has sought in the vision, necessarily puts the poem in time, as a condition of intelligibility. But my point is that the poem, as it were just in *admitting* this, in taking us back into time and the state of the poet's passive subjection to sensation (hearing and feeling, as well as seeing), and thus collapsing the dream structure, at the same time attains the kind of harmony of verbal imagery that is proper to a poem.

The tongues of the various senses in fallen man are hopelessly divided, and at least in this poem Baudelaire has despaired of rendering them intelligible one to another. He has also despaired of the attempt to achieve an artificial unity of his aesthetic consciousness by limiting it to the exercise of only one of them. But simply to express that despair so clearly as he has done, is in a measure to triumph over it.

(On the point of the impossibility of presenting anything purely *visual* in a poem, we might simply observe that even in the dream section proper, where we are supposed to have "Tout pour l'œil, rien pour les oreilles," still the actual *sound* of the words, as they are engaged in the verses, has somewhat the same importance that it has in any poetry. Only things that, if they were real, would appeal to the eye alone are presented. This is true. There is, and can be, no physically imitative use of verbal sounds — none of the "moan of doves in immemorial elms" kind of thing — since there are no trees and no birds to sit in them. But in lines like "l'enivrante monotonie/ Du métal, du marbre et de l'eau" there is certainly an imitation of a *feeling* — the arrangement of the *n* and *m* sounds, and the vowel mutations, the repetition of the *d* in "du . . . du . . . de," and so on, being indeed the principal means of communicating that part of the *sense* of "enivrante" and "monotonie" which is *emotional*.)

The poet admits, in other words, that as pure vision, as visionary reality, so to speak, the dream is insupportable. It cannot be reproduced, or re-entered. All that can be done, that has been done in the poem, is to describe it, to present an *image* of it. But, as image, it can be sustained. As image — these last two stanzas imply — the vision has precisely the same validity that a poetic representation of waking experience has. For the sensations and feelings (of waking experience) which are presented in the final section, too, can be presented only in images — of the flowing shadows, the point of care, etc. — and these then related, in a harmony of contrasts, to the images of the dream section. And this is the same thing as to say that the poet admits he cannot, as person, sustain the self-sufficiency of his dream state — but also that, by this very admission (whether it "pleases" him to make it or not), he detaches himself from the poem, and thus insures *its* self-sufficiency.

But the idea of the poem's integrity can be put best, perhaps, by one more reference to the Babel allusion. The comparison of the dream palace to Babel would make no sense at all, or would at any rate not mean the *same* thing it does, if it were not for the total complex of wit and imagery in which it is involved — the translation of the confusion of voices into a visual impression of the building's structure, the references elsewhere to the complete silence of the scene, and so on. Further, it is questionable whether the significance of the deprivation of sensibility, the limitation of the dream experience strictly to the visual, would be clear if the coda of section II, with its contrasting images of other sensations, were not there to direct us back to the "time-present" of the first stanza, the time after the dream, from which we first looked back upon the dream. The total experience or "action" of the poem does draw upon a wide range of common experience. The particular, personal experience of the dream, ironically contrary to its proud intent of making itself a universe by exclusion, is actually universalized through the poet's inescapable, allusive awareness of a larger poetic tradition. But the order of allusion is inseparable from, and is *significant* order only when read back into, the exact order of metaphor, descriptive imagery, diction and rhetorical balance, irony, which is produced here for the first and only time. Not the dream, but this, is Baudelaire's truly unique creation, and indeed that "paysage, tel que jamais mortel n'en vit."

And yet, really by the same token, we must be careful not to think of the allusions as so many measurable "units" of knowledge which the poet has gone out for and brought back then to set into the rigid context of his own statement — and that we have completed our critical duty with the allusions when we find out where he got them. For, if we are to insist upon the total inseparability of form and content, then once brought into the context there is no way of distinguishing such units. For, once more, a poem is *not* a building. Its allusive references are not blocks of building-stone, about which we can observe, 'This was quarried in Italy, this in England — note how the colors, the rough and the smooth, clash and blend,' and let it go at that. They are impulses, rather, waves of the energetic sympathies of mind and sensibility, that move continuously to and fro between poem and poem, culture and culture, century and century. Time limits our own attention to the motion. But we must be careful to leave it unimpeded.

Sonette an Orpheus,

I Teil, XX

Rilke's Singular Horse

Dir aber, Herr, o was weih ich dir, sag,
der das Ohr den Geschöpfen gelehrt? —
Mein Erinnern an einen Frühlingstag,
seinen Abend, in Russland —, ein Pferd . . .

Herüber vom Dorf kam der Schimmel allein,
an der vorderen Fessel den Pflock,
um die Nacht auf den Wiesen allein zu sein;
wie schlug seiner Mähne Gelock

an den Hals im Takte des Übermuts,
bei dem grob gehemmten Galopp.
Wie sprangen die Quellen des Rossebluts!

Der fühlte die Weiten, und ob!
der sang und der hörte —, dein Sagenkreis
war in ihm geschlossen.
        Sein Bild: ich weih's.

The *Sonette an Orpheus* is a single work. It was conceived and executed all in a remarkable rush of creative power that, for its suddenness and brevity and sureness, is one of the strangest events in the history of poetry. Each of the poems is an integral part of the volume. Yet, each is a design that comes whole in its own, individual right. How this may be, we shall hope not so much to illustrate as to discover, in a study of this sonnet of the white horse.

The obeisant, hymn style of the first line — with the conventional formula of the grammatically superfluous "dir aber," the "o" and the "sag," expressing at once an imploring attitude and a pre-condition of doubt or hesitancy on the speaker's part to approach the great "Herr," Orpheus, even to ask what he may consecrate to him — embodies the irony inherent in the question itself. The poet, in effect, is asking the god to *tell* him what to say to him, which, since Orpheus already knows it, must then seem worthless when it is repeated to him.

It is an irony related to that which we have observed in the discussion of Marvell's "The Coronet." Rilke's is just as much a *religious* poem as the older one. But perhaps we can define it more accurately here as the irony always involved in the invocation of a Muse. (Orpheus, of course, is himself a poet; but he is also the son of the Muse, Calliope.) It is the question of how the poet is to be "nothing in himself" — a mere "instrument" of the supernatural or at any rate more-than-human, spiritual power — and at the same time make the song that is played on that instrument, his poem, "something in itself" and worthy the god's *hearing* anew. This problem, or in the way Rilke handles it this mystery, of the nature of *inspiration*, is the principal burden of the whole volume of sonnets.

In saying this, I seem to run afoul of the formidable convictions of Miss Elizabeth Sewell, who takes *metamorphosis* as the key to the book. Miss Sewell's *The Orphic Voice* is an important work, which explains some important things about poetry in general and about Rilke in particular; I would not lightly dismiss even its exactitudes of terminology. And I would be inclined to agree with her that Rilke was not "inspired" to the *Sonette an Orpheus* in the sense that would be suggested by his own reference to them as an experience in "dictation." Poets are notoriously, and sometimes with malice aforethought, prone to exaggeration and inaccuracy in describing the processes of their thinking. It is a way of pinching critics, to make them wince, which is to say, a way of guarding the mysteries. But as Miss Sewell herself goes on briefly to indicate, there are other, more respectable modes of "inspiration."[1] And if I understand her (and myself) rightly, there is no great difference, finally, between what I mean by inspiration here (as power, process, and effect) and what she means by metamorphosis. I retain my term, as less troublesome at least for this particular sonnet of the horse, just because for the common reader, to whom the other word always suggests Ovid and nothing but, there is not likely to be anything occurring in the poem recognizable as *a* metamorphosis. Neither horse nor watching man undergoes a distinct change of form. But that both are inspired, carried out of themselves, into *motions* of body in the one case, mind in the other, is quite plain.[2]

One standard meaning of English "inspiration" is the literal one of in-*breathing*. Poetic exploitation of this sense in connection with the nonliteral meaning is common in English poetry. And in another of these sonnets, Rilke invests the German "Hauch," ordinarily limited to the sense of "breath" as a person's breath or as a breath or faint puff of wind, with a meaning corresponding to that of English "inspiration" as a received power — external and conceived as superhuman, by which one is intellectually and emotionally moved. It is in something of these terms that he defines singing, or poetic truth:

> *lerne*
> *vergessen, dass du aufsangst. Das verrinnt.*
> *In Wahrheit singen, ist ein andrer Hauch.*
> *Ein Hauch um nichts. Ein Wehn im Gott. Ein Wind.*
> *(I Teil, III)*

The total "poetic" elaborated in these sonnets is complex and subtle. It cannot be my purpose here to attempt a thorough analysis of that. And, obviously, I have oversimplified the meaning even of these few lines. There persists a curious and disturbing *separation* of the "du" and the "Gott." "Hauch" is earthy, human; man's breath.

---

[1] Elizabeth Sewell, *The Orphic Voice*, pp. 373-374.
[2] I might, with respect to what happens to the horse, suggest "transfiguration" as a term of compromise. But I suppose the theological connotations of this would make it hardly less, if not more, distasteful to Miss Sewell than in an opposite way she found Rilke's "dictation" to be regarding the processes of his writing.

But the "Hauch" which is "in Wahrheit singen" seems somehow not available to human lungs, either for in- or out-breathing. It simply *is* "out there," somewhere. But all the poems themselves are, in a sense, more disturbed by than concerned to settle this problem of the relationship of the inspiring power to the poet's mind, and of that mind to its natural object. It is a problem, a situation of balance, which is never forced quite into final stability.

The question with which Sonnet III (from which I quoted above) opens: "Ein Gott vermags. Wie aber, sag mir, soll/ Ein Mann ihm folgen durch die schmale Leier?" — is never answered in an entirely, theoretically satisfactory manner. One can never say, for example, quite simply that the poet is, in what we spoke of as the conventional figurative situation, himself the instrument of the inspiring power. In the lines I have just quoted, the figure suggested is more that of an accompaniment.[3] And Erich Heller, in his chapter on Rilke and Nietzsche in *The Disinherited Mind*, argues cogently that Rilke has, after all, created the god whom he invokes — that Rilke is, indeed, one of the principal modern poets in whose work we see a thorough acceptance of the fact that the older role of the poet as mouthpiece of the divine is no longer possible, that he must be now, primarily, god-maker. And I would only insist, as a corollary to agreement with this argument, that once having made the god, Rilke believes in him. Also, he did not make him absolutely out of nothing. Rilke's Orpheus, as Miss Sewell has shown, does not violate but only extends and further clarifies, reveals, the tradition. If no one is quite ready to say that the Orpheus of the Rilke poems himself *is*, before Rilke was, still the tradition, at least, was.

But, however all this may be — he is, perhaps, only the embodiment of his own impossibility — a god of some kind, name of a god, broods over the book. And we can define at least his practical, operational nature, in terms of certain recurrent motifs of the poetry.

One of these is the repeated emphasis on what may be called the receptive faculty of the poet, upon the importance, in a certain sense, of the "ear" in his equipment. This means partly, an ear for the sound of verse, for the relationship of "sound and sense." But, at the moment, I mean primarily an emphasis upon the receptive as op-

---

[3] The lines contain, in fact, multiple ambiguities. The "schmale Leier" is, in one sense, the ear itself. And "folgen durch" has also here the literal meaning of "to follow (him) through."

posed to the inquisitive, upon listening, as against questioning. Thus (cf. line 2 of Sonnet XX) —

> *da schufst du ihnen Tempel im Gehör.*
> *(I Teil, I)*

And closely related to this emphasis is that upon the imitative function. Poetic truth is *figurative.*

> *Auch die sternische Verbindung trügt.*
> *Doch uns freue eine Weile nun,*
> *der Figur zu glauben. Das genügt.*
> *(I Teil, XI)*

and again —

> *Heil dem Geist, der uns verbinden mag;*
> *denn wir leben wahrhaft in Figuren.*
> *(I Teil, XII)*

To come back now to Sonnet XX, the rhetorical question is what may be offered — that is, is suitable to be offered, dedicated or consecrated — to the master Orpheus. And the final "answer" is that only the "Bild," image, of the horse will serve. "Sein Bild: ich weih's."

Heller sees as something of primary importance in Rilke's poetic, the notion of the "once," the "emphasis . . . on the eternity of the moment here and now, the irrevocability of the one and unique opportunity and test of living."[4] He quotes, in this connection, from the ninth of the Duino elegies:

> *Einmal*
> *jedes, nur einmal. Einmal und nicht mehr. Und wir auch*
> *einmal. Nie wieder. Aber dieses*
> *einmal gewesen zu sein, wenn auch nur einmal:*
> *irdisch gewesen zu sein, scheint nicht widerrufbar.*

And there is this sense of the unique "once" about the memory of the horse. It is caught first in the way that the incident is precisely located

---

[4] Erich Heller, *the Disinherited Mind,* p. 128.

in time and place — "einen Frühlingstag,/ seinen Abend, in Russland." The details of time and place, of "setting," are not allowed to get in the way of the image to be presented, or to obscure its brilliance. There is, in fact, a certain quality of abruptness, even impatience, in this clipped phrasing, the "items" — Frühlingstag, Abend, Russland — set off in simple series by commas, with a minimal use of connectives and modifiers. It reads almost like the sparsely informational statement of stage directions for a play — Time: a Spring day, evening; Place, Russia — no more than is barely necessary to provide a frame for the essential thing, the action. But it is enough, and indeed the very curtness, abruptness, matter-of-factness, accords to fix the incident "irrevocably." Then, there, it was; no more.

And yet, as image in the memory, the incident, the action, is recalled. And this is the essential qualification of the "einmal und nicht mehr." To look back again at these lines from the ninth elegy: what has been once, on earth, *cannot* be "called back again" in the sense of revoked, cancelled out. But what this means is, of course, that it does continue to exist; that it can be, in fact, *re*called, remembered. It is the very, irrevocable "once-ness" of a thing that insures, in a sense, its eternality. (Cf. Heller's phrase in the quotation above — "the eternity of the moment.") So it is with the horse here.

About these lines once more, the third and fourth of the first stanza: the final effect of the movement we have been talking about, of the clipped series of "stage directions," is precisely to introduce, and to isolate for principal attention, not so much the fact of its having been once, but *that which* was once, the absolutely one *thing*, Pferd. "Ein Pferd." 'A horse' does not quite get it. We lose something in English that we do not capitalize nouns; but still more that our words for "a" and "one" are not the same. The movement of the line, especially with the full pause indicated by the punctuation of a long dash and comma preceding the phrase, and the multiple period following, exactly calculates this effect — that it is not simply "ein Pferd," but *"ein* Pferd." There are other significances in the stage directions: the associations of liveliness, of re-awakening, in "Frühling," appropriate both to the spirit of the horse's movement and to the sense of the recovery of the image in the poet's memory, and perhaps anticipating the later image of the surging of the horse's blood, "die Quellen des Rossebluts"; the suggestion, in "Russland," that the incident is being recalled from a considerable distance, as well as from the passage of time; the fact that it is evening, which provides a further sense of the difficulty with which the thing is, or was, literally "seen," the mysterious quality of the horse's flight. But the matter of principal importance is just the concentration of attention upon the horse.

And in the next section, "herüber," meaning principally, in the context of the recalled incident, only to or past the place where the poet watches — but suggesting also the sense of the image's reappearing now, coming over to the "here" of this moment of recollection — perhaps distracts us momentarily to the poet's own situation. But more heavily emphasized in the first three lines of this group is, again, the horse, and his oneness, aloneness. He comes from the village (where, of course, he would have been among the crowd of other creatures) now "allein" — this word picking up the "ein" of "ein Pferd," and being then strongly secured by its repetition in line 7 in such a way that it forms both an internal and an end rime with "sein." He *is*, one, unique. To be "ein," "*all*ein," is "zu sein."

But this gives us a rather too rigid impression of the horse, of the state of his being. And perhaps it would be better to say that the essential image is of an *action* — of the horse, but of the horse *moving*. It is as an impression of movement and, I think it is implied, only as such that the being of the horse is communicated, and survives in, can be reproduced from, the poet's memory. Essential to this impression, as a matter of poetic technique, is the sound pattern of the verse.

The arrangement of the last two lines in the first section, which we have discussed, in itself exemplifies the extent to which "Ohr" in line 2 refers literally to the importance of sound in the creation of the image. The following six lines bear this out still more strongly. Part of the effect, the more obvious, is that of the varied anapaestic movement, beginning after the first foot of line 5 — which reproduces, of course, the rhythm of the horse's gait. But the animal is dragging from its forefoot either a clog, or a stake to which it has been tethered,[5] so that the pace cannot be quite free and even; and in

---

5 "Pflock" usually does mean a *stake*, or *peg*. What in English is called a "clog," a heavy wooden block attached to the foot of an animal to prevent its straying, might be indicated. But a "hobble" (the word one sees most often in English translations of the poem) could not be meant. Though clumsily, the horse is running, galloping. With a hobble, which binds the feet together, this would be impossible.

analyzing the movement it is important to see that the anapaest is, as I have said, varied, and strongly so.

Line 7 ends rather abruptly with an iamb — the effect of checking reinforced, incidentally, with the internal rime "allein . . . sein," and further with the relatively difficult z — s mutation, besides the full grammatical stop at this point indicated by the semi-colon. And the next line begins again, as did line 5, with an iamb — the last syllable of which, the heavy "schlug" (heavy both in sound and sense) is followed by a secondary accent, on "sein" — before the freer movement is half restored in the last part of this line and the two following. "Übermuts," in line 9, matched by "Rossebluts" in line 11, tends to detach itself as a complete dactyl, and thus curiously to distort the rhythm, while line 10 takes the pattern —

běi děm grób/gěhémm/těn Gălópp

a central iamb between two anapaests. The restricted movement here is reinforced by the heavy g- alliteration and the final stops of -b in "grob" and -p in "Galopp," and further by the internal rime or, according to the preference of the reader's ear, near-rime which these two words from — -b and -p having in this position, of course, the same phonetic value, and "o" in "grob" permitting either [o] or the [ɔ] of "Ga-lopp." Since "grob" *means* clumsy, rough, heavy, there must be something of this sense of awkwardness retained especially in this line. That sense is carried by means of these phonic complications, which occur at the same time that the stress-rhythm of the lines (what shows up in simple scansion) is kept relatively free. The freedom must be a strong, still striving, liberty.

The g- g- g- alliteration of line 10, incidentally, clearly balances that of the v- f- f- pattern in line 6, but with a significant shift from the less obtrusive, softer sounds, to the stronger and harsher as, so to speak, the running horse comes nearer, and the precise irregularities of his gait emerge more strongly.

Further, we may observe that in the way the lines of this passage are grouped on the page, in relationship to the rime-scheme and the grammar, there is reflected the feeling of a movement at once hindered and free. With respect to rime, the four lines of the second section are a quatrain, the scheme closed, and decisively so on the -ock sound, within the section; but grammatically, it is not closed —

the sentence flowing on without a break into the next section, and not coming to a full stop until the end of the second line there, where "Galopp" assonantly and alliteratively echoes "Gelock."

The entire image, we have observed, is *of* a movement, so that it is impossible really to separate the verse movement (including even such matters as are indicated by the spacing of the lines on the page) from the other elements. We cannot speak, with any great accuracy, of a prosodic effect which simply *reinforces* an image otherwise established. But for purposes of analysis we can, now, go back to distinguish certain other non-aural effects which coöperate with the aural in securing the same emphasis on the *motion* of the horse. Beyond the fact that he is a white horse — "der Schimmel" — which makes him stand out against the semi-darkness suggested by "Abend," only two visual details are mentioned, the clog or stake he is dragging, and the name. And both of these, of course, point to the movement — the restricted forward motion of the legs, and the rising and falling of the neck. That it is the *locks* of the mane, severally agitated rather than smoothed into one curve, clearly emphasizes the character of the motion, in cadence with the hindered high spirits of the beast — "im Takte des Übermuts."

Generally, then, to move back to the problems of the poem as a whole, we can say that the fact that the horse is hindered but careless of the hindrance, which complicates the rhythm of his motion but does not stay it, makes that motion, and the urgency of his joy, only the more dynamic. And the restricted movement of the horse's feet, imitated in the subtly irregular "gait" of the verse, exactly figures the difficulty of the poet's striving here to attain a kind of devotional union with Orpheus. The horse's effort to join the inner impulse of his "Übermut" to a compelling or beckoning force without, with that which is in the distance, "Weiten," is the poet's own in making his offering. Erich Heller sees Rilke as the principal poet, as Nietzsche was the philosopher, of immanence. He associates with this the idea of the "once," and reads in both the philosopher and the poet a doctrine of the "transmutation of pain and suffering" whereby they see "in the greatest possible intensification of immanence salvation from the inglorious prison."[6] The horse here, with the dragging

---

[6] Erich Heller, *op. cit., loc. cit.*

weight at his foot, might be seen as symbolic of this "imprisonment" of the mind in immanence, and his running, despite the hindrance, despite the added pain it causes him, as the saving "intensification."

But this solves everything a little too neatly. To elaborate the phrase we used just now, there is not one difficulty which the poet has in getting to the god, and another which the horse has in reaching the meadow, the first of which can be overcome simply by projecting it in terms of the second — by, so to speak, "allegorizing" poet-aspiring as horse-running.

For this would be to make the horse unreal. And that the horse has a distinct and separate reality is absolutely insisted upon throughout the poem. We get, in the poem, and can only get, an image; but it is an image of the reality. The poet has said, we must observe, that the horse is something he remembers; it is not something he has "imagined" in the sense of inventing it, making it up, to serve as concrete representation of what was first a concept — the concept of himself in his aspiration.

The horse is distinct, first, as horse. There is no intrusion of the poet's human feelings, no suggestion that we should be interested in the horse because he is, in some way, like a man. His self-sufficiency, as beast, his eagerness to get away to the meadow which is the place of his kind, away from the village, the place of man, is precisely the ground of the poet's admiration for him.

After the passage in which he imitates the horse's running, after, as it were, the horse has gone past him, the poet empathically realizes the urgency of his blood — "Wie sprangen die Quellen des Rosse-bluts!" — and figures it as a singing, and hearing, which establishes again the communication of the remembered action to the present intention of the poem-offering. But it seems to me very important that he has said, directly, *horse*blood. If it had been simply rich blood, or mighty blood, or what not, it would have been still clear from the context that the reference was primarily to the horse and his eagerness. But that would have allowed entirely too quickly the interpretation of "blood" *merely* as high spirits, vitality, life force — and so the implication that the poet could wholly join with the joy of that urgency the delight of his admiration for it; and so, further, in this unstable identification, a possible shift of primary attention back to the poet and his situation after all, the horse again becoming only a projection of his subjective feelings — again, the figure of the easy allegory. *Horse*blood, "blood" as kind, *not* human kind, makes this mistake, or at any rate this oversimplification, impossible.

The horse's urgency sings in answer to, pursues, what the horse has heard, in complete indifference to the poet's yearning. "Dein Sagenkreis/ War in ihm geschlossen." In his mythic character, the horse is one of the beasts that come to Orpheus, charmed by his music. And for realization of the way in which he is especially pleasing to the god, already in a sense belongs to the myth, it is essential that we see the horse *as* beast. For the very mystery of Orpheus' power is, of course, that it is *dumb* creatures, dumb things, whose hearts respond to his song. The poet must make it clear (as he has, I think) that he is not claiming anything resembling this power in his own right. Rilke does not suggest that the horse has in any way responded to *his* singing, come running forth into being, into beauty, just to furnish him a subject for his poem, an object in which he can invest his subjective feelings. For so to overlook the difference between himself and the horse would be to disregard the difference between himself and Orpheus — and thus to make his first obeisance, his announced intention to *consecrate* something *to* the god, meaningless.

For, consider the history of horse and man. The poem is reverberant with silent awareness of that history. The first poem we considered in this book presented us an image from the age of, in the literal sense of the word, chivalry — the mounted man, man and horse together, as fullness and pride of life, the unmounted man, man and horse divided, as disgrace and death. And in the 19th century, a poet strangely like Rilke — in a poem strangely like this one of Rilke's, a poem of silent watching the animal beauty, of the silent singing of animal motion, "The Windhover" — could see the songless bird, still, a "chevalier" upon the mount of air. Only the bird, to be sure; only "in the air," distant and entirely silent, the image holds intact, though "plow down sillion shine." But that is still a great deal; and Hopkins could manage it, because the time was not yet quite the *twentieth* century, and because he was a Catholic priest. Man and horse, though only in falcon and air, yet could be one in Christ. But for Rilke there can be now no such "middle distance" of the sky in which to fix the image. Miss Sewell[7] has noted how "the way is prepared" for Sonnet

---

[7] Elizabeth Sewell, *op. cit.*, pp. 395-396.

asks the question: Is there no constellation of Horse and Rider? Rilke sets up two extremes, the stars and a mental image (which is of course exactly what a constellation is, a fusion of these two) and tries to bridge them by postulating a unity between real horse and real man. The vision does not succeed; the poem falls back into separation, between man and beast, between star and the figure alone, which is all we are left with at the end, enjoined to believe *that* for the time being, if we cannot do more.

And, indeed, the "way is prepared." If no constellation, Rilke seems thoroughly to have made up his mind.in the intervening eight sonnets, no man-and-horse in the stars, then back to earth and nothing but — back to horse, and nothing but, and back to man, and nothing but. The separation is so emphatic that the poem might prophesy even our own, still further alienation forty years later — sixty from the time "der Schimmel" first appeared to Rilke in Russia — when the horse has ceased to serve us even as plow horse.

But further, the horse is distinct, not only as horse, but as *that* horse, *that* beast. We will recall the earlier emphasis on his one-ness. He is going to the meadow, not simply as to the place proper for horses, but "allein zu sein." And this sense too is clearly contained in the figure of the closing of the circle — "dein Sagenkreis/ war in *ihm* geschlossen."

For the greatness of Orpheus' power is not just that he can make dumb things responsively articulate — but that to make articulate is to make individual. As we have already several times observed, his bringing these things into song is his bringing them into life — the rocks out of the total oblivion of inert thing-ness, the trees, and finally the beasts, out of their states of partial, passive vitality, still undifferentiated except as to kind, into the fullness of individual, expressive consciousness. Each thing that responds to that music, that sings with Orpheus, must respond "on its own." To sing is fully to be, and to be, is to be one.

But this is the point at which we begin to realize the compensatory value in the separation of man and beast. In this *being* of the horse, "ein" and "allein," the poet can in some sense share. *Only* as he realizes that the horse is its own thing, one, and other than himself, can he recall the horse's flight and make it the substance of his own, present praise of Orpheus. Thus the poem achieves its purpose. To consecrate anything to Orpheus — who is himself the self-sacrificing, the torn god, whose purpose is wholly to bring other things into full being, life — is just to keep oneself out of the way of that thing's motion toward the god. It is to confess that one can hold the thing, and present it, only in "Bild," image, of its passing.

(The arrangement of the lines here again at the end is important. As "weih" picks up the theme of the first line, the dropping of the last half-line yet keeps the "circle" of the image, the poem, what the poet himself has created, clear of the "Sagenkreis," the larger cycle of Orphic myth, which is not of the poet's making, but simply "given," and which is closed in the horse — to which the horse belongs quite apart from the poet's consent or intention.)

And yet that keeping out of the way, that careful limiting of the poem's intent, also promises that the image, if only an image, is a clear one. Rilke claims only to show what he has seen. Or, rather, to put it in terms that are closer both to the facts of the poem's statement, and to the idea that he avows his possession only of the blessedness of receiving, not of giving — he claims only to tell what he has heard. But, unquestionably, he has heard it well.

But this also means, I would conclude, that "Bild" in this sonnet is not quite the same as the "Figur" of Sonnet XI, in which we are asked only temporarily to believe. The "Sagenkreis" is neither more nor less closed in this poem than in the others. That it is not closed in the sense of being *ended*, is perfectly apparent from the fact that more sonnets follow this one — all still celebrating the continuing, cyclical life of the mystery. But we have made progress in the book, toward clearer understanding — and conviction. At least, Rilke has.

This is where I must finally disagree with Miss Sewell. She has said, with reference to Sonnet XI, that "a constellation *is*, a fusion of these two . . . stars and a mental image." (Italics mine.) But no. A constellation is a coming together of stars. The stars *are* in the positions they are in. The "mental image," in the sense in which Miss Sewell obviously means it, is only the way we read that positioning — as The Scales, The Bear, or whatever. Any such mental image (one of them the Lyre of Orpheus) is a "Figur," product of traditional imagination, and subject of the doubtful and tentative belief which is enjoined upon us at the close of that sonnet. Rilke would have liked to find a "Figur" of Horse and Rider among them; but regretfully cannot. And the regret is the condition of doubt which makes the final injunction tentative. Now, I am not accusing Rilke of seeking a "philosophical" exactitude of terminology. Even the "Figur" of the final lines of Sonnet XI, in which we are even tentatively to believe, has in fact primary reference to his *own* figure, of the Horse and Rider, which is not among the stars, rather than to those which are. And already by the very next poem, Sonnet XII, "Figuren" itself is beginning to take on another meaning. But what this all, obviously, is moving toward is an affirmation in the later poem (Sonnet XX) that the god has reality *apart* from the tradition, apart from any of the old stories that have been told about him, and the last "traditional" one of which (the tale of the translated lyre) had put him there beyond our ken, "among the stars." In the word "Bild," we have again, at length, the "better" word for that affirmation. It appears to me that Rilke everywhere uses "Bild" as the word for an image, representation, which is closest to the objective reality, and "Figur" for the more abstract, comparative construction, "figure of speech."

I myself have said that the poet "figures" the movements of the horse as a singing and a hearing. But this is inaccurate, a concession to conventional modes of critical thinking. No; the horse is real, and really sings. And it is *only* our ingrained habits of living outside the mythic reality, Rilke suggests, that makes our speech, our song, inadequate to interpret that song of the beast's silence.[8] For he is still saying this, that the poem is celebrative only, an offering inadequate to the reality — even the "Bild" a *mere* Bild. But, in its confession of inadequacy, the "Bild" is nearer to the truth, the reality of silence from which right speech comes, than the more pretentious "Figur." And it is by this same token that he is saying at last that *Orpheus* is real.

Embarrassing as it may be, Rilke is finding a god in this book, and really believing in him. He is not drawing upon "myths" for "metaphors," but pushing metaphor into myth — and myth as living truth, not as "poetic tradition" ("myths" plural). The strength of the

---

[8] Cf. Max Picard's beautiful words on animals. "Animals carry silence around with them. . . . They carry not only the burden of things on their backs but also the burden of silence. Animals . . . are always putting silence down in front of man. . . . Animals move through the world of words like a caravan of silence." *The World of Silence*, p. 100.

metaphor is inseparable from the truth of the myth. We may not approve of this. It may somehow "spoil" the poems for us, make them less self-complete than we imagine poems ought to be, safely set apart from the agony of belief. But, regardless of the probable inaccuracy in Rilke's description of the *process* of his inspiration as "dictation," the poems present themselves as inspired. It simply will not do for us to try and "redeem" Rilke, because we like him, for any of our contrary orthodoxies. It will not do for Miss Sewell, after all else she has said, blandly to assert that in Sonnet XX "one of earth's loveliest and earthiest creatures ('dieser Stolz aus Erde' Rilke called the horse) is offered back to Orpheus, who is in his turn, being a myth, a figure of the mind."[9] A curious sentence, anyway one looks at it — can she possibly mean to suggest that the *horse*, the "creature," is a "figure of the mind?"

But, in any case, no; "sein *Bild*, ich weih's." *Not* the horse; because, being *not* a "figure of the mind," but a god, Orpheus has already got the horse. The horse is not Rilke's to offer, nor ours.

---

[9] Elizabeth Sewell, *op. cit.*, *loc. cit.*

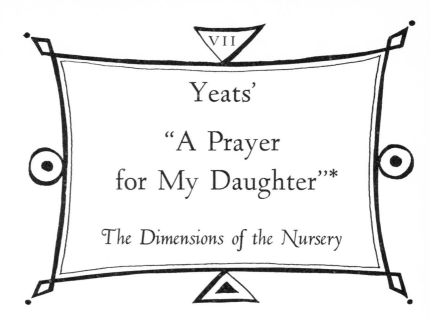

VII

Yeats'

"A Prayer for My Daughter"*

The Dimensions of the Nursery

Once more the storm is howling, and half hid
Under this cradle-hood and coverlid
My child sleeps on: There is no obstacle
But Gregory's wood and one bare hill
Whereby the haystack- and roof-levelling wind,
Bred on the Atlantic, can be stayed;
And for an hour I have walked and prayed
Because of the great gloom that is in my mind.

I have walked and prayed for this young child an hour
And heard the sea-wind scream upon the tower,
And under the arches of the bridge, and scream
In the elms above the flooded stream;
Imagining in excited reverie
That the future years had come,
Dancing to a frenzied drum,
Out of the murderous innocence of the sea.

May she be granted beauty and yet not
Beauty to make a stranger's eye distraught,
Or hers before a looking-glass, for such,
Being made beautiful overmuch,
Consider beauty a sufficient end,
Lose natural kindness and maybe
The heart-revealing intimacy
That chooses right, and never find a friend.

Helen being chosen found life flat and dull
And later had much trouble from a fool,
While that great Queen, that rose out of the spray,
Being fatherless could have her way
Yet chose a bandy-legged smith for man.
It's certain that fine women eat
A crazy salad with their meat
Whereby the Horn of Plenty is undone.

In courtesy I'd have her chiefly learned;
Hearts are not had as a gift but hearts are earned
By those that are not entirely beautiful;
Yet many, that have played the fool
For beauty's very self, has charm made wise,
And many a poor man that has roved,
Loved and thought himself beloved,
From a glad kindness cannot take his eyes.

May she become a flourishing hidden tree
That all her thoughts may like the linnet be,
And have no business but dispensing round
Their magnanimities of sound,
Nor but in merriment begin a chase,
Nor but in merriment a quarrel.
O may she live like some green laurel
Rooted in one dear perpetual place.

My mind, because the minds that I have loved,
The sort of beauty that I have approved,

Prosper but little, has dried up of late,
Yet knows that to be choked with hate
May well be of all evil chances chief.
If there's no hatred in a mind
Assault and battery of the wind
Can never tear the linnet from the leaf.

An intellectual hatred is the worst,
So let her think opinions are accursed.
Have I not seen the loveliest woman born
Out of the mouth of Plenty's horn,
Because of her opinionated mind
Barter that horn and every good
By quiet natures understood
For an old bellows for an angry wind?

Considering that, all hatred driven hence,
The soul recovers radical innocence
And learns at last that it is self-delighting,
Self-appeasing, self-affrighting,
And that its own sweet will is Heaven's will;
She can, though every face should scowl
And every windy quarter howl
Or every bellows burst, be happy still.

And may her bridegroom bring her to a house
Where all's accustomed, ceremonious;
For arrogance and hatred are the wares
Peddled in the thoroughfares.
How but in custom and in ceremony
Are innocence and beauty born?
Ceremony's a name for the rich horn,
And custom for the spreading laurel tree.

We cannot, of course, take the dimensions I speak of. It is the ultimate and incalculable human subject with which Yeats is here concerned, the mystery of one's having begotten, the solicitude for the new life which is one's own and yet not, in which one is reborn and yet must die. And it is a girl child, too; there is *that* dimension, which the father does not forget. The cradle contains the womb. Where is the beginning, and where the end?

But, confronted with such a poem, on such a subject, we can only hope somewhat to imitate in the commentary the attitude which the anxious speaker presently enjoins upon himself. It is a fortitude, courage, blend of inseparable humility and pride; the will to see that it *has* begun, and that there is no means whereby now to calculate beginning and end except the determination to know where as a man, intellectual and otherwise, one takes his own stand in the center.

It is, in every sense, a *middle* poem. It is intensely personal, intimate, and yet curiously stiff and didactic, aloof. It comes approximately at the middle of Yeats' career, and has a correspondingly moderate style, something halfway between the earlier romanticism and the later, occult realism. And, although this may well be why the poem has received little critical attention, has seemed perhaps even to many of Yeats' admirers not unattractive but not exciting, yet it can be appreciated as the source of a peculiar strength. For that "moderate" character of the style, once we have got beneath its surface, is neither blandness nor a compromising uncertainty. Actually, it is the one quality which basically distinguishes all of Yeats' poetry, and ties together all phases of his achievement, which gives his voice and his unmistakably to any poem he wrote in any period, in any mask. It is a voice profoundly honest in its immodesty, a voice daring the ages, a voice hiding consummate intellectual grace and consummate modernity under a calculated, provincial awkwardness, crotchets of old-fashioned dignity: the voice of what I should call the grand colloquial.

When sustained at such length as in the present poem, it is a voice that requires considerable patience of attention. But it is sustained. And if anything in Yeats is worth the patience, this is.

Because of the storm, and because it is his own child, with whom he is alone in a room of his own house, so that the speaker appears in his private rather than his public character, the mood is different. But this room, as we shall see, is ultimately quite as long as "the long schoolroom." And here, somewhat as in the more familiar "Among School Children," the technique is a movement from direct "dramatic" representation, the scene with the anxious father and his child in the nursery, to something altogether reflective beginning with the third stanza.

One of the principal means by which the transition is effected — from attention to the scene, the account of the actual storm, to the "excited reverie" of the major, prophetic part of the poem — is the development of the "drum" metaphor in the second stanza. There is an effect of mounting intensity from the second through the fourth line here, secured finally by the end-rime of "scream" with "stream." But the progression is not quite steady. The movement is a recurrent gathering and rushing, rising and falling, mounting toward the repeated, high-pitched and quantitatively accented "scream," and dropping back in the following phrases. This pulsing motion is partly an imitative effect; the real storm winds surge, recede and again rise, in just this way. But the ultimate function of it is to introduce the metaphor, of the drum and the dance of the years — in which the speaker becomes concerned purely, in several senses rather abstractedly, with rhythm as such, with "time."

In his "prayer," the father entertains a vision of the child's future. Moreover, as we shall observe in studying the pattern of allusion, this multiple time-consciousness, in which the future is involved fully in the present, includes also the past. The symbol for the nonhistorical, nonprogressive time sense of the poem, is the drum — musical, or to be more precise, dance time. The situation is carefully pointed up in the grammar — "I *have* walked," etc., "imagining . . . that the future years *had* come." The future is already somehow past; and the years in the image come all in a rush, not only dancing, which in itself suggests a motion self-contained, repetitive, nonprogressive, and with the performers all acting in strict unison, but also "dancing to a *frenzied* drum," that is, to a pace so rapid that the individual identity which the succeeding years have in the progression of historical time is lost.

And, in the sequence of the poem's development, the metaphor is already pushing our awareness not only forward but at the same time backward. For, in the first stanza, the father's distracted pacing of the nursery floor — the aimlessness, the restless "circularity" of his movements suggested by the close repetition of the phrase "walked and prayed" — already anticipates, at a slower tempo, the motions of the phantasmal dance.

The circumstances of the opening scene, then, serve as true occasion — not simply as a casual "background" — for the prophetic reverie. In the first place, we have here a clear, physical representation of the opposition of "inside" and "outside." The father is intensely conscious of being, with his sleeping child, *inside* — inside the strong tower, inside the room, the child lying inside the "cradle-hood and coverlid" — as he listens to the threatening voice of the storm without. If we did not have this, then the speaker's later, exclusive concern with what is in his mind, "the great gloom that is in my mind," as opposed to the gloom and threat of the actual storm, the "haystack and roof-levelling wind," his turning, within the enclosure of the room, still further within upon himself, could not come about *as* a turning, a transition. And, clearly, it is as a transition that it takes on its entire significance. But we may observe further how the descriptive images of the opening section anticipate, and in a sense control, the metaphorical pattern in the latter part.

Not all the properties of the initial setting are involved in the process of recurrent reference. Besides their function in providing two of the varied "voices" of the wind, the bridge and the tower carry traditional symbolic suggestions that are richly appropriate to the general purposes of the poem. The bridge has obvious connections with the themes of time and prophecy. And we may be conscious of the tower, not only for its values in the general tradition, but for those it takes on as a symbol used very often in Yeats' other poems. It is associated with the themes of intellectual "splendid isolation," of the aspiration of the mind beyond itself, its heaven-reaching, of a privacy also that is hard-won, arduously "built" — in this instance, of Yeats' *Thoor Ballylee*, re-built, from ancient ruins "for a girl's love," so that the mysteries of time and of sex are there too. And so on. But these two remain standing here only as a kind of signs at the entranceway to the poem, and are not explicitly referred to again.

On the other hand, the mere fact that winds of one sort and another blow throughout the poem, is an altogether obvious example of the establishment of a motif in these opening stanzas. But, among the recurrences, the one to which I would call particular attention as possibly the most important besides that of the winds themselves, and also as the most subtly contrived, is the motif of the small, protected spot, the quiet, and firmly grounded, retreat or enclosure. It is presented first in the picture of the room and the cradle, inside the house with its strong tower, and is picked up again later in the poem in the image of the girl as a "flourishing hidden tree," and of her thoughts as a bird sitting singing among the branches. Then it occurs once more in the final image of the house "where all's accustomed, ceremonious," standing apart from the noisy thoroughfares, to which the father hopes his daughter's bridegroom may take her.

The later image of the laurel tree, as enclosure image — the tree itself at first in the sixth stanza "hidden," but then in the seventh appearing with the wind blowing through it — tends to resolve the opposition of the opening stanzas. There, trees appear as an image of protection, but ineffectual — the trees of "Gregory's wood"; and again, "the elms above the flooded stream," merely as a submissive instrument of the raging wind, providing one of the threatening voices that come to the father's ears from outside the protected circle of the room. But the *mythic* tree, the laurel, furnishes an image of human dignity safeguarded both internally and externally. And the resolution, the tying together of images associated with the inside and the outside, is completed in the last stanza of the poem, where the tree as Custom ("Ceremony's a name for the rich horn/ And custom for the spreading laurel tree") is finally, in a sense, inside the house itself.

II

But further, just as the circumstances of the opening "drama" of domestic commonplace, the father's somewhat consciously overworked anxiety for the child as he hears the storm roaring about the house, set the pattern of imagery for the ensuing reverie — so, throughout the poem, there is a continuing tension between the private, or local, and the universal or traditional, a playing off of "personal" against "literary" or "learned" allusions.

In the latter class, the stories of Helen and Aphrodite, alluded to in the fourth stanza, have a sufficiently clear function as great and famous examples of the kind of bad matches made by women who, in the too exclusive service of beauty, "lose . . . the heart-revealing intimacy that chooses right." The one, Helen, is taken as a somewhat passive victim of her beauty, "being chosen"; while the other, Aphrodite, was willful, "could have her way," and did, "yet chose" perversely. But Yeats concludes his remarks on Helen and Aphrodite with the observation that "It's certain that fine women eat/ A crazy salad with their meat/ Whereby the Horn of Plenty is undone."

In the full context of the poem, the repeated reference to the Horn has a complex significance. Among other things that it has been in its varied and somewhat obscure history, the Horn of Plenty is one of the attributes of the goddess Fortuna. Fortuna seems to have been earliest an agricultural, harvest goddess. But it appears that she was from the first not merely associated with the bounty of the harvest, the goods of fortune, but somehow especially identified with, and perhaps regarded as controlling, the humanly unpredictable elements such as weather conditions that shape the fate of crops. Later, she enjoyed a reputation principally for fortune-*telling*, and for a time maintained in Italy two very popular oracles. And, since one of the earliest Greek traditions of the Horn of Plenty is that it had the power of making come true whatever its possessor wished for, it seems likely that the Horn became an attribute of Fortuna as much for this association, with foretelling the future, as for its being filled with fruits and flowers by the Naïades when it was broken from the head of Achelous, and so appropriated to the purposes of Fortuna as an agricultural deity. Moreover, Fortuna's oracle at Praeneste was the particular resort of those seeking to foretell the future of newly born children. And it is in this fact that we have the most immediately striking significance of the Horn of Plenty as a symbol in "A Prayer for My Daughter."

But, in any event, it seems in the poem generally to signify Fortune in the largest sense — of individual *destiny*. And that is ultimately involved with the problem of will, the power of moral choice, which is stated first as a matter simply of individual action in the references to "choosing right," of the third stanza, and to the "choices" of Helen and Aphrodite in the lines following, and then conclusively in the ninth stanza, where the individual human will is reconciled to the divine, the soul learning, but only when it has recovered "radical innocence," that "its own sweet will is Heaven's will." Fortune, as it is symbolized by Yeats in the Horn of Plenty, is not chance. It is, in fact, as we shall see further, directly opposed to chance — which among other things is represented rather by the symbol that is contrary to the Horn, that of the "old bellows full of angry wind." And the inquiry of the father is not, finally, into his child's "fortune" as a question of what will "happen to her," but rather into what virtues she may have to strengthen her, hold her steady, against the turbulence of chance. His concern, we may say, is not with what will *happen*, but with how she may "be *happy* still . . . ," no matter what occurs, "though every face should scowl/ And every windy quarter howl/ Or every bellows burst. . . ."

The second major symbol of the poem, associated with the Horn in opposition to the forces of the symbolic wind, is that of the tree, principally established in the sixth stanza. The identification, in the final lines, of the "hidden tree" which the father would have his daughter "become" — "O may she live like some green *laurel*/ Rooted in one dear perpetual place" — contains a veiled allusion to the story of Daphne and Apollo. The echo is appropriate in that the promises Apollo made to the transformed Daphne, that her leaves would be forever green, and used to make the wreaths of immortal fame, establish the tree in the original story as a symbol precisely of those *traditional*, enduring virtues, of "custom" and "ceremony," which the father here prays may characterize his daughter's life. The beauty to which Apollo pays his final great tribute, recognizing its superiority to that of hair and smooth cheek, the fleeting, transitory grace of the nymph's swift limbs that had first inflamed his desire, corresponds here to "the sort of beauty [he has] approved" — as opposed to the "beauty to make a stranger's eyes distraught" — which the father has prayed his daughter may be spared.

But an essential part of Yeats' daring, in many of his major poems, is the finely unembarrassed fashion in which he introduced any and all of his intimates ("And say my glory was I had such friends") to the company of the immortals. And it furnishes a considerable enrichment of our understanding of the poem — specifically of the fact that the father begins his inquiry into the blessings with which his daughter may be equipped for her future life with a consideration of *beauty* — if we have in mind the additional fact that Yeats' wife, George, had prepared shortly before the poem was written a horoscope for the infant daughter. From this it appeared that she would be, in Yeats' phrase at the time, "both good-looking and lucky."[1]

If we can to this extent identify the father in the poem with Yeats, he is "gloomy" — not just over the uncertainty of fate in general, or, somewhat more particularly, but still simply in the way of possi-

---

[1] Quoted by Joseph Hone, *W. B. Yeats*, p. 338.

bilities, from fear that his daughter *may* turn out to be more beautiful than she is wise — but he is gloomy, over the definite prophecy already made, which has aroused his anxiety because of its apparently self-contradictory promise. It helps considerably to clarify the whole burden and sequence of his reflections, if we can see him as concerned with this specific question — of how one *can* be both beautiful and fortunate, both "good-looking" *and* "lucky." Further, the allusion may be seen as introducing another element of dramatic tension in the argument of the poem that might otherwise not be apparent — having to do with the question of how one does or can "foretell" the future, with the problem, central to the entire concern of the poem, of how one consults, or knows what is, "Heaven's will." We might think of Yeats, after the manner of the device so familiar in Greek drama, as anxiously seeking in the poem the authority of an oracle — oldest and most famous for the cases of infants, Fortuna's — which will counter or somehow qualify, so as to remove the possible curse, the auguries of George.

And, if the pursuit of this reference may seem to some readers to lead us a bit "outside" the poem, there is on the other hand no getting around the essential, critical relevance of the allusions to Maud Gonne — "the loveliest woman born/ Out of the mouth of Plenty's Horn." The specific allusion in the "hatred" and "opinion" references of the eighth stanza is to the noisy contention and petty, bickering factionalism of Irish revolutionary politics in which Maud Gonne became involved, and in which the cultural and educational interests of Yeats in the movement (part of what is meant in "every good by quiet natures understood") were lost sight of. In the next stanza, the image "or every bellows burst" — i.e., and so blow out air in every direction at once — complicates the sense of the previous line, "and every windy quarter howl" — an uproar on all sides, a rushing together of all the contrarious winds on one spot. In this connection, with the reference in "every windy quarter" to the ancient conception of the squared earth — each side or "quarter" of it occupied by one of the "four winds" — the bellows becomes reminiscent of such a bag as that in which Aeolus closed up all but one of the winds to give Odysseus clear sailing, but which the foolish sailors broke open, loosing all upon the ship at once. And, looking back to the previous stanza, the bellows, the bag of wind, is used to characterize the revolutionary politics in much the same way that Joyce uses the Aeolus episode to characterize Irish journalism in *Ulysses* — as generally symbolic of a meaningless, hollow uproar, a constant shifting of positions and directions in controversy, an agitated running this way and that.

The whole image of the three lines, "though every face should scowl/ And every windy quarter howl/ Or every bellows burst" — which in their sequence exactly suggest the course of a storm's development, the gathering of the threatening clouds, the rising of the conflicting winds, the final "bursting" of the tempest — is an image of the "storm" of human passions, of course. The scowling faces are literally faces; the "windy quarters" are quarters of opinion, not of earth and air. But the significant point of distinction between this kind of storm, which the daughter may have to endure in later life, and that which is going on at the beginning of the poem, is made most emphatically by the implications of the final image here of the winds in a bag. In the episode of the *Odyssey* itself, the device of having the winds let out of a sack by the curious sailors is one that lays responsibility for their subsequent misfortunes much more clearly to their own, human folly that it would have been had they merely sailed into a storm, with or without any suspicion of a god's having stirred it up. To return specifically, in the eighth stanza, to the bartering of the Horn of Plenty as an allusion to Maud Gonne's involvement in politics, the trading for the bellows is thus precisely symbolic of what seemed to Yeats that foolish perversity of spirit whereby she abandoned the life of quiet grace and charm for which she was so greatly endowed, and deliberately raised about herself a storm of confusion, spiteful contention, and ugly accusations. And, finally, as the opposite of the Horn of Plenty — symbol of the birthright of personal, private grace and magnanimity which she traded for the noisy turmoil of her public career — the bellows is itself appropriately hornlike, but empty, ironically "full" only of "angry wind," a sorry mockery of the overflowing plenitude of the Horn.

Now, Yeats, to be sure, never mentions politics directly. The meaning of "opinion," "intellectual hatred," and so on, is not to be reduced *simply* to "political opinion," "political hatred." The moral concepts here, like the symbols of the Horn and the bellows, are broadly inclusive. There is no rigid frame of exterior reference, some chart of biographical allegory, with which we have to orient every detail of the poetic statement in order to see our way through it. But the "personal" allusions, the references to Maud Gonne as "the loveliest woman," and to her career, are essential links in the total pattern of recurrent imagery and verbal motif in these final stanzas.

We have noted that the ideal of life presented in the last stanza involves a cultivation of privacy, a retreat from the disorder and meanness of public doings, of life in the "thoroughfares." In the ninth stanza, the image was of the rigorous *trial* of that virtue of inner peace which the father hopes his daughter will enjoy, an image of the tranquillity of the soul that has driven out hatred, recovered its "radical innocence," staunchly *enduring* the terrors of whatever storms may fall about it. The final stanza is a representation of the more positively happy reward for the endurance and the militance, a picture of that calm season in which the soul may flourish in an environment and a climate it has created for itself, keeping itself quite aloof from the intemperate outer weather.

The speaker's distaste for the life of the public ways is indicated in the use of obviously scornful, depreciating words, "wares," "peddled" — an image of life sustained by petty commerce — as opposed to the suggestion of inherited wealth in the reference to the house where "all's accustomed, ceremonious," that is, handed down. In the terms of this opposition of public and private, that of the seventh and eighth stanzas is finally resolved. "Arrogance and hatred" ("arrogance" an obvious partial synonym for the sense of "opinionated") are the public vices, "the wares peddled in the thoroughfares" — opposed to the virtues of private heritage, "custom and ceremony," which are "names" for the laurel and the Horn of Plenty, and clearly recall the earlier "every good by quiet natures understood." But what I want to point out particularly is the importance of the metaphor of exchange, trade, "peddling," in the identification of "arrogance and hatred" with the public life. This also picks up a motif briefly stated in the eighth stanza, where the Horn is "bartered" for the "old bellows full of angry wind." This recurrence of image, particularly in view of the care with which the themes previously stated in the seventh and eighth stanzas have been otherwise picked up and resolved here at the last, is too exact to be accidental. And what it amounts to, for a second reading of the poem, is to suggest very strongly that the "hatred" and "opinion" in the earlier references too, the meaning of the bellows symbol there, has something to do with "public" life. Something, which we are not prepared to understand, unless we recognize the allusion to Maud Gonne and her public career.[2]

Further, we may note that the allusion to Maud Gonne and her bartering of the Horn in a sense balances the earlier example of the bad "choice" of Helen of Troy, "whereby the Horn of Plenty is undone." For Maud Gonne was a kind of Helen of the Irish revolutionary movement; Yeats makes the identification overtly in two other poems. And the advantage in recognizing the grounds for this comparison is just that it supports, by giving us a close modern parallel, one of the principal effects of the classical allusion. A good

---

[2] Cf. Cleanth Brooks on the generally-accepted allusion to Maud Gonne in Yeats' "Among School Children." Brooks rejects the reference, on the grounds that the lines in question "do not require such an interpretation." There is a difference, of course, between the situations in the two poems. In "A Prayer for My Daughter," there is *no* specific post-classical referent for "the loveliest woman" except Maud Gonne. In the other poem, the "Quattrocento finger" intervenes, between the images of antiquity and those of modernity, and Brooks grasps the finger and won't let go. For me, "a painter like Botticelli, say" is vague and inaccurate even to identify the Renaissance finger. But the main point, in any case, is that the image has both (or all three, or maybe four or five) temporal references. I suggest that Brooks simply is not willing to accept the fact of Yeats' pride. "Botticelli, say," and in another passage Aristotle and the "king of kings," presumably Alexander, are acceptable to Brooks because they belong to "tradition." But Aristotle's position as tutor to Alexander was also a part of his "private" life. This is not changed by the fact of its being an *ancient* private life. Yeats merely assumed, as he had every right to do, knowing he was a great poet or risking it, that ages hence readers (perhaps a few even sooner) would be as likely to know about school-inspector Yeats and Maud Gonne as about tutor-Aristotle or Quattrocento fingers. By ruling out the "biographical" (personal or private) allusion, Brooks has lopped off about one fifth to one third of the poem's significance. Basically the same there as here, it is the dimension of the young-old, private-public, present-past dialectic, in which "tradition" is constant *process*. To his credit, not discredit, lopped it off rather raggedly, not neatly, and I shall not say what part of the "great rooted blossomer" is thus cut away, whether "the leaf, the blossom or the bole" — maybe the roots; but as Brooks himself points out, one cannot really separate them and still have the whole tree. Or, in terms of his castigation of the biography-searcher as one who would "stop the dance" to enquire into the dancer's personal history — one is no more stopping the dance when he thinks of Maud Gonne than when he remembers Botticelli, or Helen. Once Maud Gonne *is* in my mind, she is as much there — while the dance continues — as Helen is. "How," indeed, "can we know the dancer from the dance?" (Cleanth Brooks, "Yeat's Great Rooted Blossomer," in *The Well Wrought Urn*. Harvest Books edition — pp. 183, 184, 188, 191, *et passim*.)

part of the purpose, of course, in introducing the ancient examples of beautiful women gone wrong, is simply to add a kind of " 'Twas ever thus," to the moral observations of the preceding stanza. The concluding lines of the fourth, "It's certain that fine women eat/ A crazy salad with their meat," have precisely this tone. But it is decidedly the more convincing that the universal pattern *is* universal — that fine women *always* eat a crazy salad with their meat — when we see the classical career so paralleled in the modern one.

But, in the recollection of the stories of ancient beauties, it is specifically their making bad matches "whereby the Horn of Plenty is undone." Actually, the allusion also in the figure of the bartering of the Horn seems to be as much to her marriage, about which Yeats had been very unhappy, as to Maud Gonne's public career. For the two are inseparable, really; her husband, MacBride, was one of the revolutionists. And in this way the passage parallels the reference to Aphrodite even more closely than that to Helen. The "old bellows full of angry wind" — in the oblique use of slang, a neat, typically Yeatsian slap at Major MacBride as an old windbag[3] — is in one respect simply the well-known poetic device of reducing the god to his attribute, and echoes the earlier allusion to Aphrodite's husband, Hephaestus, as the "bandy-legged smith." Thus, there is also suggested another effective characterization of the doings of the conspirators in the revolutionary movement — including MacBride — as like that activity of grubby obscurity and violence in the fabled forges under Aetna. In the modern world, our affairs are ruled over *only* by the attribute, and that the lowest; the god himself has not only fallen, but has disappeared altogether.

But this pattern of tension between the "private" and the "traditional" references is only part of a larger, single design. And to determine fully the principle of integration in the complex system of the poem's statement, we shall have to return now to consideration of its *time* sense — which is the key to understanding of large problems, of imagery and of tone, as yet entirely neglected.

---

[3] In very bad taste, certainly — since MacBride had died three years earlier during the Easter Week executions of 1916. And Joseph Hone notes (p. 339) that readers felt "some surprise" at its apparent personal and political references when the poem was published in 1920. But Yeats was never one to let "good taste" overrule the passions of his mind.

III

We dealt with the image of the wind's drum, and the dancing years, as expressive of an idea of the contraction of time, present and future, in the prophetic intensity of the poem's moment — the speaker's effort of vision. And we noted that the past, as well as present and future, is involved in this contraction. Throughout the poem, the sense of prophetic insight and conviction is secured as much by the heavy burden of preoccupation with ancient things as by the excitement of the attempt to peer into the future. Past, present, and future everywhere interpenetrate; no image stands wholly in one or the other. In a sense at the very center of the poem, the laurel tree flourishes into the hopeful future — "May she become . . .'"; and the development of its image having evoked an echo of the ancient legend, then furnishes in the next stanza a metaphor for the state of the poet's mind, and what has happened to that "of late"; but is ultimately symbolic — "rooted in one dear *perpetual* place" — of a triumph over all time.

Now, one important aspect of Yeats', perhaps we may call it, *technical* achievement here in the handling of time, is his management of tone. As an especially pertinent example of how the problem of tone is related to that of the fusion of past and present, we may consider the manner of the references to Helen and Aphrodite. There is a certain, peculiar irreverence here, a rather impudent familiarity in the way that the modern poet evokes the memory of these illustrious persons of ancient tradition. He treats them, indeed, rather as *persons* than as legendary "figures" of greatness. One a mortal, or semi-mortal, whose beauty is the symbol of the glory and disaster of a civilization, and the other the supreme goddess of beauty and love — they appear here only as two unhappy women. The language is at its mildest that of everyday, easy and familiar, and becomes finally, in the reference to Aphrodite's marriage, almost scornful.

The great misfortunes, both her own and those of the states, even of the gods, that followed from Helen's elopement with Paris, are disposed of in a phrase that rather suggests the way Yeats might have spoken of the merely private unhappiness of some contemporary woman of his acquaintance who had had an affair with a man who turned out less than he seemed. "Being chosen . . . ," she "found life flat and dull/ And later had much trouble from a fool." (For the case suggested, the nearest literary comparison would be to the situations of domestic novels, to the misfortunes, perhaps, of an Anna Karenina.) The mystery of Aphrodite's birth, Yeats uses as an excuse for treating her like some high-spirited young lady, orphaned but of good family, who having become willful and harum-scarum without the offices of a father to restrain her, perversely throws herself away and marries beneath her. The lame god Hephaestus — cunning crafts-man, designer of the glorious arms of Achilles and of the marvellous walking tables, the very patron of those arts that produce Yeats' own symbols of the soul's triumph in "Sailing to Byzantium" — is dismissed contemptuously as Aphrodite's poor jack of a husband, her "man," and "a bandy-legged smith."

And finally, there are the lines — "It's certain that fine women eat/ A crazy salad with their meat/ Whereby the Horn of Plenty is undone." The coarse and brutal sexuality of the image is unmistakable. The Horn of Plenty itself is an intricate sex symbol — both male and female, joining the properties of phallus and womb, and having been in the course of its history an attribute both of male and female deities. And the "meat" of the "fine women" is their own abused sexuality — the mere brutish flesh, that flesh becomes when it is "eaten," perversely surrendered in lust, with the "crazy salad" of an unworthy marriage — thus defiling and "undoing" the Horn's divine gift of fertility.

What is Yeats about in taking this presumptuous tone with the classical worthies? In satirical and comic poetry, poking fun at the gods and goddesses as well as the mortal heroes of antiquity is familiar enough. They are fair game. But, aside from the final, shocking bitterness of this passage, which turns the edge of any "fun" that might briefly have been suggested, there is a continuing tone of too much *earnestness* in the poem as a whole for us to accept anything as primarily an effect of burlesque. Nor will it help much here, simply to observe that much this kind of thing is characteristic of a great many of Yeats' poems. Compare, again, "Among School Children," the treatment there of the great philosophers of antiquity; and, where the seeming irreverence invades the origins of the Christian tradition, the poem "A Stick of Incense." Before we could say anything significant about similarities of effect among the various poems, we should have to determine first just how the attitude functions in each one.

But, if the effect here is not in the convention of burlesque, we might ask whether it is, on the contrary, anything like the use that hundreds of post-classical poets have made of the ancient stories — as a source of similes and analogies to dignify their contemporary subjects. Actually, in spite of the accent of irreverence we have noted, there is something of this purpose in the allusions. Like that of nearly everything Yeats wrote, at least after his earliest period, the manner of this poem as a whole is certainly the "grand manner." And the mere echoing of the great names contributes much to the establishment of that tone. The cavalier treatment here of "that great Queen," and the others, is only a certain qualification of the usual kind of dependence on them to lend something of the majesty of their presence to the proceedings of the poem as a whole. It is by no means such as to strip them completely of their dignity, or rather of their greatness, in dignity or indignity.

In the first place, of course, there simply are no means by which that could be done. The queen is still the queen, regardless of what scandals are recited about her. And, indeed, her personal folly makes history, or legend, not because it may be very different in kind from the misdoings of any woman, but simply because she is the queen. We are interested in her private life, just because she is not a private person. And Yeats is here depending heavily upon this established public character. What he is doing is only a matter of putting the emphasis upon certain implications of the ancient legends that are not ordinarily stressed in a total context of such high seriousness as this poem as a whole maintains. He is not inventing anything. But besides knowing the stories well enough to see the basis of his interpretation, we have to be fully aware that it *is* an extraordinary interpretation, that a customary attitude is being violated, or we miss the essential ironic effect altogether. Curiously, the fresh response to the traditional stories which the manner of these allusions elicits, is grounded in stock response.

Yeats, in fact, to some extent directly cues the stock response. The allusion to Aphrodite starts off distinctly in the conventional, magniloquent manner. "That great Queen, that rose out of the spray," is a phrase that betrays nothing yet of the precise turn of wit that develops in the next line on the supposed significance of her name, the legend of her strange begetting. It sounds, and must, in order that the turn may be a turn, and take us by surprise, much like any of a hundred solemn invocations of the foam-born goddess. And yet, nothing of such considerations can change the fact that the emphasis *is* put where it is, that the antique dignity *is* compromised. Presumably, the basic purpose is to "redeem the time" of the present, the modern degradation of man and his society, by holding up to it the mirror of tradition. But, if the mirror is *only* a mirror — if, in order to show how the ancient stories are "applicable" or "comparable" to present affairs, one ends up suggesting that they are *merely* comparable — then where is the redemption? If to make Maud a Helen is only to show that Helen is a Maud, then, what's she to Helen or Helen to her? What's the *good* of it all?

One might answer with the suggestion that here, as elsewhere in his poetry, Yeats is simply following the trend of much modern thought in putting emphasis upon the traditional *symbols*, rather than upon the mere "stories" of ancient myth with their gods, goddesses, and heroes. Aphrodite and Helen, Hephaestus and Paris, are devalued; but the Horn is not. The real value or virtue does reside in the attribute, after all, not in the person, divine or mortal, who for a time possesses it. But to read in such a "doctrine," at least at this point, short-circuits the processes of the poem.

Yeats "devalues" the stories, perhaps, but at least he does tell them, at least evokes our recollection of them. And an irreducible part of the interest of them is that they are *old*. "Custom and ceremony," celebrated in the final stanzas of the poem, are not simply vehicles for truth; they are a part of the truth. And their due observance, if the words have any of their usual meaning here, is somewhat a matter of pious *awareness* that what one does is old — a holding onto certain usages consciously and deliberately in consideration of, and respect for, the fact of their antiquity. The continuing and inescapable irony of the allusions to Helen and Aphrodite and their men, is that their stories at once represent a violation of "ceremony," identified in the last stanza with the Horn — to make the "crazy salad" of their capricious marriages, the Horn is quite literally "undone," its contents of fruits, flowers, and vegetables emptied out — and are a part of it. The legends themselves are a portion of the tradition, the heritage which is to be preserved in the house where "all's accustomed, ceremonious." Yeats' introducing them into the poem is itself a ceremonial usage, although curiously inverted.

But if we look a bit further, the irony is resolved. I said that "custom and ceremony" are not simply vehicles of the truth — i.e., the moral truth, of the nature of innocence and happiness, which the father reflects upon in his daughter's interest — but a part of that truth. But, to be more precise, they are a part of it only as parent and offspring are one. The image of the storm's being *"bred* on the Atlantic" is the first of a series of figures in the poem on the motif of *birth.* Aphrodite is alluded to as "that great Queen that rose out of the spray." Maud Gonne is "the loveliest woman born/ Out of the mouth of Plenty's horn." And, finally, the question is put — "How but in custom and in ceremony/ Are innocence and beauty born?"

Now, setting aside the question of what is meant by "beauty" here — I am coming to that later — "innocence" has been introduced in the preceding stanza as a quality that the soul "recovers" when "all hatred [is] driven hence," and as that whereby the soul knows itself to be "self-delighting, self-appeasing, self-affrighting," and knows that "its own sweet will is Heaven's will." That the innocence is "recovered" is important; and, in an echo of the plant imagery of the sixth stanza, where the laurel is *"rooted* in one dear perpetual place," it is *"radical* innocence." There is an overtone, in other words, of the theme of the restoration of Eden, the recovery of a traditional, lost age or state of happiness. Or, correspondingly, in terms of the poem's survey of the daughter's life from infancy to maturity, it is a reclaiming and perfecting in the woman of that innocence of the child which permits her to sleep on through the storm, and now again "though every face should scowl/ And every windy quarter howl/ Or every bellows burst, be happy still." This unmistakable cyclical structure of the poem, returning us at the end to the beginning — a design that is further secured, of course, by the final vision of the infant daughter's marriage — makes everything a matter of return, restoration, recovery. Nothing is, but what was.

And yet, the idea of self-sufficiency remains in force. The state of mature, perfected innocence is one that is supremely individual. It is *born* of "custom and ceremony," the observance of what was, but its ultimate realization is not simply a return to that matrix. Innocence here at the last — in the soul "self-delighting, self-appeasing, self-affrighting" — would seem to be nothing more or less than uncorrupted will, the enjoyment of a supreme, unrestricted capacity for choice. In terms of the distinction we made earlier, it is self-determination, determination of one's own "fortune" as opposed to the external forces of evil "chance," the happenstance of environment, whose symbol is the winds. Radical innocence consists simply in the soul's having, and knowing that it has, full individual responsibility for its destiny. It should be noted that the word in the poem is "can" — not "will," or even "may." "She *can*, though every face should scowl/ And every windy quarter howl,/ . . . be happy still." There is no certainty, or the father is incapable of determining with certainty, that she will be happy. He is able to say only that she can be, if she so wills it. To pin the matter down, Yeats is careful to include among the things of which the soul is capable, besides its being "self-appeasing" and "self-delighting," also its being "self-affrighting."

If we have followed this argument at all rightly, it throws a little more light on the meaning of the allusions to Helen and Aphrodite, and also, for it is very similar again in this respect, the reference to Maud Gonne. To be born out of the Horn of Plenty, as was "the loveliest woman," or once to possess its blessings, as Helen and Aphrodite did, is no guarantee of happiness. For one, perhaps the principal one, of its endowments is just that power of will by which the soul can if she chooses destroy, "undo" or "barter" away, the Horn itself. One of the legends of the Horn, as we have earlier noted, is that it had the power of making come true whatever its possessor wished for. And its virtue turns out like that of the "wishing ring" or other talisman in folk stories, beneficent only if the wish is wise, malign if, as on the part of the "fine women," it is vain and greedy.

And, with a brief consideration of one further pattern of significance in the imagery of stanzas six and seven, we can come now to a final definition of the function of these allusions, and their manner, in the total strategy of the poem. Actually, the poem is a good deal more "about" poetry itself than might at first appear.

The tree here is a laurel. The twig which Apollo broke from the branches of the transformed nymph and put in his hair is, with his lyre, the attribute of the god associated most closely with his office as patron of poetry; and the fame of achievement, of which he made the laurel wreath the sign, has come to be primarily the achievement of the poet. According to some renderings of the story, one of the promises he made to the tree was that he would hang his lyre among its branches. And, further, the image here is of a bird singing among the branches of the tree.

The singing bird is probably the most common of all symbols of the poetic imagination; certainly, it is one to which Yeats has frequent recourse. Moreover, although the first reference here is to the daughter, and the qualities of mind and temper he wishes for her — "May *she* become a flourishing hidden tree/ That all *her* thoughts may like the linnet be," etc. — the tree image is developed straight through the next stanza (the phrases "dried up" and "*choked* with hate" clearly continuing the metaphor of plant life) with a shift of attention to the poet's own situation. "*My* mind, because the minds that *I* have loved,/ The sort of beauty that *I* have approved,/ Prosper but little, has dried up of late,/ Yet knows. . . ." This, before it is turned finally to minds in general — "If there's no hatred in *a* mind/ Assault and battery of the wind/ Can never tear the linnet from the leaf."

The concern of the entire poem may be seen ultimately to be just with "man," the life of man's mind, with what is true of "*the* soul." The situation of the poet's mind is merely exemplary, an epitome. But so also, then, although more extended, is the attention to the character of the girl and her fate a particular focus for what becomes a universal insight. The imagery of the poem justifies, or demands, an assessment of its central problem as one of an *ars poetica*, as clearly as it warrants any other approach to its significance.

The implication of the lines, then, is that the virtue in the uses of "ceremony" and "custom" — access to the good plenty, and a perching place in the tree, of poetic tradition — must also be finally an individual virtue. The practice of the art must be firmly grounded in consciousness of the past, and secure against the flux of what are merely "current" affairs — the "assault and battery" of the confused winds of purely contemporary opinion and prejudice, the mischance of what has happened "of late," of having one's notions gone temporarily out of fashion. But it is not enough simply to hang on. The linnet's "business," the business of the poetic imagination, is "dispensing round [its] magnanimities of sound." The bird must sing. (The image recalls, by contrast, that of the wind's "screaming" among the trees, in the second stanza. There, the tree was only the passive instrument of the wind; but here the voice of magnanimous thought, the bird from within the tree, cries down the wind.) And like that of the birds in "Sailing to Byzantium," the song must be one not only of what is "past" and "to come," but also of what is "passing," simultaneously. For — we have noted that the tree is "rooted in one dear *perpetual* place" — the whole purpose of the preservation of tradition, the recovery or restoration of the past on which the inquiry into the future depends, is not to retreat from one time to another, but to triumph over all time.

The poet may find evil the days, the chance of circumstances, upon which he has fallen. But he must at all costs avoid, as "of all evil chances chief," the error of retreating into inarticulate resentment and hatred of his age for its disfavor. (The word "choked," I suggested before, with "dried up," continues the metaphor of plant life. But it is brilliantly ambiguous in referring also to the shutting off of breath, stilling the voice — of the bird, the mind. In the image, especially as it is first stated, the bird and the tree are hardly separable; rather like Keats' nightingale, the bird is invisible, referred to only as a voice, "magnanimities of sound," issuing from the tree. The tree is not only itself "hidden," but hides the singing bird.) For the speechless poet is no poet at all. He must have "magnanimity" enough to go on singing, in the time that is allotted to him, however bad a time it seems. And as magnanimity usually, and especially in the present figure of the bird of thought's "dispensing" its notes, implies generosity, the nobility of returning favor for slight or injury received — the song must be one in which the time is not held in contempt, but redeemed. Which, for one thing, means deigning to *use* the familiar idiom of one's time, as an essential condition of any purpose to improve that language and the attitudes it embodies. Which, for another thing, means putting one's personal, contemporary experiences, even one's friends and enemies, dead or alive, into the poem side-by-side with the images of tradition.

Dante did it. Both of these things. Why not, then, Yeats? The poem becomes a versified treatise *De Vulgari Eloquentia*.

And here we are, again, with the question of Yeats' patronizing tone in the allusions to Helen and Aphrodite. He disposes of their affairs already with the same slangy modernity in which he recalls the folly of Maud Gonne's career. Already in the first reference, Hephaestus is a humanized caricature of himself — before, in the characterization of MacBride and the revolutionaries, the degradation is complete and he appears in *de*humanized form, reduced to his attribute the bellows. What is it? It is a matter of Yeats' reconciling, or utilizing, controlling as a device of poetic form, the tensions between his total consciousness verbal and otherwise of the past, and his consciousness of the present. The brash treatment of the ancient worthies is a way of expressing the long view of the ruin he sees about him now, the decline of his age, the ignominy of his people, the repudiation of "the minds that [he has] loved, the sort of beauty that [he has] approved." The kind of perversity of will that the new Helen, Maud Gonne, has exercised, that characterizes this age and its abuse of the Horn of Plenty, its abandonment of the values of traditional usage, has been many times suffered in the past and many times survived — for so long, indeed, that the pattern of perversity, of ruin and degradation, is itself traditional. The tendency of man (or woman, as man) to dishonor and demean himself is an inseparable part of the very earliest legends from which we derive our notions of what constitutes his honor and his greatness. And the realization of this continuity of the paradox — not simply *recognition*, but realization, an embodying of the recognition in just such an expressive form as the poem, both old and new, its "style" at once traditional and unconventional, grand and familiar, detached and intensely personal — is itself the consolation against the poet's dismay at the latest manifestations of the folly. That itself is the consolation, against his fear that it may be repeated in his daughter's future life, against the despair that might otherwise be engendered by the very knowledge that it has so long a history.

Yeats, in other words, offers himself consolation in his own ability to "make it new," out of the old. The virtue of custom and ceremony, for the poet as for the man, is an individual virtue. The poet too must not simply "observe" custom and ceremony, but practice it. To the extent that such practice is a keeping of tradition, an imitation of the older practice of the art, it is rather an imitation in active principle, than in effect. Simply reciting the old, honored names, in vain repetition, will not serve. The myths of Helen and her lover, of Aphrodite and Hephaestus, of Apollo and Daphne, must be recreated. They must be made a part, as we have seen them made here, of a context in which they have never appeared before, the stories and their symbolism "interpreted" in a fashion never precisely anticipated.

And, if this should seem now to leave the poet with a little *more* responsibility than he ought to be saddled with, we can only agree. We can say, with Yeats, that it is after all not *he*, except as one member of his society, who has degraded the language — man, and his language. All he is doing, in the poem, is trying to use what he has been left with — make the best of it.

The question on which for a time we seemed stuck dead center, was how the past was to *redeem* the present, if both seemed only to insult each other. But, of course, it precisely *is* that the past must be also redeemed, at the very first and least in the sense of *recovered*. And how else are we to call it back, except in the language of the present? That, we seem somehow at the time to have forgotten. But a still better way of putting it, is to say that we had simply forgotten the *future*.

For the reference of the will, of which we have spoken, of choice, and of making and doing, is to the future. We had temporarily forgotten again the *sexual* character of the Horn. We can be content neither with truce nor even with platonic friendship between present and past. The past must spill its seed in the present. They must be married, and yield up increase, to the future. Even the great Horn is of no virtue if it is not somehow emptied, though we should wish it to be properly, and not to furnish the crazy salad for the obscene feast of the fine women with their "meat."

But, increase of what? For one thing — and this is also at least a partial answer to those who would see Yeats as following a strictly symbolist doctrine with regard to the virtue of the mythic tradition — for one thing, poems. Just that. The Horn cannot be left to lie silent and entirely mysterious, in the oneness of pure potentiality. If the gods and heroes had not seized it, used it; if we hadn't the poems, the stories of their doings, how should we even know of the Horn? In dreams? But dreams, too, must be told.

The poem, then — that is the increase, the yield. What does one do when one's Maud has finally and irrevocably rejected him, turned out to be with a vengeance *only* a Helen? If one is a Yeats — and maybe realizes that she has left him partly *because* he is Yeats, only a poet — one writes, one makes, one "does," a poem. The poem may, as we have said it does, envisage a "triumph over all time." But, first of all, it is the choosing and the making and the doing, the gesture to the future.

And, if someone should still impudently ask, 'but what *good* is it'?

The poem? That, perhaps, is the unanswerable question. But, we have already come a long way, at least far enough to assert that this question, now, is only the question — 'What good is *poetry?*' Not, at least, any longer 'What good, *for* the poem, this poem, is the marriage of past and present?' We know that. Even the division; for, of course, without first the division there is no joining together. Vive la différence! We even have some idea what good — for the poem, the gesture to the future — the disappointment of love is. The division not only of time, past and present, but the division of man — man-woman — we know the good of that, for the poem. For the poem, the two divisions are identical. And, from certain further considerations, *of* the poem, there may yet be a hint of an answer even to the unanswerable.

IV

The argument that the poem's statement contains something of an aesthetics, or *ars poetica*, obliges us finally to account for its use of the word "beauty." For Yeats, in reaction from his bitterness over Maud Gonne, did not only write a poem. He married another woman. He had a child. And the poem is written to the child, or "for" her.

The word occurs three times in the noun form "beauty"; once as an adjective, "beautiful"; and once in a synonym of the adjective, "loveliest." The subject is first introduced in the opening line of stanza three. Taken alone, as one at first has a tendency to read the verse unit, the line seems deliberately self-contradictory — "May she be granted beauty and yet not." The sense that immediately appears, when we follow the syntax into the next line, is of course that the father wants her to have beauty, but not too much of it. Beauty is not in itself evil, but it is not a terminal good; it is by nature inferior to the good of other, moral qualities. And, when considered a "sufficient end" by those who have it in excess, it becomes evil by blinding its possessor to that other, superior good — of "natural kindness," and "heart-revealing intimacy."

But it may be that the apparent self-contradiction of the first line is calculated to point up an implicit distinction between *kinds* of beauty, only one of which is being condemned for the effects of its excess. The construction "and yet not beauty to make . . ." is, in any case, elliptical. And the missing words, "such as," may be taken as easily to mean "of the *kind*" as they may be to mean "so *much* as." The prayer, that is to say, is not just that the daughter may be spared such excess of "beauty" that it will "make a stranger's eye distraught,/ Or hers before a looking glass" — but rather, that she may not have too much precisely of that sort of beauty which appears on the deceptive surface of a looking-glass, in short, beauty of physical person.

The imagery of eye and mirror here belongs to the general pattern of opposition between "inside" and "outside" that we have noted before as recurring, in various forms, throughout the poem. The evil of great physical beauty is that it tends to reduce one to seeing other people, and being seen, even by oneself, only on the surface, on the outside; whereas all true goodness is "intimate," lies inside in the "heart." But what I want to note especially here — following from the mirror image, where the woman makes her own exterior the object of her superficial, admiring sight — is the ambiguity of the phrase "heart-revealing intimacy." "Revealing" continues the motif of "seeing"; and this intimacy (in a meaning related to that of "intimate" as a verb, to hint, to suggest) is a power of *in*sight, by which one looks into the "hearts" of others. But — completing the notion of a capacity for real affection as opposed to the illusory experience of self-infatuation, the narcissism represented in the mirror image — "intimacy" implies also a mutuality of action and response. It is a "revealing" or exposing of one's own heart as well as the discovery of another's.

Thus, we begin to see how the "inwardness," the self-sufficiency, which the father prays will characterize his daughter's life, is yet not an exclusiveness of temperament. It is a sense of one's own worth. But, motivated no more by pride than by timidity, it is still an openness of nature. It is the paradox that is implicit later in the image of the tree, where the mind is both "hidden," living apart and sufficient to itself, and yet full of thoughts that are entirely generous and outgoing — freely "dispensing round/ Their magnanimities of sound." So also, the poet warns himself, in the following stanza, of the danger of the mind's becoming "choked" that shuts itself away to nurse its hatred. And we have noted previously how the final stanza, with its image of retreat—the daughter entering the house that stands apart from the noise and confusion of the thoroughfares—yet pictures that house as so generously proportioned that it contains the "spreading tree." Outdoors and indoors become one; the life that is most quiet and secluded is yet most selfless and open.

In fact — so complete is the soul's triumph over the fear of its position being damaged by the assault of the external and temporal forces of chance — the state in which it "learns" its mature self-sufficiency bears the same name of a quality of being which is first attributed to the source of the natural storm that beats against the house at the beginning of the poem. The sea — constant symbol of eternity in the poetic tradition, undisturbed in its essentially changeless state by the storms that agitate its surface — though "murderous," maintains its "innocence." Correspondingly, the soul trained in the changeless usages of "custom and ceremony" is innocent of harm from the winds of time and chance.

But what I have been working toward is a way of accounting for the fact that "innocence" appears here at the end, in the final perfection of its birth or re-birth, with a twin. "How but in custom and in ceremony/ Are innocence and *beauty* born?" Now, if we take the "beauty" of stanza three to be undifferentiated — and see that what is being called "innocence" in the concluding stanzas, that whereby the soul knows the self-sufficient capacity of its will, must be inclusive of those virtues of "natural kindness" and "heart-revealing intimacy that chooses right" which the father fears his daughter will lose if she is made "beautiful overmuch" — then the twinning of innocence and beauty, at the end, must seem a strange inconsistency.

But if I am justified in the interpretation I have offered of an ambiguity in the ellipsis of the opening lines of the third stanza, and the supporting effect of the mirror image, there is no inconsistency. It is an essential part of the poem's effect, simply, that for a time there *appear* to be an inconsistency. The conflict at the beginning of the reverie, between "beauty" and "the heart-revealing intimacy that chooses right," is basic. The father's anxiety is centered precisely in this — in the fear that one cannot be, at once, so beautiful as it is prophesied his daughter will be, and capable of "choosing right." He fears that she cannot be both beautiful, and blessed with that unimpaired vigor of will which is defined at last as the power of "innocence," and as "happiness" — true good fortune. And it is essential to the effect of calmness in the final stanza that it seem hard won, that we appear to have "come a long way," from the gloom of the opening conflict, to witness the joy of this reconciling birth.

But the grounds of the final resolution, at least on a second reading of the poem, may be seen as I have tried to suggest in the first statement of the problem. For the implications there, of a distinction between kinds of beauty, anticipate a more direct phrasing of this idea in stanza seven — "My mind, because the minds that I have loved,/ The *sort of beauty* that I have approved,/ Prosper but little, has dried up of late." Recalling again the allusion to George's prophecy, what Yeats does is not so much to invoke an oracle which contradicts hers, as to find another which will allow an *interpretation* of her auguries more to his liking.

I mean that what appears at first as opposed to beauty, or the excess of beauty — "kindness," "intimacy," everything that is summed up in the final concept of "innocence" — is actually, all along, itself a kind of beauty. We might easily take certain phrases of these early stanzas — "natural kindness," and all the talk of "hearts," and how "hearts are not had as a gift but hearts are earned/ By those that are not entirely beautiful" — just with the usual homely and somewhat sentimental connotations which such diction carries. If one did this, then he might be further tempted to reduce what I am saying Yeats has offered himself, as an escape from the "dilemma" of his wife's prophecy, to some cliché like "handsome is as handsome does." But the question is — as always when one attempts to reduce poetry to saws and sayings — whether we *can* take the familiar phrases, in full context, with only their usual connotations.

The word "heart" appears twice in the same line of the fifth stanza — "Hearts are not had as a gift but hearts are earned/ By those that are not entirely beautiful" — following the line, "In *courtesy* I'd have her chiefly *learned*." The closeness of the context argues, I should think, a significant association. "Courtesy" is apparently the means by which "hearts are earned." And the choice of the word "courtesy" — with its sense not only of dispensing favor, but of doing it in a certain, rather formal and dignified, disciplined manner — is a crucial point of diction. "Courtesy" is, derivatively, the politeness of the "court." And there is everywhere here, both in this stanza and the next, in the ideal of behavior which the father would recommend to his daughter, a suggestion of "courtliness." She is not to go and search out objects of her kindness; but rather the "poor man, who has roved, loved, and thought himself beloved" must at last resort to the fixed seat of that kindness, come to gaze upon it as upon a seat of state. The favor of her thoughts is to be "dispensed," and the dispensing is of a sort that carries a sense of her knowing the value of what is given. It is "magnanimity," the kind of generosity that proceeds from an awareness that it is beneath one's dignity to be ungenerous. *Noblesse oblige.* "Courtesy," then, implies good nature, but formalized in good manners. It is something, precisely, that has to be *learned,* an intellectual discipline of the moral and social impulses of kindness.[4]

This, then, is the sense in which Yeats would see in the things of the "heart," "kindness" and "intimacy," an aesthetic value. In the practice of "courtesy" these motions of the heart are no longer simply *feeling,* undirected and instinctive emotional impulse, but take on a definite *form.* So formalized, the usages of personal morality become "beautiful" — or ugly, as in the distortions produced by "hatred" and "opinion" — in much the same way that a ritualized expression of religious feeling demands an aesthetic response, is to be judged for its "beauty" as well as its "sincerity," the two becoming finally impossible to disjoin in practice, if not to distinguish.

We may note also that the line "from a glad kindness cannot take his eyes" makes "kindness," the revelation of the "courteous" heart, an object of the so-called aesthetic sense of sight. We remarked earlier that the word "revealing," in the seventh line of stanza three, "heart-revealing intimacy," continues the metaphor of "seeing." It makes "intimacy" a power of *in*sight, a showing forth, or discovering, of something previously hidden from view. But the image here, of the "poor man who has *roved* . . ." gazing upon the heart in the full state of its courteous kindness, recalls with singular sharpness the first image of the third stanza — "and yet not beauty to make a

---

4 The rime word with "learned" is "earned" — "Hearts are not had as a gift but hearts are earned." This, with the "business" of the third line of stanza seven — "And have no business but dispensing round/ Their magnanimities of sound" — significantly anticipates the contrast of images, of the life that is sustained by petty commerce, trading, "peddling," and of that enjoying an inherited wealth, which we have noted in the final stanza. As "courtesy" and "magnanimity" clearly must belong to the things of "custom and ceremony," their usage is something handed down. Their practice cannot be a matter of "trade"; their business is "*no* business." And yet, "earning" is involved. The sense is that in every generation these inherited moral and social virtues must be recovered, restored, as individual virtue — just as the poet must, by his individual effort, reclaim the wealth of tradition, his traditional "rights."

stranger's eye distraught." The effect is very clearly to have the true beauty, of courtesy, now wholly displace the superficial, physical beauty. The essential *difference* of the new image from the first is secured by the fact that it is "eyes" here, the sight as it were clearly focused (in the plural, perhaps also suggesting the attention of all the senses, intelligence, the man becoming "all eyes"), and in full, fixed gaze — as opposed to the "eye," which in looking "distraught" with desire, wild and glancingly, upon physical "beauty," is in a sense not *seeing* anything at all. Yeats would seem to suggest not only that there is a kind of "beauty" ("the sort of beauty that [he has] approved") in the forms of moral usage, in "courtesy," "charm," "a glad kindness" — but ultimately that these are *more properly* called "beautiful" than are the face and body of a woman, since, by exciting desire, these latter "distract" the senses, rather than concentrate them in that rapture which is aesthetic perception.

Now, the "poor man's" fixing his "eyes" upon "a glad kindness" is still, in a special sense, *only* a metaphor. And, emphasizing that the revelation of courtesy is, in fact, *insight* — holding still to the motif of enclosure (the root word *cohors*, incidentally, means "an enclosure" as well as "court" in other senses), keeping our attention upon the essential inwardness of beauty — the poet, having briefly opened to view the "glad kindness" of the heart, immediately restores the sense of privacy in the image of the "hidden tree" and its inhabitant presence which is manifested now, not by anything seen, but only by the overflowing "magnanimities of *sound*."

Further, this sound is the manifestation of "thought," and, in the next stanza, where in the second line the reference occurs to "the sort of beauty [he has] approved," the attention shifts definitely to the region of the "mind." As we have previously noted, but in somewhat different terms, there is throughout the poem a progressive concentration of attention inward — the inquiry, level by level more deeply searching, moves from observations primarily on the superficiality of physical beauty, from the face and the body, into the "heart" (through stanza five), then into the "mind" (through stanza eight), and finally into the "soul."

(The concentration, we have taken care to observe in the remarks on the final echo of the sea image and on the house of the bridegroom and how it contains the laurel tree, is not a narrowing. The "soul"

— and, of course, what Yeats ultimately means by "soul" is something that involves all the vital faculties — is in the fullness of its innocence least of all constricted. But it is, by its own will, contained. In the sixth stanza, what might be called the "garden" passage of the poem, and especially in the lines "Nor but in merriment begin a chase/ Nor but in merriment a quarrel," Yeats beautifully catches the sense of innocence and its delight. It is freedom — the freedom of play, of a child's game, or, the syntax may indicate, of the merry "aimless" flutterings and chasings of birds — which the father hopes will always characterize his daughter's intellectual life, "all her thoughts." Yet, there is an image of containment. The movement of such innocence — imitated in the repetitive verses — is "free," precisely in that there is no impulse to go beyond the limits of the "game." Like that of children's play, or of the chase of birds among the trees, it is a movement only "to and fro." As a projected ideal of adult behavior — even for a woman — this might seem indeed rather too well, even impossibly and absurdly "contained." Life, of course, is *not* a game. But, also of course, the passage has to be taken in context, immediately, in that of the strengthened images of bird and tree in the following stanza. The final sense is just that the father would have his daughter never to pursue any thought, any idea, relentlessly — with that extreme devotion to a rational conviction that finally becomes the enslavement of the mind in "opinion.")

The beauty in the motions of the heart is in the form, the order, those motions take on in the ritual of "courtesy." But this order has so far been described in terms of its *effects*, upon the beholder. The implication of the shift of attention from "heart" to "mind," is of a searching, farther in, for the *principle* of that order. The order of the heart, of "courtesy," is seen as an extension of the order of the mind, of the rational principle. And — "an intellectual hatred is the worst" — it is in the perversion of reason, its enslavement in the service of some prejudice, in "opinion," that the growth of the moral life, its flourishing into beauty, is choked off at the roots. There is one step further, of course, into the "soul," and the paradox of its knowing innocence. Yeats finally, here as in many of his poems, refers the principle of reason itself, the power of understanding, to some harmony of the individual *will* with the universal, which, setting aside the terminology of his fully developed occult system, I suppose we may call a variety of intuition. This, it appears, is the true "root" of the matter — where "the soul recovers *radical* innocence," and simply, no matter how, "learns . . . that its own sweet *will* is Heaven's *will*."

But again, such learning, the intuition of an ordained harmony, is only possible "considering that, all hatred [has been] driven hence." The recurrence of the word "hatred" referring us clearly back to the previous stanza, where "intellectual hatred" is equated with "opinion," the implication is that the establishment of intellectual order and harmony, the elimination of rational bias, is a necessary preliminary to the act of intuition. The order of reason is in no way in conflict with that of the "radical innocence." Rather, the rational order is, in principle, but an extension of the universal order, "Heaven's will," that the soul in its recovered innocence discovers, "learns" — and so, in a sense, an extension of innocence itself, just as the order of "courtesy," in which also one must be "learned," was seen to be an extension of reason's own.

We may reverse the order of our description of the gradually deepening "inquiry" of the poem. Toward the supreme enlightenment, the vision of Heaven from its summit, the ruined tower must be rebuilt, level by ordered level.

And seeing, then, these concepts — of the soul's wholeness, "innocence"; of the order of the "mind," reason; of "courtesy," the rationally disciplined, ritual "beauty" of the "heart" — as linked in a kind of circular chain, or better, in a system at once circular and vertically extended, the spiral stairway of the tower, we discover the inevitability of the final reconciliation of the "opposites," beauty and innocence. They are, after all, "twins," actually only two different expressions, embodiments in two different orders of usage, of the same principle. And, as "innocence" is that by which the soul discovers its harmony with "Heaven's will," or Fortune, so Yeats finally resolves the distressing, apparent self-contradiction of his wife's prophecy, that the child would be both beautiful and fortunate.

But we led into discussion of the meanings of "beauty" from consideration of the fact that his own mind and his own work, as poet, are as much the subject of Yeats' anxiety in the poem as is his daughter's fate. It is the relationship of these two concerns, for the "life" situation and for "art," that is the central, though only in one central passage overt, theme of the poem. The conflict of values *within* the realm of concern for the daughter's personal life, between "innocence" and "beauty," and their final reconciliation, epitomizes the larger struggle, and its resolution, in which that entire class of values, the moral, is opposed to the aesthetic. In the way that he answers the question of how his daughter may be both beautiful and happy, innocent, Yeats also proposes a way out of the dilemma that is raised by the very fact of his making such a personal, domestic concern as this the subject of a poem at all — a way of avoiding the necessity, as another of his poems puts it, to "choose perfection of the life, or of the work."

Or, we can put it in other pairings of terms used earlier — public and private, or public (or *traditional*) and personal. But it is immediately apparent that simply shifting terms is not going to solve the problem. The reality of the problem — something probably not even susceptible of logical analysis — is precisely why we have to keep shifting the terms. E.g., the poem is a "public" utterance, but it upholds an ideal of "private" virtue as against the enslavement of the mind in "public affairs" — and does that exactly as a means of assuring its public character; while, on the other hand, the "public affairs" got into the picture in the first place as a matter of private concern, and, though eschewed, still has to be somehow really brought *in*, to complete the dialectic as real operational principle in the poem. And "traditional" is not of much help, even as opposed to "personal" — because, as "custom and ceremony," tradition is offered precisely as an ideal of personal life. And so on.

And my first point of conclusion would be simply to repeat in explicit summary what I have implicitly insisted upon throughout the essay — the *poem* does much better in handling the oppositions, the "terms," than we can do with them in the abstract. Just in using them as words, *not* "terms," the poem is even more precise, more *philosophical*, than we are when we turn them into terms. It is all there, together; public and private, traditional and personal, past-present-future. All that we can try to do, as I have tried in the essay, is to follow. The poem does, in fact, so interweave its themes, its images, of "myth" and domestic "reality" — that it is impossible for us to understand the song we hear in the grove of Apollo's laurel unless we remember the wind that blows through the elms and Gregory's wood; impossible to read the oracle of Fortuna without the auguries of George, or hers without Fortuna's; impossible to reach the house "where all's accustomed, ceremonious," and understand the question "How but in custom and in ceremony/ Are innocence and beauty born?" by any route except the private way of the father's pacing on the nursery floor, avoiding all "thoroughfares" of critical presupposition — "opinion."

Not, of course, that we fully "understand" even then. A poem does not *solve* problems, any more than formal philosophy does. But it does *prove* them, in the event and trial of its own action; it proves, at least, that they *are* problems. And then, the words having been fully exercised, brought forth to display their rich and supple strength of meaning, they retire again to the center of silence whence they came. A harmony is achieved. The mind rests.

It rests, except for one thing. That is, that when in order to understand the references of the poem we have to learn something of "Yeats himself," the man who was the poet, we inevitably encounter the fact that *he* did not rest, with having got it all into the poem. First, he wrote more poems. Always, this is true, that the mind rests — the poem, so to speak, permits it to rest — only then to propel us out of that one center of silence, to other poems, other words which in their turn are to create their own silences. For silence has many centers. "To morrow to fresh Woods, and Pastures new."

But this is not all. In Yeats' case, the retreat to Thoor Ballylee, the marriage and the offspring, were an attempt to fulfill what he considered the highest conception of the poet's office. It was no squeamish withdrawal, in bitterness and defeat. The retreat represented an effort (one that we have already seen was superbly realized) to make the life available to the poem. But, conversely, it was just as obviously an attempt to push the poem into life, to surround himself with living forms of the poetic symbols, the tower and trees, the usages of "custom and ceremony." The reconciliation of the two orders of beauty was to be achieved there too. The life was to be the poem.

Impossible, of course. But, I submit, no more impossible than any other ideal of life. It had richness, strength, answerability. It is only a kind of impossibility that is tried less ofen than the kinds most of us try. And what it, in any event, suggests — what will not let the mind rest — is that the images of the poem are not *just* images. It suggests, that the *problems* of the poem are not just problems. It suggests, that the poem touches on truth, not, "an order of truth," but truth.

Very well, and we have heard all *this* before. But, raise an eyebrow at it, and my point is that we do not raise it just at Yeats, at the forgivable weakness of the man. We raise it at the poet, and at the poem. Do we dare presume to "forgive" that, the poem? For, once again, it is all there too; all thoroughly inside the poem, its outsideness. All the suggestions, all the rest that will not let us rest, compose its rest.

The great, traditional symbols that the poem venerates are like Shakespeare's star, "whose worth's unknown, although his height be taken." They remain apart, untouched, their meaning never fully realized in that of any cause, however large, and however shrewdly calculated and self-contained, for which their influence is evoked. "Ceremony's a name for the rich horn,/ And custom for the spreading laurel tree." Just one, *a* name. The mystery of this unity, of tree and horn — for, of course, the horn too is symbol of poetry, of sound in silence, as much as the laurel — is not contained in the unity of names. But and lest strident Symbolists strut, even at last too soon — the patrons, whose attributes the symbols are, are *never* named. We have dared to name them — Aphrodite, Apollo, Hephaestus, Fortuna herself — but Yeats is more cautious, more modest, more awed. In insult or in praise, for to the gods what praise is not equally insulting, he has stood in fear. Awe there is too in his not naming George, Maud Gonne MacBride, Anne his daughter; but the awe of such gallantry serves the awe of truth, serves the gods that are in them. And that not-naming is in the poem.

This prayer, this poem, is only one way of the invocation. "And for an hour I have walked and prayed/ . . . / I have walked and prayed for this young child an hour." But precisely to define the wholeness that is proper to that hour, the unity and completeness, the singularity of its dedication to the child, we must understand with the prophetic father that it is only an hour. For he knows that at last he must give her away, to the bridegroom. Her rest too, while his mind god-possessed of the Horn walks the enormous nursery, is secured in his unrest.

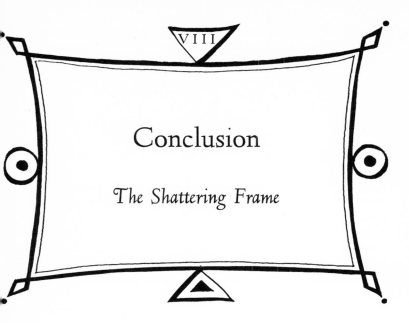

Conclusion

The Shattering Frame

My main purpose in the preceding seven chapters has been to explicate, or illuminate, seven different poems. If I have done that at all successfully, the book as a whole has its principal justification.

But this design, the limitation of each essay to the study of one poem, in itself attests my acceptance of a certain critical doctrine. Further, I have at the end of each chapter said, in one way or another, that there is no means of defining the poem itself, and so of grasping its significance, except in discovering that exact, total order of relationships among its parts that no other poem duplicates. In the last part of the opening chapter, I attempted to show that even so-called variant "copies" of so unsophisticated a poetic fiction as a folk-ballad may have differences that make the final effect of one quite unlike that of the other, that even here one can work with the single text in its distinct entirety, and not identify the poem with some one element of its plot or theme that it shares with any number of others. The principle of this approach informs still more firmly the succeeding studies. And the book remains after all, I think, a part of the apologetics of that *school* of critical activity which recommends such an approach.[1]

But, while acknowledging that the method does embody what is, in a literal sense, a doctrine, one might ask whether it has been followed here in a way that could be called, as much of the practice of the school is charged with becoming, *doctrinaire*. I have espoused, specifically, the view that poetry is an art; that art is knowable only as the work-of-art, unique and entire; and that the primary act of criticism, therefore, is in contemplation of the single work. This basic thesis of the "explicationist" movement, as I accept it, is not subject to modification. Efforts in recent years to relegate explication of individual poems entirely to the status of classroom exercise — as though it were simply "outmoded" in the concerns of professional criticism, as though it were an indifferent "technique" to be taught and learned — betray a fundamental indifference to the nature of the poetic art. There is no "higher criticism" of literature — no variety of *Kultur Kritik*, no History of Ideas, no study of the "mind" of the poet individual or typical, no location of the poem in rhetorical tradition, no criticism founded on principles of psychology, anthropology, or mythography, nothing grounded in the sciences of language analysis and symbolic, no combination of these — which is

---

[1] What is the school, and who belongs to it? What are its essential doctrines? These are vexed questions. I have here and there used the terms The New Criticism and The New Critics, but only for want of better ones. "They" have been called everything from "the new Scholastics" through "the new neo-Classicists" to "the new Romantics." The validity of any such definition will much depend upon whom one is reading, and why. I have tried to confine my attention here to certain *issues*, and have chosen in the latter part of this chapter two critics, Cleanth Brooks and William Wimsatt, who seem to me answerable for views contrary to mine on some of these issues. In most assessments of the school, Brooks is recognized; to some readers, Wimsatt may not look like a New Critic at all, and he is certainly not, in practice, an "explicationist." Others generally recognized are T. S. Eliot, I. A. Richards, R. P. Blackmur, John Crowe Ransom, Eliseo Vivas, Allen Tate, Robert Penn Warren, Robert Heilman. I cannot be concerned in this book primarily to present my view of what any group of such formidably independent writers might have in common. As I see it, there is a *tendency* among all of them to support one or another set of "lost" values — values in one way or another opposed to the ostensibly dominant values of scientism and materialism in the modern world — and to appropriate poetry as the vehicle of their favorite losses. Implicitly, my remarks later in this chapter, and in the Preface, may refer to and criticize this general tendency. But I should hesitate to define it as anything more than a tendency. For me, it is the specific issues that are important.

valid without specific evidence of its grasp of the whole, single work. I do not mean that all such books must actually include full-dress explications of different works. But if there is any suggestion of contempt for explication, any suggestion that the author's assertions are founded on a merely "assumed" or ostensibly obvious, unproduced reading of any single poem referred to, then the book immediately and so far invalidates itself. On the other hand, there is a real question whether the explicationists themselves have not in the past at least partially invalidated their own work, and invited the attacks upon their influence, by defining "the poem" too narrowly for their critical purposes — and by hedging about with "dogmas" of irrelevant, theoretical assertion the practice of their essential faith.

When one proposes, as I have done in each of these studies, to read a poem for its individual order, he is proposing in some sense to stay "inside" the poem. But, in what sense? Where, or how, is one to draw the line between what lies "inside" the poem and what "outside," and so within or without the legitimate province of one's critical concern?

Perhaps I should explain, immediately, the meaning of my pretentious sub-title for the book — the use of the words "text and context." The text, let us say, is what is given, what confronts us on the page. This is not ultimate Text [1], what would be wholly "given"; but it is as close as we are likely to get to it. "Context" we are accustomed to using, sometimes confusedly, in two different senses. It can refer to what in some way seems to lie "outside" the poem — the tradition, literary and otherwise, the poet's life and other writings, etc. Or, "context" can mean what I prefer usually to call poetic *syntax*, the specific order — grammatical, logical, recurrent-metaphorical, order of motif, order of tone, order of sound when heard mentally or otherwise — which the poet seems to have created with the words for the first and only time. (It is this latter context to which we refer familiarly in saying that a passage should not be taken "out of context.") I do not know that I have always succeeded in doing so, but I want to effect a fusion (I trust not further *confusion*) of these two senses of "context." For neither of these — Context [1] nor Context [2] — is in any sense *given*. The "given" thing, the text, actually sends us in search of both "contexts" in much the same way and simultaneously. But when they are found, and complete themselves in each other, then and then only does the pseudo-Text [1] begin to disappear, and become *meaningful*. In other words, the two contexts together yield a final "text" — Text [2] — which is not given, but taken, apprehended. It is this Text [2] with which we are critically concerned, which we strive to get at, and in regard to which we can at length speak only of "text" and dismiss "context." Or, according to our interests, having apprehended the text, we can dismiss *that*, and concern ourselves only with Context [1] or Context [2]. (The varieties of "higher criticism," so long as they do not continue to call themselves that, or to parade mightily as "Scholarship," might then be legitimately occupied with aspects of Context [1]; and the varieties of "practical criticism" and of literary pedagogy with aspects of Context [2].) But, for any purpose, Text [2] is extremely hard to "get at," and we are always thinking we have got at it when we have not. With ultimate Text [1] we cannot be concerned. For it exists only in silence, and therefore is, if not unknowable, unthinkable.

But, beyond this much, I cannot "explain immediately" the subtitle. It is that, in fact, which the whole book is intended to "explicate." And to that end, it would be better if we proceeded now in less abstract and more familiar terms, if not less difficult ones.

Whatever else it may be, one is used to hearing from almost all sides, a poem is an arrangement of parts of a language. But this is already a hard and complex matter — because, for one thing, the words of a language are always changing their meanings, and from one time to another being combined with other words in certain habitual phrasings of a people's speech, the alterations of which habits reflect changes in social, intellectual, and other attitudes and preoccupations.

One of the principal ways in which the poet's use of language differs from that of other, we may say "professional" masters of the word, is just that instead of "loading" it in one direction of practical persuasion as the political orator does, or on the other hand stripping it, for conceptual precision, as the scientist or the formal philosopher attempts to do, he exploits as wide a range of its values as possible — its reflections of manners as well as its embodiment of ideas, its many-shaded colorings of emotion and attitude. And, as a part of this, he may be aware of the effect of time, and complicate the sense of his statement by reviving words that have passed out of common use before his period, or older meanings of common words. But to whatever end, of wit, or merely of a calculated quaintness of style, such usage depends for its effectiveness upon a communicated consciousness that it *is* a revival, that it is counter to, or divergent from, the contemporary idiom.

Clearly, then, any poet, at any time, and writing with whatever individuality of style — even the poet who is, by the standards of his own time, deliberately "old-fashioned" — must somehow take over into his work, not only some of the language habits that are embodied in distinctly literary conventions and perhaps in philosophical or other discursive systems in which he may be interested, but many of those that belong to his society and his intellectual age in general. And any critic, reading the poem in a later period, cannot avoid having his understanding — even his very attempt to recover the sense of the past usage — conditioned, however subtly, by the climate of his own linguistic environment. Changes even in the sounds of words, the manner in which they are pronounced, may profoundly influence the conditions under which the reader's mind encounters the poem.

And the effects of *time*, in this large and obvious sense of the reference to differences of periods or "eras" of intellectual, linguistic, and literary history, are not the only hazards of criticism. My having included here two "foreign" poems, one in French and one in German, only intensifies the difficulties attributed to time; these are languages, after all, within our own, larger historic "community" of speech, and we share with the Germans and the French a common intellectual tradition. But even in studying a poem written in his native language, and more or less in his own period, the critic may find that his having had a different education from the poet's, and having lived under different social conditions and in a different place, will make it necessary for him to try to *learn* the poet's idiom.

The "miracle of communication" is, we know, somehow accomplished. We do read, and understand, and enjoy remarkably substantial agreement upon the meaning of many different kinds of poems. Americans read English poets, and French and German. We read Andrew Marvell and John Milton, in some senses as easily as we read Yeats. In short, we read each other. But the enormity of the difficulties under which this miracle is brought about, the enormity of the fact that it *is* a miracle, cannot be exaggerated.

One of the recurrent complaints against the modern explicationist critics, is that they try to read all poems in the same way, specifically, with indifference to the period of their origin. We are urged that we must try, when we read Milton for example, to comprehend the "mind" of the 17th century. And so we must.

The efficacy, it should by now be clear, of Mr. I. A. Richards' famous experiments with his students in the reading of wholly "anonymous" poems, is pedagogical.[2] Such an approach cannot be pursued as the method of final, mature reading. When it is done by the conscious critic — pretending that he does not know the period of the poet's career, as well as the facts of his particular education and interests, his beliefs, the extent and character of his reputation, etc. — it is *only* a pretense. And though the pose may be valuable as a temporary device to avoid premature *distractions* of interest from the present integrity of the poem's single statement, its self-supporting "syntax," yet it must be finally acknowledged as a pose. The temporarily excluded facts, such as we have mentioned, must eventually be recognized as an essential part of our critical situation when confronting the poem — indeed, as a real part of the poem's own, whole context. (See the preliminary remarks on Contexts, above.)

The trouble with the position of Cleanth Brooks, for example, on the "heresy of paraphrase," is just that it does not go far enough. It is not that we should refuse to have the poem "reduced" to its paraphrasable content. There simply is, if we are to argue the total integrity of form and content, no such thing as the "paraphrasable content." In so far as this content would be presumed to include (besides Yvor Winters' "motive" of the poem) the facts of the poet's identity, his period character, and so on, it is, precisely, *content*; it is, as we view it, contained in the poem. The poem "contains" all its references. A poem like "Lycidas" contains all that it recognizes of the 17th century culture, and of the personality of the author; and these recognitions are inseparable from our recognition of the poem.

Again, we are asked to recognize the mind of the 17th century, and Marvell's or Milton's mind, as expressed in their poems, as part of the period mind, the language of the poem as part of the language

[2] To Mr. Richards himself, of course, it is clear, has been for a long time, and perhaps was in some sense from the first. But for many others, this cannot be said. When they somehow "know" it, often they still do not know *why*, and the knowledge continues to embarrass them.

of the era, the poem as part of the period culture. But would it not make more critical sense to reverse the formula, and speak of the culture, rather, as part of the poem?

For we learn to read, after all, *in order* to read, to read the works that are written in the language. Moreover, whether it is our "own" or a foreign language that we are learning, we learn to read *by* reading. That, too, is an essential part of the "miracle." We have to take the plunge sooner or later; and probably in the end it is best to have made it sooner, and in as deep a place as possible.

The basic difficulty with the historical approach, as usually practiced, is that it takes too static a view of culture. The great poem, like "Lycidas," any poem worthy of the name indeed, does not simply reflect a culture, but makes it. The poem *is* the culture. And the best we can ever do, by way of "locating" one of these makings in its period, for our better understanding of it, is to draw *analogies* between it and the other makings of the same period, the works of other poets, and other philosophers, painters, musicians, explorers, believers.

Further, the static concept of culture entertained by the historicists (I think, for example, of Rosemond Tuve) ignores the prophetic character of the poet. What poet ever presumed to address only his own age? It is the essential distinction of the poet's vision that he looks before and after, that he speaks to the future and to the past.

By the same token, moreover, it is only in so far as we ourselves are poets, only so far as we are able to view the past as the poet does, addressing *ourselves* to it, in a sense re-making the past, that we can in the 20th century adopt the point-of-view of the 17th century reader. In effect, the historicists ask us to do this, to make ourselves over, by dint of sufficient research into the culture of the period, as men of the 17th century. But can the research ever be sufficient, for this purpose? Specifically, I mean that this very passion for accuracy and completeness of historical research, this notion of the possibility of a total recapture of the past — *recherche du temps perdu* by scholarship! — is a peculiarity of *modern* Western culture. It belongs all but exclusively to the 19th and 20th centuries, and would be, by all the evidence, alien to the mind of 17th century man. By the very notion of doing such a thing, making ourselves into the complete man of the past, we are already debarred from accomplishing it.

But I mean also, just that culture flows, continuously, though backward and forward. And we need something — by no means all — but something more of at least that part of Mr. T. S. Eliot's and Mr. Ezra Pound's kind of criticism, which emphasizes the *usefulness* of research — reading the older poets primarily for what can be turned to account in *modern* poetry. It is a kind of criticism that is good for critics, as well as for poet-critics. No critic of the literature of any past period ever made much sense of that, who had not at the same time a lively interest in the poetry of his own time. (I have elsewhere stated my position with regard to Mr. Eliot's prejudices against certain favorites of my own among the older poets; at least for me, if not as I suggested he might be for Eliot himself, Milton is a good deal more useful than Eliot ever wanted to give him credit for being. But the virtue of the critical principle is not compromised by particular shortcomings of the mind that avows it.)

The idea, then, of the scholarly conquest of the past — conquest of our own minds, to the point of being able to transform ourselves into men, poetry-readers, of the past — is an illusion. We not only cannot do it; but if we propose to read poetry as poetry — that is, as involved in the flow of culture, old poems becoming the property of new — we ought not even to try. But it is, though illusion, a grand illusion; it has been tried, whether or not it ought to have been; and the accumulation of knowledge, the effort of research expended in pursuit of the illusion, is a real part of our intellectual experience as modern men. The opposed truth, therefore, also follows: that, if we cannot be men of the 17th century, yet precisely as men of the 20th century we cannot "unknow" the historical knowledge our age has accumulated; we cannot, even, merely wish away the historical attitude. We can only hope to transcend it, with another from which we see man in his art as always, continuously and creatively involved in the historical process, at the same time that he observes it — thus to do away with the static concept of disjunct "periods" of culture, each with its self-contained "mind" which we are supposed somehow to recover intact, merely by observation.

Nor, again, will such still rather grudging concessions as Mr. Brooks' (p. 236, footnote, *The Well Wrought Urn*) to the historicists — admitting that one must "start outside the poem," in recognition of its "unit meanings" — serve to establish the transcendent attitude. For this is, actually, just to accept and repeat the fundamental, historicist error, of regarding the poem as merely receptacle or mirror of culture, rather than what is making the culture, what is "containing" it as part of its own, vital structure. Once more, Brooks seems to me refuted here on the terms of his own doctrine of the unity of form and content. If there really is such a unity, if the poem means only and exactly what it says, and the way of saying is indistinguishable from what is said — then how are we to determine these borrowed "units" of meaning?

Another common prejudice of the historicist attitude, and again usually at the expense of the explicationists, is to identify the poem with its physical text. Professor Fredson Bowers, in his book *Textual and Literary Criticism* has greatly amused himself at the vagaries of New Critics like John Crowe Ransom and Delmore Schwartz — who respectively exercise their ingenuities on a wholly imaginary manuscript text, and a printed text known to be corrupt. But the implicit argument of Bowers' essay — that most of the fundamental problems of criticism might be solved if only we could be sure we had the "pure" physical text of the poem before starting to read — must provoke another, more melancholy amusement still. For, by Professor Bowers' own evidence, *all* texts are corrupt and corruptible.

The view of the absolute sacredness of the physical text is, again, a product of the strictly modern, 19th and 20th century, development of methods in historical scholarship, in conjunction with the effects of the older, but still definably "modern" art of printing. The scholarly method was first employed primarily in the study and "establishment" of ancient texts — by virtue simply of their age, in some sense the easier to establish, of course, to "fix" permanently — but has recently been extended, with even greater attitudinal severity, to the examination of modern works. The scholars are eager to establish, once and for all, the authentic texts of poems that have hardly aged a critical season beyond the poet's death, thus to prevent the slightest chance of errors of interpretation. (The attendant anxiety, to get and preserve permanently all the variants, and manuscript "working" texts, besides the final "established" one, might suggest an opposite motivation, the desire to keep the critic in perpetual uncertainty. But I prefer the more charitable interpretation.)

But it appears that modern printers are hardly more reliable than the mediaeval scribes. As it happens, the text over which Mr. Schwartz tripped up, so much to Bowers' edification, is that of Yeats' "Among School Children," in the 1933 American collected edition. But regardless of whether he is dealing with an ancient or a modern *poem*, the text is modern just in so far as it is designed to be presented to a modern audience; and the soberest and surest textual scholar, once he presents his finished copy, is at the mercy of the drunken typesetter, with whom the poet probably has more in common than he has with the purist scholar.

The perfection of the methods of historical scholarship, including those of "textual criticism," is, as I have said, the paradoxical pride of our incomparable modernity. The like of it, no other civilization has produced. It is, as far as it goes, already a wholly admirable accomplishment. Yet, even if by some unimaginable further development of these techniques to the point of excluding any probability of errors in technical judgment, plus the evolution of a printer's union selflessly devoted to the sacredness of the texts entrusted to them for transmission — if, by whatever means, we could ever be sure of getting to every reader always and only the one, true text of any given poem, always and only the "right" words of the poet — still, they would be, *only* words.

It is surely significant that the poet (T. S. Eliot) who writes:

> . . . *Words strain,*
> *Crack and sometimes break, under the burden,*
> *Under the tension, slip, slide, perish,*
> *Decay with imprecision* . . .

and that:

> . . . *one has only learnt to get the better of words*
> *For the thing one no longer has to say, or the way*
> *in which*
> *One is no longer disposed to say it* . . .

is the poet of *our* age, precisely the age of the most acute historical awareness and the most exacting methods of historical scholarship, perhaps the final phase of "The Age of Gutenberg."

Let us, by all possible means, have the "right" words not the "wrong" ones. We want, if we can get them, the words the poet wrote, not those of a careless editor or printer. If the poet himself, between editions, changed his mind about certain lines — then we want the ones he composed when in his "right" mind concerning them, whether earlier or later in his life. We have faith to judge even of that. But, with all these "rightnesses," right understanding is still quite another matter.

II

But if it is apparent, then, in view of the general instability and complexity of language, and specifically of poetic usage, that literary criticism can never be an exact science — and yet if we are to insist, as do the critics especially of the school to which I am indebted for my basic method here, that it ought to be a science of some kind, a discipline — the question about determining the limits of the poem becomes still more urgent. Let us attempt to rephrase it more narrowly. Of all the possible, manifold "meaning" that a single word appearing in a poetic text might have to a given reader — say, the word "jacks" in Shakespeare's sonnet 128 — as specifically denoting a certain object; as part of a metaphor there; but also as having an etymology known to the reader that itself involves a rather complex metaphorical process in the development of the common speech; and again as reflecting perhaps a certain set of social and economic attitudes, characteristic of the poem's period of composition, with which the reader is also familiar; or even, it might be, as having certain strongly marked private associations for him, reminding him always, whenever he encounters it, of some incident of his personal life — what parts belong to the poem as I want to identify it, and what must be, in so far as possible, temporarily excluded from one's consciousness as critically irrelevant?

The "answer" to that question, implicit in the way I have handled the texts of poems in these essays, is that *nothing* is automatically excluded — but that the test of final relevance is just in whether any meaning attributed to one word, one phrase, can be shown to be compatible with all the significance one allows to all the other parts of the text. I suppose if "private" *means* "private," if the total configuration, the history, of each individual human consciousness is distinct from every other, and there is no metempsychosis by which Shakespeare himself may live again in one of his readers, then private associations can hardly produce anything that will meet the requirements of the review of the poem's syntax. If "jack" always recalls to my mind the face of a friend, or the image of a mule, or that of a device for lifting an automobile wheel clear of the ground, then, once having duly entertained the image, allowed it to put in its appearance and be recognized, I am simply obliged to exert my will and respectfully request it to retire. "Meaning," I have said, is meaning *toward*; and the relationship is at best unstable, but any sane man can grasp the fact that he is at least *primarily* the listener, not the speaker, when he reads a poem. But anything that can meet the test — as, for example, recalling the etymology of "jack" could be one of the best ways of getting at, in Shakespeare's poem, the full sense of the metaphor of the young woman's hands being "kissed" by the "saucy jacks," the keys of the virginal, and the complexity of the speaker's attitude toward her display of her musical skill, his "jealousy" — is admissible. One brings to the reading of the poem everything that he knows, every faculty of his sensibility. And he is only "wrong," at one point or another (or concludes that the poem is in error, disordered; but it is most becoming in the critic to give the poet the benefit of any doubt), and must discard something of his impressions, when among the various meanings he has elicited from the different parts of the poem there appear to be conflicts or divergencies which he cannot by appeal to any discoverable, further pattern of tonal contrasts, of irony, of adherence to a literary convention, or whatever, resolve.

To return briefly to the question of the change of meaning which words may undergo between the time that a poem is written and the time that it is read, and to my admission that one can never quite escape the effect of the linguistic climate of his own time, never fully "recover" the language habits of an earlier period — theoretically, there is nothing sacred even about that one court of historical scholarship to which most explicationists still habitually defer, the NED. Always, we must start with the "given" text. And if one is to insist upon this "given-ness" and entirely disdain the "intentional fallacy," he must allow the possibility of instances in which the single poetic usage has somehow, whether wittingly or unwittingly on the part of the poet, anticipated a later development in the general practice of the language. Apart even from words which are the distinct "coinage" of the poet (Milton's "pandemonium"), one must admit the possibility of a situation in which he could simply take some "common" word in the poem as he finds it, that is, with its now accumulated meaning, read it in some sense later than those that should have been available to the poet, and still find it quite compatible in the full context of the poem. It is only that such instances are extremely rare. And, ordinarily, one will simply find it most convenient, when he is tempted to attribute a certain meaning to a word, that he try to determine whether it commonly had that significance in the poet's period. For, if it had not, the chances are that following up the suggested meaning in the context will sooner or later lead to an irresolvable conflict.

It seems to me, further, that the method allows to the reader this same liberty, and only this restriction of obligation to the total context, in his reaction to any systems of ideas involved in the poem. I have already observed, or implied, that "knowing the language" in which a poem is written means also to know the systems of ideas to which it may refer. I have insisted that these references are an integral, inseparable *part* of the final text. Later, I shall have something more to say about the problem of "belief" in poetry; and about "intention." But in so far as beliefs may be embodied in public, traditional "systems" they are available and thoroughly relevant to criticism. One cannot read Marvell's "The Coronet," for example, without knowing something about Christian tradition and theology; and the more he knows, the better. In the course of reading the poem according to the method I am recommending, one may go as far afield as he likes in pursuit of its systematic references — into the history of religious belief in Marvell's own time, into theological studies, into mythography and the history of the relationship of Biblical symbolism to the symbolism of other religions. He may do all of this, provided only that he does not *stay* afield, but brings all back finally into relationship with the other elements of the poem's particular order, with the pattern of shifting emotional attitudes there, the pattern of word play and imagery, and so on.

I have said, "traditional or public systems." But, in this connection, the essay on Rilke's sonnet presents an instance in which it is advisable, or even necessary, to make some reference not simply to a traditional system of beliefs, but to a particular system (*as* system) which belongs primarily to the one poet. We must recognize, as part of the obligation imposed by our view of the poem as "containing" cultural history, the fact that in the 20th century, with the breakdown of traditional systems — of what may be called a public community of belief and of recognition of the community symbols — it has become more and more the burden of the poet to create his own "frame of reference." Thus, I spoke of a "poetic" which is elaborated in the book of sonnets as a whole, in order to explicate the significance of the present *image* of the horse's movement in this particular poem — as it embodies a set of attitudes on the subject of inspiration, the dedication of poems to an inspiring power, and the faculty of the imagination as a faculty of receptivity. Orpheus, the "Herr," is mentioned directly in this poem, and so is his function with relation to hearing, the ear; and we come back finally to attend just to what he has to do with this particular image, of the horse. But we have the same liberty, or obligation, to look aside for some information about him especially in the rest of Rilke's volume, since he is clearly not just the Orpheus of *ancient* tradition — or, for that matter, with due caution, into Heller's book for commentary on the "ein," or Miss Sewell's on the "Orphic voice" — as we have, if we do not already know, to look in the Bible to find out who it was who wore the crown of thorns that Marvell mentions, or in one of the fathers to learn something about the sin of pride.

In short, these matters are not "private" in the same sense that my friend's face, the mule or the automobile jack, are private meanings of "jack" and therefore unavailable, inadmissible in a reading of Shakespeare's sonnet. Again, I am listener, not speaker; *my* privacy must yield to the poet's, in any event. Later, if face-of-friend and mule and wheel-lifter once again assert themselves, I am at liberty to write my own poem about them, even to incorporate an allusion to Shakespeare's "saucy jacks," publish it, and see how it fares in the world along with Shakespeare's effort. But that would *have* to be, later. But further — beyond this question of distinguishing privacies, speaker's and listener's, a task which at more complex levels of critical activity is attended to far less often than it ought to be — by the very fact of its *systematization* the modern poet's "private" system of beliefs becomes publicly available. I should hope that my essay here is some evidence that the predicament of the modern poet, of modern man, is not after all so bad as it is painted, that even in such a case as Rilke's the "miracle of communication," through the walls of the "inglorious prison" of the artist's immanence of being, is still possible.

Nor do I, speaking of word play and imagery in connection both with Marvell's and with Rilke's poem, find that the method necessarily enforces a preference only for certain kinds of poetic effects. There is a sense in which all poetry is metaphor — just in that it always involves a nonlogical, imaginative or intuitive, transfer of the poet's impression of things in one order of reality into context or juxtaposition with his impressions of things in another order without consideration of what "necessary" or, better, *logically predictable* relationship there may or may not be between the two. In this sense, Wordsworth's poem "The Solitary Reaper" is just as metaphorical as Marvell's "The Coronet." In the essay, I have attempted to show how, in an adaptation of this sense, it can be regarded as even *more* metaphoric. But, according to the terms of rhetorical definition to which most of us habitually defer, there is in "The Solitary Reaper" hardly any one figure of speech that can be called *a* metaphor, or even a simile. There are no strict tropes — except, perhaps, the one from common speech, common in everyday usage as in poetry, of the heart's "bearing" the music. There is, I suggested, an implicitly figurative usage in the phrase "vale profound"; but it is not a fully developed metaphor. The references to the two birds, in their respective situations, the nightingale and the cuckoo, are "metaphorically" brought into the context of the speaker's admiration for the girl's song; but in the way they are presented, they do not qualify as ordinary *metaphors*. (Wordsworth does not say anything like — "Ah, Nightingale, that sings in the desert of my heart.") And yet, in the study of this poem, we have managed to stay within the structure of its interrelated effects, although they are effects for the most part of a different rhetorical kind from those Marvell achieves in his poem (including much more not-saying as well as saying), just as strictly as we stayed within the extended conceit that binds together the diverse elements in "The Coronet."

Also, in studying "The Coronet," I made much of a certain kind of syntactical ambiguity, in the multiple reference of the pronouns in the last section. The syntax of "The Solitary Reaper" presents nothing of this sort. But the word order there is no less self-contained, but only grammatically less intricate, than in Marvell's poem. And, although as a matter of taste I may prefer poems which exploit such capacities of the language as Marvell's is built on (I am not sure that I do), there is no theoretical reason for the preference, nothing in the defined character of the approach that would dictate it.

Whether the emphasis is to be upon effects of one kind or another, depends just upon what the particular poem offers. In the essay on Rilke's sonnet, I put unusually strong emphasis upon the sound structure of the verse. These and other prosodic effects are important in all poems. And, strictly speaking, if one is to insist upon the individual order of a poem as *total* order, he ought to provide a complete prosodic analysis as part of the explication of any poem. But, if it is impossible, just because a poem is words and words are rhythmical sounds, that these elements can be eliminated from any poem — as some standard elements, in a plain sense, *can* be, "The Coronet," for example, getting on without any of the element of setting, or "scene," which all the others to some extent include, or pretend to include — still, obviously, the sound structure, the movement of the verse, is not important in the same degree in one poem as in another. In Rilke's poem, the image is *of* a movement, not just of the horse, but of the horse running; thus, one cannot speak of the image, the "Bild," without discussing the prosodic pattern of the lines in which that image is presented. But in other poems there may be no such imperative.

The essay on "Lycidas" illustrates one way in which a knowledge of a system of poetic convention must be utilized to secure attention to the individual order of the poem. We simply cannot understand that individuality unless we have first, or at the same time, observed the use of conventions. And in the study of Yeats' "A Prayer for My Daughter," it is equally necessary that we recognize, not a "system" of conventions like the pastoral of "Lycidas," but in another sense a *conventionality* of tone, attitude, in particular phrases. The essential irony, in a passage like that referring to the birth of Aphrodite, depends upon evocation of the attitude conventionally associated with such a phrase as "that great Queen, that rose out of the spray" — evocation of the "stock response," as I called it earlier — so that this attitude may then be startlingly played off against the entirely different one, of mocking familiarity, in the lines following.

But perhaps the best illustration of the general principle I am trying to define, of the proper relationship between what the reader "knows" (or thinks he knows, prior to reading the poem, roughly Context [1]) and his sense of the individual order of the poem (roughly, Context [2], or "syntax"), is in the effect of the Babel reference in "Rêve Parisien." The final "meaning" of the name as applied to the palace of the dream vision, can be discovered only in the full context of the poem, only as one brings back to that what he has gone out to recover from his previous reading. Its precise meaning is apparent only when we have related the reference to the fact that the present scene is entirely silent, and further to the imagery which in its turn has suggested allusion to traditional conceptions of the infernal regions, and this again to the ambivalence of the speaker's attitude toward the work of his dream. Whatever diverse meanings "Babel" might have elsewhere, we have to read and define it here in the full light of the poem's "feu personnel." But, simultaneously, one has to know what the word alludes to — the Biblical story, and, the more *fully* we are to read the framework of associations in which he involves it, also other poetic uses of the story.

Finally, in the study of "A Prayer for My Daughter" I have accommodated, besides the literary and other learned references of the poem, a range of significance, that of the personal allusions, against which the method from which mine derives has sometimes seemed to enjoin an absolute prejudice. It is true that in reaction against the excesses of a certain kind of biographical scholarship that had reached its widest influence at the time the American branch of the explicationist movement was established, the exponents of the new doctrine developed a strong intolerance for anything suggesting the direct involvement of the poet's personal feelings in his work. They looked exclusively for "universal," or "traditional," values. The poem was supposed to be entirely free from any reflection of the personality of the author, entirely detached from its occasion, and so on. And when the poem (that is, their critics were for a time inclined to say, any poem other than certain contemporary ones or those of the English Metaphysicals) contained hints of personalism, either these elements of its statement were elaborately explained away, or such a poem was simply ignored, left unstudied.

The attitude, in fact, still persists in the critical practice of the school — not only determining the direction studies of any poetry may take, but to some extent, although not so severely as it was once supposed it had to, restricting in the first place the choice of poems for consideration. (It is undoubtedly significant that, although Yeats himself is a poet much honored by the movement, the praise is given almost exclusively to the poems of the late-middle period, where attention to the mechanics of the symbolic system can obscure the importance of its being a *personal* system. So far as I know, my essay here on "A Prayer for My Daughter" is the first more than cursory glance at this poem, whereas full-length studies of both the Byzantium poems are commonplace.) It is an attitude, moreover, with which I myself obviously have still some general sympathy — even in the final intent of my Yeats chapter.

I have, after all, chosen poems to study that may well seem to some readers significantly alike in one respect or another. There are two "circular" poems, Marvell's and Rilke's — even "Young Waters" is such in a sense; three that involve versions of the song-within-the-song, Milton's and Wordsworth's and Rilke's; two that balance scenes of common reality against a vision, Baudelaire's and Yeats.' And, besides whatever these and other features that might be pointed out may indicate about the rule of my choice — that I wanted poems in which the "architectonics," the self-containing or self-sustaining order, would be plainly apparent — I have in every essay stressed the elements of the statement that do, whether one wants to call them "universal" or "traditional" or not, refer to what can be termed matters of public knowledge. In a certain sense, every poem has an order; there is no such thing as an un-ordered work of art. But there are some in which it is almost impossibly difficult to get at the principle of that order; and others in which it is so obvious, provides so superficial a grasp of any reality, that it must seem hardly worth bothering to define; and poems that utilize mainly private experience are likely to be the worst offenders in either of these ways. In *not* including poems that are off-balanced in this direction, I have implicitly avowed a standard of communicability and one of general acuteness and objective awareness. When I have spoken of *order* in a poem, I have meant an order whose principle can be explained by someone other than the poet himself in private conversation, or by his psychoanalyst, that has been communicated, in short; and one that organizes a view of some rather large area of the world intellectual and otherwise that we all live in, and organizes it, what is more, profoundly, on more than one obvious level. To this extent, I acknowledge my acceptance of the anti-personalist or universalist attitude.

Hand-in-hand with this, though at first glance they might seem to be at variance, goes my obvious tendency at least to *emphasize* most strongly what I have called the individual "syntax" of the poem, or Context [2] — at the same time that I have argued it has to complete itself in Context [1]. It has to be emphasized, because it does somehow lie nearest the *center* of the poem, and is the area, so to speak, of the study in which we are most likely to go hopelessly wrong. It is here that we discover, at length, what the central motivating principle of the poem is, and thereby, which elements (prosody, visual imagery, pattern of allusion, etc.) are of greater and lesser importance. A sure criterion of excellence, in my mind, is the ability of a poet to create this syntax — that whereby we recognize not just his poems, as distinct from the poems of other poets, but by which each of his own is distinguishable, which keeps his poems as we say from "collapsing into each other." The great poet gives himself, all but entirely, to each work he undertakes. Again by this means, then, the poem is "universalized." It stands alone, in the public domain.

And yet I think that the customary mode of critical statement that recognizes these criteria can, and must be, liberalized. I should like to pursue a bit further the specific issue of "personalism." If we are not simply to ignore such a poem as "A Prayer for My Daughter," and leave it to the biographical sentimentalists as "their Yeats" — and yet are strictly to insist that every element of the poem's statement be accommodated in the order of internal relevance — then we will have to find some way of accounting for the personal references. For the references are undeniably there. They are there not as excrescences, or digressions, but fully and vitally involved in the total complex of imagery, attitude, and symbolism, inseparable from the final significance of any part of the poem's statement, their meaning lying no more "outside" the poem than does the meaning of the references to Helen and Aphrodite or to the Horn of Plenty. But the problem of "accounting for" has bearings much beyond the question of how to read this one poem, or even to read all of Yeats. It has bearings, at the very least, upon the whole predicament of *modern* poetry, and therefore of modern criticism. We have to find some way of accounting for — as "matter of public knowledge" — the modern poet's myth of himself, the way in which he has become, perforce, the hero of his own poem.

Poetry in our age has tended to become more and more strictly identifiable with *lyric* poetry. The method of the explicationist critics, with certain modifications, is not necessarily limited to the study of works in this mode. But, with their emphasis upon the grasp of the single work, they have in general followed this tendency of the development of the art. And yet, they have usually refused recognition of what once was regarded as the essential characteristic of the lyric — its personalism. They have talked of the "dramatic" structure of the poem, and so on, pushing toward denial of the genre distinctions. And while it is unquestionably true that any poem, lyric or otherwise, is "dramatic" in the sense that the poet puts on a mask, adopts a *persona*, to speak the lines — yet there is some sense, that we ought I think to define more clearly, in which we can "afford" not to know anything about Shakespeare the man, but cannot allow the lyricist the same anonymity.

The 16th- or 17th-century lyricist perhaps disappears the more easily behind his work, just because of the greater stability of public values in his period than in ours. (One must say even this much with reservations, however. The modernist tendency, to collapsing the genres, most definably "began" in the 17th century, of course. Milton's poetic career, in some way obviously an attempt to stem the tide, is ironically the best proof of the impossibility of doing so. And the longer I think about his work, in all the forms, the greater importance the problem of "personality" assumes.) But even if the "quest for anonymity," the very eagerness to assume the *personae*, is itself also an attribute of the modern poet — so that the critic is only, again, following his lead in shying away from personal elements in the poetic statement, and speaking of the lyric as a "dramatic" mode — still we should not miss seeing how readily the tendency of this eagerness reverses itself, with the masks of the poetry being worn back into the life, to establish a new and yet more intense, super-personalism. The quest for anonymity, in other words, is only a reverse expression of the well-known "quest for identity," for a means of reaffirming the reality of the self and of personal values. And for the great modern poets like Yeats and Rilke, their poetry is thoroughly a way of life, an embodiment of the myth of themselves.

The late 19th-century French symbolists, taking their cue somewhat from Baudelaire, attempted for a time the creation of a poetry which should be totally unintelligible — structures of words that, like the creations of certain modern sculptors and painters (Moore and Picasso) seeming to stand completely outside time and nature, demonically compelling, should defy us to perform any "criticism" except an act of mindless and eternal not-contemplation, of total surrender, of an "entering into" the work without hope ever of emerging. I cannot say how nearly realizable an ideal of dehumanization[3] this may be for the plastic arts; everyone who has attended an exhibition of such works must remember at least the very real *fear*, with which he looked upon each of these insufferable presences, that if he stood too long he might never be permitted even to move on to the next, for the legend borne by each one is the same, *lasciate ogni speranza voi ch'entrate*. But for poetry, anyway, by the very nature of language, it is impossible. The desperation of the effort is understandable. These poets were the first to feel the terrible need, which afflicts us yet more sorely now, to re-establish what Max Picard calls the relationship of speech with silence, to restore the word to recognition of its origin in silence. But this, simply to deny language its history, which is to say its intelligibility, its value as means of communication between one human being and another, was not the way to go about fulfilling the need. The effort to "use words as if they had never been used before," as Symons said of Mallarmé, worked out or seemed to work out in only a very few of the symbolists' own poems. The words, almost as if of themselves, persisted in forming sentences. Yeats, truth to tell, never even tried it (his own "symbolism" was from the first of a different order — which may have something to do with Symons' dropping the dedication of his book to him in the 1919 edition); Eliot dallied with it but briefly, likewise Pound (whose mature unintelligibility is of a different order), and likewise Stevens; today, it has been everywhere abandoned except in minor quarters. And, by virtue of their avowed standards of intelligibility and traditionalism, the explicationist critics of our time might seem to applaud the abandonment, to join with the great 20th-century poets in setting themselves against the forces of dehumanization.

But — my point, to repeat, is that the personalism, or "superpersonalism," of a Yeats or a Rilke, their development of private systems of symbolic reference, is *not* the same thing as that earlier French attempt at the creation of a totally depersonalized, inaccessibly virgin *language* — the critics' insistence upon the anonymity of

---

[3] The term, of course, is from Ortega y Gasset's *The Dehumanization of Art*, an essay which keeps getting awkwardly in the way of everyone's effort to read or look at any modern art-work again and know how he really feels about it, or say anything either. One feels somehow tremendously excited, even "persuaded," by Ortega's insights. But (he says plainly that works of art as such do not interest him) his ineffable superiority to his subject-matter makes it impertinent to ask — persuaded to *what?*

the poem, its thoroughly detached and self-contained "dramatic" order, has its own curiously dehumanizing and deadening effect. They would speak of the poem as if it had come into being, or ought to have come into being, without an author. Every poem, regardless of whether it is old *or* modern, is set apart like the sculptures, totally outside time and nature. As if fearful that an author might have left something unsaid, some loose ends of meaning dangling, something subject to future change of interpretation, they have simply expelled the poet — supplying then with criticism what is necessary to fix the poem in eternal, changeless significance. And with the poet, of course, they have expelled also all future readers. But, *die Sprache ist das Haus des Seins* (Heidegger). And that "Being" is *man's* being, which is in time and nature. We can talk about the *poet's* anonymity; but there must exist a person to *be* anonymous. The *poem* is anonymous only in so far as it expresses the poet's will to anonymity. In their apparent failure to recognize this, the critics are precisely not modern according to the modernity of the great poets themselves, and cannot claim their patronage.

III

But this brings us, finally, to the problems of belief and intention. I have tried, so far, to restrict myself principally to questions of *knowledge*. How does the poet's knowing enter into the statement of the poem? What must we know, and what attempt to "unknow," in order to read the poem? The statement I have made about Marvell's "The Coronet," for example, that one must know something about Christian tradition and theology in order to understand such a poem, is a commonplace of the more responsible explicationist criticism. But if this might satisfy most of the complaints of pure historicism, there still remains the troublesome question, posed both by the religious and the anti-religious critic, the relativist or positivist: how are we to reconcile, not our religious knowledge, but our religious interests and convictions, our moral-theological insights,[4] which are never a matter simply of rational knowing, with our aesthetic appreciation?

The standard answer would be something as follows: One cannot

---

[4] I am not, of course, speaking of Moral Theology in the technical sense.

read "The Coronet" without knowing something about Christian tradition and theology; and the more he knows, the better. But he can either *be* a Christian, or not be, when he starts to read the poem, and can have whatever his position was in that respect changed or unchanged when he has read it, without affecting the critical situation. For, indeed, if one concentrated upon the Christian elements in the poem exclusively for the satisfaction of agreeing or disagreeing with what they embody (or *probably* embody) of Marvell's religious convictions, then he would necessarily miss, or have to ignore, to put down as annoying irrelevance, the whole elaborate system of extended metaphor, the imagery of the "crown," with which the expression of these convictions is here involved. Or if he were a Roman Catholic, and were looking only for confirmation or contradiction of his position on certain points of doctrine, and found that Marvell is perhaps strongly Protestant in addressing Christ as "thou who only could'st the Serpent tame," pointedly transferring to Him the role of the one who stands with his foot on the head of the serpent, in divergence from the traditional representations of the Blessed Virgin in this attitude — again, if he stopped there, he would probably be "right" about Marvell's being earnestly of the "other persuasion," and is at liberty to think that persuasion is, in the order of religious truth, a persuasion in error. But he would meanwhile have missed the entire "rightness" of Marvell's metaphoric conceit, the "logic" by which the crown of flowers that was meant to replace the crown of thorns on Christ's head, becoming entangled with the serpent, must be finally put under His feet.

It is a good answer, in its way. It is intellectually tolerant. It recognizes the "structure of values," the "structure of attitudes," in the poem — both aesthetic and theological — and only asks that they not be improperly confused, the one narrowly prejudged in terms of the other. Implicit in it, in so far as it contains a defense of Marvell's poem with its expressed view of life as a "good" poem or a "successful" poem, is something like T. S. Eliot's broad-minded criterion of tenability — the demand only that a poem, to deserve our recognition and praise, be "mature, and founded on the facts of experience."

But it is an answer which, the more I examine it, seems itself not to be "founded on the facts of experience" — at least *my* experience, both in reading and writing poetry. For, although it scrupulously and rightly avoids *confusion* of aesthetic and religious values, there is a real question whether it does not enforce a false and impossible *separation* of the two orders.

If this is our answer, we are still talking as if Marvell were not really *interested* in the religious experience which is "dramatized" in the poem, or, if interested, interested only in religion *qua* aesthetics, so that the prejudgment is merely reversed. We all know what mischief is worked in the opposite direction, when aesthetic problems are prejudged in terms of religious conviction; but there has been in modern criticism scant concern for avoiding the contrary error. Such a divorce of the two orders of value as we have attempted becomes, sooner or later, only another confusion — in one direction or the other.

To put the difficulty another way, if this is our answer we are still talking as if the religious interest of the poem were only a matter of knowledge, as if belief were, after all, the same as knowledge. But, I have already insisted, there is a difference. Knowledge may lead to belief, and further knowledge flow from belief. But knowledge is only something we have, or have not. If we do not have it, we may *desire* it; if we do have it, we may in some instances desire to be rid of it. But belief is volitional.[5] And Marvell's poem is instinct with the excitement of belief — with, rather, for it is always such, the excitement of the will, the effort to believe.

This volitional excitement is the only conceivable impetus to the "making" of the poem, and it is inseparable from the completed order of its verbal action, its "drama" in the only legitimate sense beyond the wearing of masks. I assert: if I do not share that excitement, I am not reading the poem, I am not understanding it. We must have done with the modern reversal of Coleridge's formula, with the effort to read poetry in a state of "the willing suspension of *belief*."

If someone reminds me now that Marvell wrote poems, more famous than this one, to a contrary intent — that is nothing to the point. For as soon as we make that observation, we have already gone "outside the poem" and I am free to put my own interpretation

---

[5] In the whole, earnest, learned and in many ways illuminating debate of the English Institute Essays for 1957 on *Literature and Belief*, no one seems to be making this (as I think it) basic distinction between knowledge and belief. Fr. Walter J. Ong's distinction there between "belief *in*" and "belief *that*" (after Gabriel Marcel) barely skirts the issue, but nothing more.

on the facts. He was not, simply, so single-minded a man as Milton, for example. The pull of belief, and doubt, took him at one time and another in opposite directions. But the strength is the same in each instance.

Parochial standards of doctrinal "agreement" — Catholic vs. Protestant, etc. — are not, of course, in court. One can be, professedly, either Christian or atheist, Catholic, Protestant, or Jewish, and still understand the poem. But he cannot, not believe, or not want to believe, anything relevant to what Marvell believes, or is trying to believe. What occurs, I think, when we read a poem is that we discover active analogies to our beliefs; and the discovery is a test, a proof by combat, of our strength in believing. The analogy may in general tend either to complement or to reverse our convictions (convictions are attained and defined, solidified beliefs, which we impose upon ourselves or attempt to impose upon others, in practical situations of proposed action where we consider it dangerous to engage in active believing); but the important thing is that belief is *engaged*, the conviction is no longer quite adequate to the verbal occasion. We may feel that we wrestle with angel or demon; our prize may be a blessing or a curse; but we wrestle — we do not merely engage in, or observe, a dance of "attitudes," we do not simply "agree" or "disagree" with the author, we do not find his positions, his holds upon us, merely "tenable" or "untenable." We admire and judge his performance, according to the vigor and complexity of the test it provides for our own, real, volitional interest — again, our believing. And our beliefs, we, may be permanently changed. A total "conversion" from the reading of one poem would be rare. But in some measure we *risk* conversion every time we read a poem of any complexity.

Belief, then, is radically involved with understanding, with the vital *interest* which is understanding of poetry. But what of the merely non-Christian poem? I should have to say, simply, that if such a poem exists — not, note, the *anti*-Christian poem, but the thoroughly non-Christian, or extra-Christian poem — then it would be impossible for any Western reader to understand it. It would be, in the most radical sense, unintelligible. I am not certain that such a poem does, or can, exist. Further development of studies in comparative religion may make finally intelligible to us the poetries of Eastern and primitive cultures which now — even when we know, in the simplest practical sense, perhaps, the "languages" in which they are composed — are perhaps incomprehensible. But, to repeat, *if* such a poem, a poem that simply does not engage our beliefs, finally exists — then, it is unintelligible. Otherwise, the question is irrelevant — because, at least within our own, Occidental culture, no such poem does exist. Rilke's poem about the horse, for example, or Yeats' about his daughter, are perhaps *anti*-Christian poems; but they are not extra-Christian. Even the pre-Christian Greek or Latin poetry — aside from the truth or falsity of any Christian theories of the specifically "prophetic" character of Homer or Virgil, say — is not extra-Christian, just in the sense that we have to recover it from the vantage point of two thousand years of Christian civilization. And the situation is similar with any poem, I should think, in the strictly Hebraic tradition, whether ancient or modern, and even for an orthodox Jewish reader — since his entire sensibility cannot but be shaped by his consciousness of Christianity as an outgrowth of the Hebrew tradition, and of the breaking apart of the two religions.

We do have poems, of course, both old and modern, that are non-Christian just in that they are, superficially, non-*religious* in subject. Wordsworth on daffodils, for example. It would require, no doubt, a lengthy and ingenious argument to prove that the implicit aesthetic in this poem, and therefore its intelligibility, is one derivable only from the experience of Christian culture. But I think it could be done. And even if it could not, even if we are to suppose that there are certain sentiments and predispositions of our nature which are not touched by our specifically religious experience, and a poetry answerable to this part of ourselves, this strictly mundane "soul" — the case of my central argument would not be altered. For, in order to understand the poem about flowers, just flowers, and the response of the "heart" to the remembered sight of them, we still have to *believe* in something, in the possibility of "glee" in nature, in man, that he *has* a "heart," or is at any rate capable of thinking that he has. There are only, then, some poems that do not specifically, in a form recognizable to all readers, raise the "problems" of belief — i.e., the problems of religion. There is no such thing as a non-believing poem; and no such thing as a non-believing reader, a non-believing criticism.

But I am interested primarily in making my point with reference to those poems, and those criticisms, that *do* specifically engage the problems of religious belief. I have said that Yeats' and Rilke's poems may be regarded as *anti*-Christian, but never as extra-Christian. The same is true of certain systems of criticism. Not only the relativists and the positivists, and the pure historicists, but those of late who have been most confidently and condescendingly detached from the whole controversy over "The New Criticism" — the anthropological and mythographic schools, the Jungians, and even still the Freudians — are not exempt. The religious philosophers, Christian and Jewish, although often wrongheadedly, are currently dispelling with great vigor any illusions these schools might once have had of providing simply a total *escape* for modern man from the preoccupations of his traditional beliefs. Belief in the archetypes, let us say, as providing the "real" significance of works of art, may or may not be proved finally compatible with Christian truth. But it is a belief, nonetheless, and answerable to the beliefs of the artist expressed in his work; it is a belief, moreover, that is incomprehensible except as something arising, whether in benevolence or antagonism, from the main stream of the Hebrew-Christian tradition, as surely as the New Criticism itself arises from that stream. There is no escape from the fundamental problem of criticism, simply in substituting one "set" of beliefs, or representational forms of belief, for another. The basic question is: whether belief, as the volitional act of believing, is or is not an inextricable part of the poetic statement. I say that it is. And there is no escape from their enemies for the Christians among the New Critics, either, simply in congratulating themselves on the beautiful irony of the fact that it is not, after all, *they* who want to keep injecting the problem of belief into critical discussion, that they are precisely the ones who have most rigorously insisted upon keeping clear the distinctions between "literary" and "extra-literary" considerations, between "literature" and "apologetics."

(I am thinking, of course, specifically of Cleanth Brooks at this point. But he has a host of followers and compatriots — Protestant and Catholic, and a good many who are not especially Christian but simply not anything else particularly, except gentlemen — all of whom will stand shoulder to shoulder on this issue when they may be divided on practically everything else. And it is true, I think, as Mr. Brooks has often pointed out, that the staunchness of their "anti-apologetic" stand as critics tends to be measurable in direct proportion to the hardiness of their orthodoxy as private citizens.)

A closely related, perhaps identical problem, is the problem of "intention." Earlier in this chapter, I myself have tried to make clear the view that we can read only the "given text" of a poem, that our comprehension and judgment of the poem must be based on that alone. I have insisted, in qualification, only that we are obliged to recognize the conditions under which it is "given," as part of the giving. If Mr. W. K. Wimsatt's famous definition and repudiation of the "intentional fallacy" in criticism means only this — that we are not to impose upon the poem our preconceptions of the author's intent, according to our knowledge of his biographical character or of the character of his age in literary history, etc., or that, if we have no special preconceptions, we are mistaken to suppose that we must acquire some, look up the "facts" on the poet's life and times, his reputation, the "occasion" of the poem, before even beginning to read, that we must consult, finally, the particular order of the poem's statement to apprehend its significance, and not be running off after allusions and sources for their own sakes, in the hope of making the poem mean something less, more, or other than what it says (with due allowance for not-saying as a way of saying) — then I entirely agree.

But if it means — as I suspect it does, at least in effect or tone, at least in what *it* leaves unsaid, whether or not this was part of Mr. Wimsatt's own, unspoken intention in writing! — that the poet really does not "intend" anything, then I demur. There is so much talk of the critic's burden of responsibility, his "public" office in judging the worthwhileness of the poem, so little of the poets except with regard to their general *irresponsibility* as critics, and practically none of poems except for scraps of illustration. What it all comes to, after much elaborate hedging, is that we had *better*, when we can, let everything except the text alone. Critics can be called to account, must be prepared to defend what they have said (Mr. Wimsatt is never so gleeful as when he *is* called to account, even if it is only by another critic, Mr. Coomaraswamy, or whoever); he is responsible; in short, he *intended* something when he spoke. But the poem drops from the lips of the poet, and thereafter must go its way in the world alone; the poet is *not* responsible, even while he is still alive; in short, he did *not intend*. (We are assured that the poem, too, is thus a "public" thing. But, somehow, "public" with respect to the critical statement gets around to meaning exactly the opposite of what it meant with respect to the poem. The critical statement is "public" to the extent of its responsibility; the poem, to the extent of its irresponsibility. I see, of course, what Mr. Wimsatt "means"; but it is not exactly what he *says*. One has to supply so much out of solicitude for the "intent," and gets a bit tired after a while of doing this for the critic, when he is forbidden to do it for the poet.)[6]

In a later chapter ("Poetry and Morals," p. 100 especially), we discover Mr. Wimsatt's suspicion that the poet may be *saying* something, after all. But what or how is still not very clear. Poetry has, at least, "a tendency to an assertion." But, since "in-" seems to have been earlier eliminated, I would like now another prefix for that "tendency." And I can hardly imagine what it would be, unless "pre-".

It comes to that, does it not, after so much and all — precisely the Socratic-Platonic position? The poet *pre*tends.

The objectionable quality of so much of the New Criticism (not only Mr. Wimsatt's brand of it), which its enemies have felt but usually been unable to put their hands on because of their own parochial prejudices and sentimentalities, is precisely this — that it leaves us an image of the poet as pretentious meddler with thought, dressing himself in the borrowed finery of ideas upon which he has no just claim and to which, therefore, no sense of final obligation. Or, the poet is a Pretender, a king without a kingdom. Or, he is always tending, toward something, making elaborate gestures toward truth, but always stopping short, again, *pre*tending, never intending.

I vastly oversimplify, of course. I am necessarily in the position, everywhere in this final chapter, of merely seeking the best way to impose my "convictions," in one of those "practical" situations, as I put it, of proposed action, when it might be dangerous to engage in active believing. Mr. Wimsatt actually loves poetry, of course; he knows a great deal of it, and about it. (And the same is true of Mr. Brooks, naturally.) But, I don't want to make matters worse by seeming to patronize either of them — Wimsatt's final and over-riding concern, regardless of his love for poetry, is just the overriding and final concern of Socrates-Plato himself. His love for it is indistinguishable from his suspicion of it; and the big question for the critic is what to "do about" poetry. Poetry is a charming lunatic loose in the world; for all its charm nonetheless lunatic, for all its lunacy nonetheless charming, and you can never tell when it is going to be "up to"

---

[6] W. K. Wimsatt, Jr., *The Verbal Icon*. The chapter on "The Intentional Fallacy" is actually a collaboration, of course, with Monroe Beardsley.

something. It does not "intend" to do any harm; occasionally it might even do some good. But it has to be watched, and that is the job of the critic. The central chapter in *The Verbal Icon* is the one on "Poetry and Morals"; and Wimsatt's criticism is fundamentally a mor*alistic* one. (I know that he says it is not; in "The International Fallacy" and elsewhere. But, then, he says so many things on every issue — and usually by way of qualified assent and dissent to what everybody else for the last two or three thousand years has said on it. One has to sift things down. And besides, any applied system of intellectual rigor is always a higher kind of morality.) The critic is the policeman of literature. A bemused, wise, Offissa Pupp kind of policeman (I risk the allusion in a serious context, since *Krazy Kat* was written up in *The Sewanee Review*) hopelessly trapped between a lover and beloved (poet and people) who are constantly betraying and reversing their roles, and sometimes, just sometimes, wondering if it *all* really is just an action within the self-enclosed universe of the comic-strip (read "university"), if somewhere out there, it may be, there are a real people and a real poet who don't give a real rap about each other, or him either. But, a policeman.

But, speaking of the university, a curious further thing *is* that this image should have been created by the critics — most of whom are also professors — as instrumentation of the desire to preserve a "place" for the study of poetry among the academic disciplines. It is a curious maneuver, since it seems calculated finally to have exactly the opposite effect. There has been much talk of the humanistic "values" of poetry. But values which are reduced, in the very terms of their defenders, to a matter of assumed "attitudes," values without belief or intent, which are locked up within an impenetrable structure of mutually paralyzing "tensions" (again, no *in*tention) which is supposed to be the poem, values which we dare not even assert were "meant" by anyone, an author, since we cannot know who that was — in the end, these are not likely to appear values at all to the hardheaded realist, in or out of university administration. We may be for a time left alone to play our little game of value-ball, this terminological pitch-and-catch, on the implicit plea that at least (unlike certain other disciplines) we "do no harm" with it. But eventually it must become plain to anyone that doing no harm is pretty much the same as doing no good; and that, however innocuous, it costs money. If we had the courage to assert that they are *real* values, that experience of poetry *as* work-of-art can and does really *change* people, perhaps our values would be driven out anyway; maybe even the sooner driven out. But I doubt it. And who, in any event, would not prefer to be discharged as a troublemaker rather than a do-nothing?

I know very well the sense in which the poem is self-sustaining. I am confident I have shown that in the preceding chapters. I know also the sense in which it must go its own way in the world — that we cannot forever be running back to the author, or to anyone else, to ask him what he meant. These are facts, and there is a glory in them, an intimation of immortality. But there is a melancholy too, a shudder of mortality. The man was there, and is no longer — one man, a man, *that* man. And once we lose our sense of that melancholy, once we grow so accustomed to his not being there that we no longer know or care that he was there, once we have trained ourselves to call that melancholy a vulgar sentimentalism, then we have lost also the glory of his not being there. We have lost ourselves. We have lost the meaning of the poem, any poem. And we might as well lose our posts.

But, however all that may turn out, the burden of *responsibility* of statement has been preëmpted for criticism, not poetry. That is why Mr. Wimsatt can speak so confidently of "fallacies." Poetry itself, since it does not intend, is lunatic and irresponsible, illogical in the first place, cannot be "fallacious." But, as if "therefore" (?), criticism can — since it is responsible. It does intend, does, at least intend, to be logical. Similarly, when Mr. Brooks speaks of "normative judgments" — a cautiously fancy word for "*value* judgments" — and of the right of the critic, which must be defended, to *make* normative judgments, it turns out that he means only his right to judge which poems are good or bad. The term "value," once again, has been subtly shifted away from the poetic statement to the critical statement. We still don't know whether the *poem* makes "normative judgments," or does anything else with or of real value. And, what is more, the shifting has been done again within the context of a struggle for *academic* privilege. The critic is the professor-critic. And his right to "normative judgment" is to be preserved so that the study of literature will not be turned over to the history department or the sociology department.

But, another of Mr. Brooks' favorite terms gets us a little closer to the heart of the matter. Wimsatt's "fallacy" — although it is in the interest of a moralistic criticism, smacks of logic, wants to reduce poetry in the end pretty much *just* to what can be ascertained of its possible moral impact, and criticism to the job of logically policing that — is also a term finally grounded in religion, of course. The "morality" is ultimately an orthodox, Christian morality — and the trouble with the way he uses it, almost interchangeably with "religion," is that it tends to *reduce* religious as well as poetic experience, as subjects of intelligible discourse, to morality and only morality, and morality in turn to logically definable moral *principles*, so that he has got either us, the poet, or himself, I don't know which, coming and going. But "fallacy" is theologically cautious. On the other hand, Brooks' "heresy" (the "heresy of paraphrase," etc.) is most beautifully, aptly, incautiously *theological*.

Have I seemed earlier to accuse myself of the famous "Arnoldian heresy," speaking of heresies? Well, perhaps. I have said, if that is by any stretch Arnoldian, something to the effect that poetry *is* religion, or *is* religious. Certainly that. This seems to me quite a different thing from saying that poetry is a substitute for religion. My statement does not want to put either Poetry (poets and poems) or Religion (the church) out of business — it simply does not want *ipso facto* to exclude the poet and his writing (for which he is responsible) from the realm of Grace. I assume that religion as a whole, i.e. the affairs of God and man, as well as the Church, are not mine to dispose of; and at least in that respect I am more cautious than Mr. Arnold, if in others more reckless. But I leave the possible charges against myself to be prepared by another court.

In any event, Mr. Brooks, for all his anxiety to expel the Arnoldian heresy, has by the very use of that term "heresy" permitted something that looks to me very like the original to smuggle itself in again by the back door. (I mean, of course, his *habitual* use of the term, not just for Arnold's error.) *Poetry* is not to substitute for religion; this is "asking poetry to do more than it can or needs to do," etc., etc. But criticism can, it seems; it can, and does, in acquiescence to the collapse of traditional faith, preëmpt the theological terms. It sternly expels "heretics" from the True Church of Criticism.

"Something very like the original," I said. But is it not some yet more frightful offspring of the old? Does Brooks not, in locking up the value in poetry, which amounts to the same thing as denying it, ask poetry to do still *more* than Arnold asked of it? He asks it, really, to do what religion itself cannot and never could and never will do, until the end: and that is, to remove the mind from the agony of belief.

We worship a false god, and pretend to ourselves that because we have admitted he is false we are not worshipping him, and therefore are not to be held responsible for the appearances of our actions. But we want to be supported and vested, at public expense, for the continuation of these curious gyrations before the empty altar.

But I fall to railing, and the railer rails always at himself. Somewhat more soberly, then — I have said that I suspect what is behind all this is the lingering fear on the part of the critics that Plato was right, that the poet is in fact thrice removed from truth, a "mere" imitator, a pretender. This is another way of saying, that in all the talk of distinguishing the methods of poetry, the poetic use of language, from the methods of "science," or "philosophy," and therefore the poet's "purpose" or "mode of truth," from those of the scientist and philosopher — there is a lingering, wistful Rationalism. They fear, or hope, that somewhere out there — if not in science, then in "philosophy," at least surely in theology — there is yet a realm, and yet verbal, of purely rational discourse. And though for old times' sake, they would like to keep the poet around — at least until, remembering the consequences of premature efforts in the past to push him out, they can be sure of the auspices for expulsion — meanwhile, they propose to supply the deficiencies of his rationality with the rigor of criticism itself.

But the sad truth is that the anti-rationalist revolution of the late 18th and 19th centuries was radical and irreversible. And the only kind of "criticism" which can result from a failure to face this truth, is itself the most patent imitation — imitation *of* an imitation. Mr. Wimsatt, to do him justice, is not most of the time actively moralizing. (Sometimes, "justly" or not, one wishes he would be.) But when he is not, he is getting ready to do so with what looks to me suspiciously like the kind of activity that much of the rest of modern "philosophy" is up to, and which he himself would find abhorrent if it were applied to anything other than the already concededly worthless materials of poetry: i.e., historicising, epistemologizing, a little covert logical-positivizing — in short, moving energetically about the boneyard of Rationalism, tidying up the discredited value systems. He is cheerful, even gay at moments, he hums, and whistles his own metaphors as he works; and they are bright, astonishingly fresh with crotchety, homey newness. But he is not fooling anybody, least of all himself I should think. For, those metaphors — they are at their best when they are offered quite consciously. Somehow, he *knows* better than to be doing what he is doing, that "work." And that is the curious thing.

Plato did not, although he suspected, of course, and therefore started telling stories when logic failed him. But we do. The realm of pure, verbal rationality simply does not exist, anywhere available to man on this earth — not even in formal theology. And so long as we persist in the dream of it, and try to sustain poetry thereby, with the imposed rigor that is most of all alien to *its* nature, we are slowly but surely strangling it, and turning over more and more of its proper influence to the mindless forces of pseudo-art, of "entertainment." The rigor of such criticism is the *rigor mortis* of poetry.

Or will cat poetry, whom we feel so sure of — about whom as Mr. Wimsatt says "professors of poetry know too well what [it] is — a way of ordering our impulses" — not be strangled, but turn tiger, as "pre-Homeric" as you please? (*The Verbal Icon*, p. 279). I have already suggested that I think poetry *is* the tiger. And impulses that think themselves too well ordered have a way of getting disordered with alarming suddenness. We flatter ourselves to assume even that we will be there when the sociologists come to turn us out of our offices.

But I doubt, actually, that we will have to face either such unpleasant alternative. The dangers especially in the academic situation have been much exaggerated. At least in my university, and I suspect it is the same at others, there is no immediate prospect of anyone's turning anyone else out. And I have, on my own, still somewhat overdrawn my differences with Wimsatt and Brooks on the subject of our solicitude for poetry.

The very inconsistencies and evasions on their part, or unconscious shiftings of terms, that I have pointed out, argue a real division of mind. I do not mean, a division between Brooks and Wimsatt — although there is that too, which shows up very plainly in their efforts at collaboration — but an ambivalence of attitude in the thinking of each. The evidence for what I have said about the explicationists, in general, as die-hard rationalists, could be interpreted quite differently. Perhaps it is, rather, that they have believed in the supremacy of the imagination, but have been afraid to say so. Both Brooks and Wimsatt somehow do, at any rate, fear the poets. (There is probably some conscious irony in Wimsatt's remark on the professors and poetry.) Wimsatt's weapon, to subdue the fear, is his rather more outspoken if elaborate moralism; Mr. Brooks' is likely to be most often a concealed principle of *decorum*, as that which supervenes when he refuses to recognize the allusion to Maud Gonne in "Among School Children." And the fear in itself, however misdirected, is sane and healthy. It is well to fear all users of the word. I fear Mr. Wimsatt and Mr. Brooks.

But, although the poet above all is fearful, are we right to find his fearfulness malevolent? Or, better, is he whether in benign or malevolent aspect, necessarily the lunatic, as we have been taught for centuries to believe? It is at least worth the risk of thinking, that the anti-rationalist revolution is not a "sad" truth, but a glorious one.

The 18th- and 19th-century theories of imagination — when first, in the fustian words of some historian-of-philosophy that stick in my mind, "Imagination was rushed in triumph to the abandoned throne of Reason" — were in many ways miscalculated and over-enthusiastic. But precisely what the obvious inadequacy of the metaphor here reveals, is the folly of thinking that the nature of man himself, the nature of the "government" of his being, is changed by alterations of theory concerning it. We gain, or hope to gain, only occasional new *insights* into our nature. And, while I trust I am not recommending any simplistic revival of the older conceptions of the imagination, to try to make them cover a situation of our experience which we know very well they will not, yet I cannot see any real reason for the near-despair of a statement like the following from the closing paragraph of *The Verbal Icon* (p. 297):

> What then is an adequately serious view of poetry? I submit that this has always been, and remains, difficult if not impossible to define with any rigor. What is the formula by which we shall recognize the metaphoric capacities of language and the moral importance of valid linguistic expression without surrendering our conception of truth as a thing beyond language, without yielding to the lead of the idealistic symbolists, the ritualists, and the myth-makers? I confess that I do not clearly see the answer. I have not found the book in which the answer is permanently and

canonically formulated. But I insist that this question is a real and important one — and not only for more dogmatic Christians and less dogmatic Christians, but for all persons who are interested to inquire into the norms by which they live.

I say "near-despair" because, although the paragraph ends with insistence upon the fact that it is a "real and important" question, there is the assertion at the beginning that presumably the same thing (the thing questioned) is "difficult if not impossible to define." To be faced, in any human situation, with an issue "real and important" but at the same time even seemingly "impossible" is to approach despair.

The whole paragraph is a well-nigh impenetrable, logical and syntactical thicket, and mined with conceptual booby-traps. One moves cautiously. But there is some version here of the legend of Miss Stein on her deathbed. It would help considerably to "see the answer" if we could only remember what the question was.

If I read the passage at all rightly, the really important question is contained wholly in the first sentence and a part of the third. How can we have "an adequately serious view of poetry . . . without surrendering our conception of truth as a thing beyond language?" At least for *me* (perhaps I should say to avoid undue presumption) this is the only vital question. It is, at best, difficult. But Wimsatt makes it "difficult if not impossible," precludes any possible answer, with the impossible *conditions* he attaches to its statement.

He wants an "adequately serious" view of poetry — but it must be at the same time a view "defined" with "rigor." The first phrase would seem momentarily to mean a view adequate to the seriousness of the thing viewed; certainly it ought to mean that, at least primarily. But, of course, since the seriousness of poetry is of a nonrigorous order — it has rules, but there are always situations coming up in which luck and native ingenuity have to be called upon — there *can* be no adequate (comprehensive) view of it which is at the same time determined to be rigorous. One cannot, to be sure, adequately play tennis while wearing an overcoat and hat and carrying a cane — it is, "difficult if not impossible." Also, he wants a "formula" by which to "recognize the metaphoric capacities of language and the moral importance of valid linguistic expression" — what would require, no doubt, much sedulous and sedentary activity in the study — but at the same time is beckoned away by some phantoms called "idealistic symbolists, ritualists, and myth-makers" who want him to "yield to their lead" and follow them who knows where. If I were in the same predicament (which I don't believe I am), I would opt for the phantoms; it sounds more fun, anyway, and scarcely more likely to take me to perdition than the other business of hunting for the formula. (One thinks of another famous study, and the search for a "formula." Who, exactly, called those phantoms up, in the first place?) And finally, there is the gloomy admission that he has not "found the book" where the answer to his question might be "canonically formulated." "The book," and "canonical"; it is all beginning to look, indeed, most ominously familiar. Let us devoutly hope, "dogmatic and less dogmatic Christians . . . and all others," that he never *does* find that book.

Of course, there is still that otherwise tormenting undertone in it, the suggestion that in some way he *knows* there is no "book," no "formula," not even any "rigor" — and that, in fact, this is somehow just what he means to be saying. But to talk of undertones at this point is not going to help much; and neither will an outburst of impatience, however honest.

If one were willing to state the question in the reduced form I suggest, however — clearing one's mind at least temporarily of all distracting intellectual, moral, theological, and professional precommitments — then it might yield up an answer almost of itself. How can we have "an adequately serious view of poetry . . . without surrendering our conception of truth as a thing beyond language?" I am not sure that I like, still, that word "conception." But I have *faith* in such a truth; I believe in it.

For the sake of the argument, however, I will let that pass, and presume further only that we are speaking of something that, although "beyond language," is yet somehow *available* to language, that can be apprehended *through* language. Otherwise, it could hardly be the proper concern of a book on literary criticism. And now, finally, if that is what is meant, where or how do we apprehend such truth if not in, or through, the language of poetry itself?

Is this not exactly what we mean when we say that the language of poetry is primarily evocative, suggestive, that there is something more "in" it than what is "said"? At any rate, this is finally what *I* mean, when I say that poetry "intends." It "intends" or "means" to say, more than it says.

If that is the highest purpose of language, as I think it is, to express the truth that is beyond language, then the poetic is the truest and most proper use of language. It is not authorless, but it reveals the person of the author who is beyond himself, who by "meaning," "intending," becomes the *thou* to my *I*, who, in other words, communicates with me. And no matter how many of the thou's within him he projects, the *personae*, they are all still his, and become my thou's.

Will not the "adequately serious" view of poetry be the view that recognizes just this nature of the language of poetry, as that which most yields the "meaning," the truth, that is beyond language?

Now, I am sure that to many it will seem I am being capricious in thus appropriating "truth" to that kind only of "meaning" which is a *person's* "meaning" — "intention," "meaning to, or toward." But it seems to me, on the other hand, no less capricious, prejudicial, although it is more time-sanctified, to want to appropriate "truth" to the other kind of meaning — the "meaning" of propositional statements, the specific "truth" of which can be supposedly verified by review of the purely rational order of the statement, without reference to the speaker as person.

Perhaps I am being capricious. But I should only like to find some way of reminding us that there *is* this intentional meaning of "meaning," and truth, and that moreover it has something to do with the other kind. Poetry is not all the first kind; it contains also propositional meaning. But we keep forgetting that "rational" discourse has its small portion of the poetic, too, and that it had better have, or it will cease to be meaningful.

I say forthrightly that I consider the first kind of meaning, the kind most proper to poetry, superior. Its truth is superior. In terms of Mr. Wimsatt's opposition in the Epilogue chapter of *Literary Criticism*: I say that the verbal "making" of poetry is "saying-seeing" in its highest form.[8] It is a shadow, only, of God's meaning. But so also is our rationality a shadow of God's reasoning.

Because we are recurrently weak-minded, we need the other kind of language — what Wimsatt calls the "full conceptualized discourse of science and philosophy" — to lead us along by the hand, and "explain" things to us, between the times when we are aware of our need for the higher truth of poetry, and when we are strong enough

---

[8] William K. Wimsatt, Jr., and Cleanth Brooks, *Literary Criticism: A Short History*, p. 753.

to bear it. Philosophy is our good nurse. But when she hints, as nurses are wont to do, that her own may be the higher truth, then she is the wicked nurse. And it is high time that we made her confess her wickedness.

With all that we now know of the psychological bases of thought, we ought to begin to be able to break through the rationalistic prejudices, and to re-evaluate the problem of poetry and meaning. The great contribution of Sigmund Freud, for a major example, was not that he prodded the monster of sex out of hiding, but simply that he showed us we cannot *think straight*, i.e., talk straight. But we might seem to suppose that this means we are forbidden to think at all, and so keep sullenly going around in unvarying circles. But, to return one last time to Wimsatt of *The Verbal Icon*, it is I think that rationalistic "rigor," that freezing of the mind in a conceptualist order of thinking, which makes him put the "idealistic symbolists, ritualists, and myth-makers" all in the same group of beckoning phantoms.

In the perspective established in the paragraph I have quoted, it is impossible to tell just who, or what, all these may be. Nor would it help much to look back at previous chapters of the book. Martin Foss, the anti-symbolist of the chapter "Symbol and Metaphor," for all I know, may by the end have got to be an "idealistic symbolist" in Wimsatt's mind. But it is everywhere apparent, anyway, that Mr. Wimsatt does not think much of the *pretensions* to differences among such groups which are made by the writers themselves. He will carefully, tolerantly, and with much admiration for their varying "strategies," sift the pretensions. But, finally, they *are* all the same to him; they are the ones, whatever they call themselves, who want to take one or another aspect of what he recognizes as the *poetic* use of language, and set it up, outside language as Wimsatt wants to comprehend language, as having real powers in the world of reality. In short, they all want to make a *god* of language.

But what is most interesting to me, on the previous page (278) he has mentioned Yeats (along with Melville) in a context that would suggest Yeats' alliance with such god-makers. But in my chapter on "A Prayer for My Daughter" here, I made a considerable point of the fact that it seemed to me Yeats was in that poem *specifically* showing an anti-Symbolist tendency. Moreover, I think this is, despite what might seem to some readers contrary evidence in other poems, the general tendency of his work — even where there is not, as in "A Prayer for My Daughter," the particular situation of a "conflict" between the gods and the symbolic attributes. I think, further, that there is in all poetry this necessary tendency, only to *seem* to make the symbol an independent reality, the better to activate it as source of expressive language, language as medium of human communication. I think that it makes some considerable difference whether one puts the final emphasis upon the symbol or the myth.

I think, in brief, that this is a crucial issue for the whole problem of poetry and belief, poetry and reality. And if we are interested in that, not in the preservation simply of tidiness in the rationalistic system of thought, we would do well to attend to some of the claims of differentiation among the varying schools of thought on symbol, myth, and ritual, and not be so anxious merely to "dispose of" them.[9] There may be something more here than a chicken-and-egg problem. It could be the egg with which Yeats proposed to "alter Plato's parable." And in that hope, I for one would be quite happy to "yield to the lead of" practically anybody for as long as necessary. For the phantoms are not phantoms, but men, and no man in the name of

---

[9] Because it is a history, and a collaboration, on both counts the less accountable, I have for the most part preferred not to make reference to statements in the book *Literary Criticism: A Short History*, by Wimsatt and Brooks. But the Introduction to that volume indicates the chapters for which each of the authors has principal responsibility. And it should be pointed out that in Chapter 31, "Myth and Archetype," Brooks has made a notable contribution to the needed effort I speak of: "to attend to some of the claims of differentiation among the varying schools of thought on symbol, myth, and ritual." (This is reflected somewhat in the Epilogue chapter also, which is primarily Wimsatt's.) And, while acknowledging that Brooks has been laudably careful not merely to "dispose of" these schools but to understand and appreciate them, I would also assert my general agreement with his resistance to the reductionist tendency of many of these thinkers — the tendency, on *their* part, to try to dispose of *poetry*. Certainly we can only applaud the closing statement of that chapter (p. 720), that the important thing about Yeats is that he was a poet, not that he was a maker of myths. But it seems to me that here, no less than in his earlier writings, Mr. Brooks is still avoiding the crucial problem of *belief*. He still wants to treat the symbolic system of A *Vision* as merely a *convenience* to Yeats in the writing of poems, and to avoid any recognition of the possibility that either these symbolic values or others that the poems themselves developed, independently of the prose study, were values in which Mr. Yeats really and truly believed. In other words, Mr. Brooks rightly wants to preserve the poet and the poems, but he wants to dispose of the man. Here as elsewhere, the statement moves toward final emphasis upon the *structure* of the poem, regardless of its intentional validity, regardless of the *truth* of poetic expression.

any theory from Rationalism to Ritualism leads me to conviction against my will.

We have been, then, so concerned to avoid the "extra-literary" in recent criticism that we have unduly restricted the intra-literary. To return to the pair of terms with which the purpose of this discussion was first defined, we have been so afraid to stray outside the poem, that we have blinded ourselves to half of what is inside it. The purpose of this entire volume of studies has been to suggest means for enlarging the intra-literary vision. Or, it has been to yield up what seemed to me the falsely confining frames of theory to be shattered, so what we might begin to discover what is the real frame of the poem, and even how that might contain the yet more curious frame of man and his language.

There is one step further, of course, where all frames shatter. And I can only hope that, after all I have said, it will not seem in any event impious, if I return us now for that just to the poem itself.

IV

But, I say now "we," or us — and often in another context, in the course of the discussion, when I have spoken of "the explicationists" or of "The New Criticism," it has seemed six of one and a half dozen of the other whether to say "we" or "they." I avowed at the beginning my membership in the school, so far as it may be legitimately supposed to exist. (See again the footnote on p. 152, at the start of this chapter.) And I am duly proud of what contributions I have made in the past to its literature. One of the essays in this book, on Milton's "Lycidas," is in its present form as much the work of another and prior member of the school as it is mine. And if, in this final chapter and elsewhere, I shall have seemed to single out Mr. Brooks, who has been both my teacher and my collaborator, and others (especially Mr. Wimsatt) of those I like to regard at least as intellectual friends, for especially severe criticism, I trust it will be apparent to everyone that the severity is the greatest mark of my respect. I have never made a practice of preaching at anyone unless I thought him in at least as advantageous a position to preach back.

I would not attempt now to minimize the importance of my differences with them. I have changed my mind about poetry, radically changed it, during the past few years. I did not know quite how much, even until the final revision of this book. As a result, it may seem in some quarters that I have hopelessly alienated myself from my former alliances. And yet, I have had no aspirations to become, as another friend wittily put it when I talked over with him some of the ideas expressed here, "the Whittaker Chambers of the New Criticism." The analogy, although flattering even in the patently false hope of notoriety that it holds out, will not work for two reasons. The first is, that I have never been in any sense, willingly, an undercover agent, that I have made no secret of my alliances, but published them as often as I could find anyone agreeable to putting them in print. And the second reason is, that I do not wish now to repudiate them, at least in the sense of eagerness to go over to any other definable "camp."

I trust it is abundantly clear, from this entire book, and especially from this final chapter, that I regard with as much suspicion as ever the claims upon literature of pure historicism, of *Kultur Kritik*, of the psychological and other "therapeutic" schools which in pandering to the psychic ills of the public age pretend to be talking about art. Even when I spoke of my willingness to "yield to the lead" of scholarly studies in myth, ritual, and symbol, I did not mean that I was ready to start reading poems according to any approach that might be systematized by any of these writers. I continue to regard that sort of thing, when it is good, simply as scholarship. And scholarship is the servant of criticism. Nor have I, with my remarks on poetry and belief, proposed to turn literary criticism into a branch of religious apologetics. "Apologetics" is not and never was the real issue in any dispute of modern criticism, simply because the devaluation of religion has gone hand in hand with that of poetry; but the red herring has been industriously dragged back and forth between opposing factions.

Implicitly, if not overtly, I have meant also to condemn all varieties of "impressionism" in criticism. I do not consider the studies of the poems in this book in any sense impressionistic. Literary criticism is, in the truest sense, a discipline of the mind, and one not to be confused with other disciplines, although it draws upon them. It can be pursued even as an academic discipline. But I have suggested only that the academicians, *including* the explicationists, have a way of coming to love the instruments of truth, their terminological rectitude, more than truth, and the precincts of their own, special truths, more than the world of truth. Nothing that I have said here is meant wholly to invalidate the readings of poetry which have been supplied in the past by the explicationists — including myself. I found that if I had the "Lycidas" essay to do over, for example, if it had been mine wholly to change as I pleased, except for a few matters of emphasis and terminology for description of effects there was not much I should want to alter. There is a great deal I might like to *add*, and perhaps one day when I can get the poem again in clearer perspective, I shall — but not much to change.

I say only that we have succeeded, usually, in spite rather than because of the rigor of our methods. And in so doing we have been neglectful of our duty both to the poetry and to the academic community — which latter stands today in far greater need of re-definition *as* a community, as community or universe of discourse, than of further multiplication and defense of disciplinary distinctions. Also in that interest, I have tried here to clarify the "meaning" of poetry, in the only, multiple meaning of meaning that any longer makes any sense to me.

And yet, there is no "broadening" of the subject required. The great and continuing advantage of the explicationist method is just that it shows us we can never fully understand, never fully explain, any true poem. The whole book has said this, that poetry is enough. But how to name it, only?

Literary criticism is a discipline. The essays in this book are all meant as examples of what Coleridge called "genial Criticism." But the master discipline is poetry itself. And we are obliged to insist that if Coleridge is right also that poetry is to be "enjoyed," still, enjoyment does not mean rape, does not mean the seizure of the poem simply for the satisfaction of one's preconceived intellectual interests, in utter licence. But, further and finally, and I have also insisted that poetry is the largest and most liberal of the disciplines of language, this then means that enjoyment is love — that state of affection in which enjoyment is indistinguishable from understanding. And the true lover, our true critic, is not jealous of his prerogatives in the enjoyment of the beloved. He will not make her the instrument of his vanity before the world. But rather, he will recognize the infinite superiority of her greatness to his, and her presence will *be* his world. And merely to enter into that world, with all it contains, he will be himself content.

BIBLIOGRAPHY

I. Texts of the Poems

"Young Waters"
Sargent, Helen Child, and George Lyman Kittredge, eds. *English and Scottish Popular Ballads*. Cambridge Edition. Boston, Houghton, Mifflin Co., 1932.

"Young Waters" (second version)
Buchan, Peter, ed. *Ancient Ballads and Songs of the North of Scotland*. Edinburgh, 1828; version of "Young Waters" from Buchan's collection reprinted in Child, Francis James, ed., *The English and Scottish Popular Ballads* (III). Boston, Little, Brown and Co., 1864.

"Lycidas"
Poems of Mr. John Milton. London, Humphrey Moseley, 1645. Reprinted in Brooks, Cleanth, and John Edward Hardy, eds.; *Poems of Mr. John Milton: The 1645 Edition with Essays in Analysis*. New York, Harcourt, Brace and Co., 1951; London, Denis Dobson, 1957.

"The Coronet"
Margoliouth, H. M., ed. *The Poems and Letters of Andrew Marvell* (I). Oxford, The Clarendon Press, 1927.

"The Solitary Reaper"
de Selincourt, Ernest, ed. *The Poetical Works of William Wordsworth*, (III). Oxford, The Clarendon Press, 1946.

"Rêve Parisien"
Crépet, Jacques, ed., *Œuvres Complètes de Charles Baudelaire* (VI). Paris, Louis Conard, 1930.

"Sonette an Orpheus," I Teil, XX
Rainer Maria Rilke, Ausgewählte Werke (I). Leipzig, Im Insel Verlag, 1938.

"A Prayer for My Daughter"
Collected Poems of W. B. Yeats. New York, The Macmillan Co., 1945.

II. Works Cited

Abrams, M. H., ed. *Literature and Belief: English Institute Essays, 1957*. New York, Columbia University Press, 1958.

Brooks, Cleanth. *The Well Wrought Urn*. New York, Harcourt, Brace and Co., 1947.

Brooks, Cleanth, and John Edward Hardy. *Poems of Mr. John Milton: The 1645 Edition with Essays in Analysis*. New York, Harcourt, Brace and Co., 1951; London, Denis Dobson, 1957.

Bowers, Fredson. *Textual and Literary Criticism*. Cambridge, The Cambridge University Press, 1959.

Buchan, Peter, ed. *Ancient Ballads and Songs of the North of Scotland*. Edinburgh, 1828.

Child, Francis James, ed. *The English and Scottish Popular Ballads* (III). Boston, Little, Brown and Co., 1864.

Clapton, George Thomas. *Baudelaire et de Quincey*. Paris, Société d'édition "Les Belles Lettres," 1931.

Darbishire, Helen, ed. *Wordsworth, Poems in Two Volumes* (incl. *Poems Published in 1807*). Oxford, The Clarendon Press, 1914.

Gordon, Caroline. *The Malefactors*. New York, Harcourt, Brace and Co., 1956.

Heller, Erich. *The Disinherited Mind: Essays in Modern German Literature and Thought*. New York, Farrar, Straus, and Cudahy, 1957.

Hone, Joseph. *W. B. Yeats, 1865-1939*. New York, The Macmillan Co., 1943.

Hubert, J.-D. *L'Esthétique des "Fleurs du Mal": Essai sur l'Ambiguïté Poétique*. Genève, P. Cailler, 1953.

Knight, William, ed. *Journals of Dorothy Wordsworth*. London, Macmillan and Co., Ltd., 1930.

Ortega y Gasset, José. *The Dehumanization of Art, and Other Writings on Art and Culture*. Garden City, N. Y., Doubleday and Co., Inc., 1956.

Picard, Max. *The World of Silence*. Chicago, Henry Regnery Co., 1961.

Richards, Ivor Armstrong. *Practical Criticism: A Study of Literary Judgment*. New York, Harcourt, Brace and Co., 1946.

Sargent, Helen Child, and George Lyman Kittredge, eds. *English and Scottish Popular Ballads*. Cambridge Edition. Boston, Houghton, Mifflin Co., 1932.

de Selincourt, Ernest, ed. *Early Letters of Dorothy and William Wordsworth*. Oxford, The Clarendon Press, 1935.

Sewell, Elizabeth. *The Orphic Voice: Poetry and Natural History*. New Haven, Yale University Press, 1960.

Starkie, Enid. *Baudelaire*. London, Faber and Faber, 1957.

Symons, Arthur. *The Symbolist Movement in Literature.* New York, E. P. Dutton and Co., 1919.

Van Doren, Mark. *Introduction to Poetry.* New York, William Sloane Associates, Inc., 1951.

Wasserman, Earl R. *The Finer Tone: Keats' Major Poems.* Baltimore, The Johns Hopkins Press, 1953.

Wimsatt, William K., Jr. *The Verbal Icon: Studies in the Meaning of Poetry.* Lexington, University of Kentucky Press, 1954.

Wimsatt, William K., Jr., and Cleanth Brooks. *Literary Criticism: A Short History.* New York, Alfred A. Knopf, 1959.